NOTE BY TONY ORCHARD : 16/6/97

ELEANOR JANE BOARDEN

NEÉ ORCHARD

BAPTISED 30 December 1827
IN MAWGAN IN MENEAGE Cornwall
D/O WILLIAM ORCHARD + HIS

WIFE, JANE.

D1784846

CHANGING TIMES
AND FORTUNES

CHANGING TIMES
AND FORTUNES

A Cornish Farmer's Life
1828–1904

by

John Rowe

Retired Reader in History
University of Liverpool

with Introduction by
Philip Payton
Director, Institute of Cornish Studies
University of Exeter

FIRST EDITION – 1996
Cornish Hillside Publications
12 Hillside Road, St Austell

To the Rowes
Constance, Gareth and Jeremy
and the memory of
Austin and Mary

© John Rowe 1996

ISBN 1 900147 02 5 Paperback
1 900147 03 3 Hardback

Typeset by Kestrel Data, Exeter

Printed in Great Britain by
Short Run Press Ltd, Exeter

Foreword

John Rowe needs no introduction to students of Cornish history. The author of two seminal works, *Cornwall in the Age of the Industrial Revolution* and *The Hard-Rock Men*, (the former happily in print again, and in extended form), as well as countless other articles and papers, it was John Rowe who more than anyone established modern Cornwall as a major focus of historical research. In fact the pen-picture of Cornwall in the nineteenth century, drawn so skillfully by Dr. Rowe in his many works, still largely informs our understanding of issues and evens in that all-important period of Cornish history.

In this book, John Rowe turns his attention to the life of a Cornish farmer, John Boaden of Skyburriowe in the Meneage district of the Lizard peninsula. Born in 1828 and departing this world in 1904, John Boaden lived in an extraordinary age. His life spanned the whole of the Victorian era and more, from the agitation that preceded the Great Reform Act of 1832 to the era of high Imperialism and the chastening impact of the South African War. He was perhaps typical of the Cornish tenant farmer of the period, his pre-occupations and concerns – from Methodism to the price of corn, to emigration and public service – characteristic of his social and cultural background in a remote corner of Cornwall. But unlike most of his peers and contemporaries, John Boaden left a detailed account of his life when, well into his 'seventies' and troubled by an encroaching blindness, he painstakingly wrote his autobiography.

The autobiography is the raw material for this book; the historian's art has enabled John Rowe to take, set alongside other evidences and survivals, place the whole in a wider context, to give a vivid picture of the life of John Boaden and the Cornish times through which he lived. The result is an eminently readable but scholarly insight into a way of life which has all but vanished and yet has profoundly influenced the condition of contemporary Cornwall that we have inherited.

For the student of agricultural history there is much in this account that is of importance but it is as a work of social history that it will be especially welcomed and remembered. It is easy to imagine that rural, nineteenth century Cornwall was wrapped in a cocooning timelessness, disturbed only by the passage of the seasons – a stark contrast with the ceaseless change of today's world. The experience of John Boaden shows that change was also an ever-present fact of life for our Cornish forebears, in the last century, faced with a range of new technologies and ever-widening opportunities offered by emigration to new lands.

There were the 'Hungry Forties' and the potato blights which, notwithstanding all the recent attention afforded to their impact in Ireland and Highland Scotland (in marked contrast to the silence with which Cornwall has greeted their centenary), hit Cornwall hard and led to riots and threats of riots as angry mobs forced 'fair prices' for bread at Helston, St. Austell, Callington and elsewhere. There were, too, difficult days for agriculture in the late 1870s and 1880s, when not a few Cornish farmers (including kinsmen and colleagues of John Boaden) forsook their native land to try their luck in the perhaps more favourable conditions of the midland and eastern counties.

Amidst this adversity we see the character of John Boaden emerging, strengthening and adapting. One of Dr. Rowe's achievements in this book is his ability to portray the human detail of John Boaden the man, against the background of these wider themes. For example, emigration came to dominate Cornish life in the nineteenth century, but John Boaden's autobiography, in the sensitive hands of John Rowe 'depicts', as he puts it, 'with rare poignancy the actual uprooting of a Cornish emigrant family'. This was the Orchard family, one of whom – Eleanor Jane Orchard – had formed a relationship with John Boaden; the lovers remained true to one another for the five years in which Eleanor was in South Australia, and when, in 1855, she returned to Cornwall they were, at last, wed. It sounds a romantic story, yet John Boaden's account of Eleanor's return has a certain prosaic ambivalance shocking the reader:

'Her appearance was somewhat changed beyond a little by the Australian sun and sea air. She had also a new set of artificial teeth, quite an uncommon thing in those days, given by her father, costing sixteen pounds.'

Likewise, John Boaden's reaction to the completion of the Royal Albert Bridge at Saltash in 1859, linking Cornwall's railway to the rest of the British system, was similarly equivocal:

'we got connected with the rest of the Kingdom, an advantage difficult to estimate'.

Years later, when he had been elevated to the status of County Councillor, John Boaden was depicted by the West Briton as a taciturn but shrewd pragmatist: 'a Home Ruler, a prominent Wesleyan, total abstainer, practical agriculturalist, of sound judgement, unpretending in manner', a judgement itself not without reason.

John Boaden speaks to us across the years in the tones of a Cornishman; even today his attitudes and turns of phrase ring true, with an authentic Cornishness to which we cannot fail to note and to warm. That John Rowe is also so firmly and unmistakeably rooted in Cornwall must be a key in part to his success in bringing John Boaden alive for us. Dr. Rowe's twin credentials as historian and Cornishman have combined to present us with a fascinating window on farming life in Cornwall in the nineteenth century.

Philip Payton
Reader in Cornish Studies and Director
Institute of Cornish Studies
University of Exeter
September 1995

Preface

In recent years there has been continuing and often controversial interest in the countryside and its problems. Many books have dealt with rural life, several advocating 'going back to the land'. Some authors have described farming satirically, others suggest that in the 'good old days' things were much better. Yet what was rural life really like during those bygone times? Agrarian historians seem to concentrate overmuch on legal deeds or on statistics of production and prices. Social historians give impressionistic rather than realistic accounts of former days. Many concentrate on squires and labourers and neglect the intermediate classes, the working land-owning yeoman farmers and the tenant farmers who might lose their leaseholds at the end of a fixed term of years.

Several years ago a descendent of John Boaden's drew my attention to his manuscript autobiography. Boaden was a tenant farmer who lived in the Lizard district of the Meneage from 1828 to 1904. An unusual individual in some respects, he was a farmer all his life and shared the common fortunes of the Cornish farmers of his time. While his individual traits and talents enabled him to prosper when others failed this only shows that in Victorian days, as now, there are farmers and farmers – able or incompetent, fortunate or luckless. His memoirs reveal him as a very orthodox Wesleyan Methodist of that school which made teetotalism a dogma of faith. It matters little whether one shares or abhors his beliefs and religious creed, but it was those farmers who had faith, faith of one sort or another who best survived the long period of agricultural depression from 1875 to the end of the Victorian era.

Boaden wrote his reminiscences in the style of a nineteenth century Methodist sermon, but revealing that, first and foremost, he was a farmer living through a fascinating period of British agricultural history. His account is the basis and the heart of the following narrative. Certain parts of the story of his life have been expanded by material drawn from contemporary newspapers and other sources, for he did not give a full account of his middle life, but concentrated on his boyhood days and his latter years. His life vindicates the Victorian gospel of individual self-reliance and personal responsibility as the key to material success and well-being. His memoirs stress family values: farming is a family business. Pragmatism is evident – the weather affects agricultural fortunes as much as any economic considerations. Nevertheless economic conditions are important; even in the so-called golden age of high farming, between the Crimean War and the last Disraeli administration, too much was being taken out of the land and not enough capital was put back into it.

In his farming career Boaden experienced good, bad, and indifferent years, but like some farmers he made the most of the good and escaped much of the damage caused by the bad weather in 'catchy' seasons which, after all, are normal in Cornwall. Damage by late frost or summer storm to standing crops has always been a matter of blind fate which cannot be reduced to scientific analysis. Even more unpredictable was the incidence of epidemic foot-and-mouth, or pleuro-pneumonia, and his neighbour not have a single casualty; one farmer might lose all his sheep from 'rot', and the next lose only two or three. Such vagaries make it seem no significant omission on Boaden's part that he never gave details of the acreages he tilled or the numbers of livestock he kept, while he only mentioned a few changes in the price of farm produce. As today the price of corn and beef could vary every week; only abnormally high or low prices or pronounced upward or downward trends aroused discussion or concern and even less so when smaller tenant farmers had but little to sell since often they consumed much of the produce they raised themselves.

'Cash flow' was not a term current in Boaden's time, although it was certainly a reality. The most vivid consideration of tenant farmers, proverbially, was whether or not their corn mows would pay the landlords' rents. When corn prices slumped at the end of the Napoleonic wars the British Parliament, in which landowning classes were predominant, passed 'Corn Laws' imposing protective practices designed to restrict importations of cheap foreign grain. Opposition to these laws grew with the increasing political influence of manufacturing interests and urban consuming population, culminating with the crisis caused by the failure of potato crops, most devastating in but not confined to Ireland, which brought about the repeal of the Corn Laws demanded by the long agitation of the Anti-Corn Law League of Cobden and Bright. Landlords and tenants alike had to adjust themselves to a new situation; most immediately a method of doing so was the adoption of more economical practices of production; labour costs could be reduced by mechanization in the harvest fields; already scythes had largely replaced reaping hooks or sickles and in the 1850s reaping machines started appearing to be followed by sheaf binders and more devices for threshing out the grain that flails had, in the past, been the way of providing farm hands with indoor winter employment. This advancing agricultural technology provided British farmers with the means of harvesting and marketing their corn in the home market earlier than supplies could be shipped in by sailing vessels from the Black and Baltic Seas and, rather later, from the prairies of North America. Nevertheless the rent of a tenant farmer still had to be found; dependence on the corn mow alone was risky; diversification was resorted to and, along with it, there intensified in John Boaden's case an ambitious determination to obtain for his family their own farm or farms whereby to continue in the way of life to which they had been bred.

There were as there always have been unsolved problems in farming and rural life. John Boaden met many difficulties in his long life, perhaps solving more of them than some of his fellow Meneage farmers. He made mistakes, but made the most of his life according to his lights, possibly inspired by those Noncornformist preachers to whom he delighted to listen expounding the parable of the talents. Like many successful men, he had his critics. When in retirement he devoted himself to public life some suggested that he had the traits of the contemporary Poet Laureate, Tennyson's, 'Northern Farmer' who, riding along on his business occasion, deep in thought, declared:

'Doesn't thou 'ear my 'erse's legs, as they canters awaay?
Proputty, proputty, proputty – that's what I 'ears 'em saay.'

Times have changed since John Boaden's days and farming has

been transformed. Many of the characteristics of farmers and aspects of their lifestyle, however, endure, and it is a lifestyle with its own peculiar rewards and compensations. There are, too, rewards and compensations in writing of it, and of them the greatest is in thanking those who have helped, and my own indebtedness for help is a great one. The late Mr. H. E. Boaden and the late Mrs. A. Boaden first drew my attention to and allowed me to use John Boaden's memoirs, the manuscript of which is now in the Cornwall County Records Office at Truro, whose staff are unstintingly helpful in assisting harvests of research. Mr. and Mrs. T. Boaden have given me access to other family records.

To Mr. Andre Thomas I am indebted for his painstaking photography of the Meneage scene around Skyburriowe, a task performed in much less than perfect weather. Appreciating how these scenes have changed Mr. Thomas also reproduced the old photographs used in this book and even obtained a contemporary view of Trelowarren with an identical cloud cover to that depicted in an engraving of 1824 in F. W. L. Stockdale's *Excursions in the County of Cornwall.*

Roger Penhallurick kindly drew the map of th Meneage district, and allowed me to use photographs of late Victorian farming in the collection of the Royal Institution of Cornwall.

Many helped in the research of this book: the late Claude Berry and the staff of the West Briton, the staff of the University Libraries of Liverpool and Cambridge, and of the Morrab Library in Penzance and Angela Broome of the Courtney Library in the Royal Institution of Cornwall.

To farming friends in Cornwall and elsewhere I owe a great deal – this after all is their history.

Dr. Philip Payton kindly read the manuscript and wrote the foreword. I am grateful to Charles Thurlow, my publisher, for his interest, enthusiasm and encouragement in transforming the manuscript into a book. Finally above all I am indebted to John Boaden himself – without his memoirs this story would never have been told.

John Rowe
Rock Mill
Par
September 1995

Contents

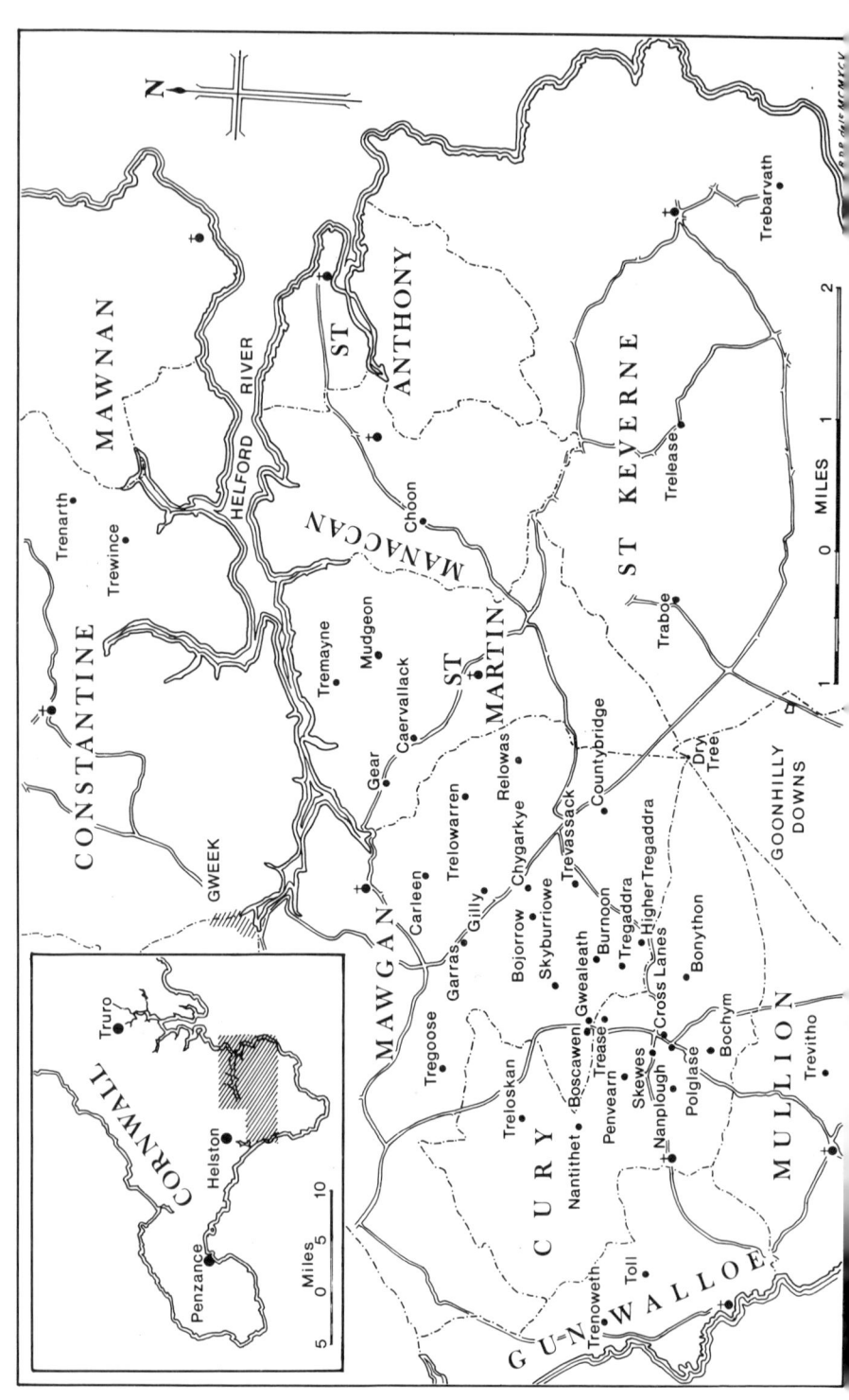

1

Setting In Meneage

A week before his seventy-third birthday, conscious of the burden of his years John Boaden began to write his life story. He had worked hard most of his days, retiring from farming eight years before, and now, partially blind, expecting soon to be bereft of the helpmeet he had married five and forty years before, he opened a thick black-covered exercise book and, slowly, wrote

'believing that the time will come when my children will be interested and may be profited to know the history however brief of their parents; at present their attention looks forward rather than backwards, but age generally alters this, and then if there is no written record, death will have put it beyond our power to give the information. Now on this 22nd August, with failing eyesight growing dim, I write and my dear wife ill in bed (Lady Vyvyan just gone up to see her) all this admonishes that what I do I shall do quickly.'

What better motive could a man have to write his auto-biography? To many John Boaden's life may seem uneventful. In 1901, however, respectability had not become the most decried of all virtues, nor had winning by hard, unremitting, honest toil a reasonable affluence on which to end one's days in ease, come to be regarded with suspicion or derision.

The world that John Boaden knew has gone. He knew his earlier days would be more interesting to his children, but did not foresee that a later generation might welcome more about his middle age and later days, nor that a day would come when hardly anywhere in the land would a squire's wife visit the sick wife of an old

1

tenant farmer because tenants and squires were vanishing races of men.

John Boaden's story was that of a tenant farmer, of a member of that rural class which in the Victorian age had lived between comfort and hardship, and which, rather than the few independent freeholders farming their own estates, should be regarded as the backbone of England in those times. Only a legalistic precision of definition denies them the title of yeoman, yet, until the end of the nineteenth century, the way in which son succeeded father as tenant on the same farm shows their status was more secure than the term tenant now suggests.

The Boadens lived in the Meneage, the southernmost peninsula of Cornwall, a region of indifferent soils and of an equable but fickle climate, where seedtime might be late and harvests not infrequently fail. During John Boaden's own lifetime, too, other forces than those of nature made the position of the small farmer insecure.

Even in 1828, when John Boaden was born, farmers and land-owners were looking regretfully back to bygone days, when agriculture had been the main source of wealth to the most influential classes of society and of livelihood to the greater number of the people. The story of cottagers drifting away from the countryside to become 'wage slaves' in new industrial towns, of independent yeomen farmers dropping into the ranks of struggling smallholders and landless labourers, and of squires and landowning aristocracy losing control of government to a new plutocracy of business, commerce and industry, has often been told. Many, however, still managed to get a living from the land, and quite often succeeded, by sheer hard labour, to gain rather than lose wealth and social standing. The general picture of rural decline in the century following Waterloo was true enough, yet, there were few years in which a strong-armed and 'long-headed' farmer could not keep up a reasonable standard of life, and even save money. Still, it was a century of change, and farming felt the impact of change more than other callings.

The world John Boaden knew seemed to be turning upside down when he began to write his reminiscences. He could dimly recall the beginning of Victoria's reign, but now the Victorian era had ended and its sunset had not been one of tranquil skies but lurid with bloodshot clouds of storm. In South Africa, where one of

Boaden's own sons had recently gone, the Boer War showed Englishmen that their hopes that war and its attendant miseries had been banished from the earth were vain delusions. Furthermore there were misgivings about the justice of the war, misgivings accentuated in Cornwall by knowledge that the very presence of so many Cornish miners on the Rand had been, in part, responsible for the Anglo-Boer conflict.

Religious faith quietened any doubts that troubled John Boaden. His staunch Methodist faith which had helped him to withstand material difficulties and misfortunes, dominated his autobiographical sketch. Intending it for his own family and, taking it for granted that they were familiar with the districts in which he had passed his life he did not describe it, and it seems likely, too, that his religious faith led him to neglect the setting of this world in which he had lived.

Apart from visits to local markets and sales, a trip now and again to Helston, Falmouth, and one or two other towns on some business or other, and one or two brief holidays, Boaden's life, until he retired from farming, was mostly spent within the district of the north-western Meneage between Cury Church on the west and St. Martin's Church in the east; even with a detour to Garras and Mawgan it is easy to stroll over the whole ground on a short winter's afternoon.

In boyhood, John Boaden knew the Cury side best. A footpath from Trease, his birthplace, joined the road from Cury Cross Lanes to Cury White Cross at the lane entrance to Penvearn Farm. At White Cross hamlet there were dame schools and a carpenter's shop had been turned into one of the first Methodist chapels in the Meneage. It was not a picturesque district, having the appearance of a barren upland, although only about two hundred feet above sea level. Salt winds from the Atlantic, less than two miles away, had been too strong for trees save tough thorns and twisted oaks to grow except in the sheltered valleys, whilst closely cropped pastures accentuated the impression of barrenness.

Trease itself was built in the side of a hill, sheltered from the south-westerly gales, facing on the opposite side of the main Helston-Lizard road, Trenoweth Farm. Down below was the stream making the boundary of Cury and Mawgan parishes, and the farmsteads of Boscawen and Gwealeath, whence a footpath across four fields led up over the crest of Boscawen Hill to

Skyburriowe, the farm where John Boaden spent most of his working life, and beyond that again a steep valley with a stream crossed by a ford and footbridge up to Worval where Boaden had gone in retirement.

The hills and valleys in this small area indicate the complex geology of the Meneage which contains some of the oldest rocks in Britain: In the district south of the Helford only the serpentine rock is utterly infertile. Some farmers in the old days, however, hardly realised the break between the serpentine masses and the ajoining geological formations, and saw no reason why it was impossible to grow wheat and barley in one spot when those crops were flourishing less than a stone's-throw away. The variety of soils meant that only tardy, and at times costly, processes of trial and error proved the best means of using the land. The experience of a few seasons' farming however showed which fields scorched in dry years and which became quagmires in rainy times, while old time farmers, too, profited from trace elements in the soil long before scientists gave them a name.

Skyburriowe today is not the house in which John Boaden spent most of his life, for that old thatched-roofed house was destroyed by fire a year or two before he retired. The high- sounding name only means barns, although that suggests the fertility of the lands lying below the southern downs. The site itself is a shallow coombe, the bottom being rather 'stoggy' in wet seasons, and it lies in a sheltered spot where there was a good supply of water. The streams here drain away to the Helford creeks, whilst those on the other side of Boscawen hill – which is barely two hundred and fifty feet above sea-level – flow to the Gunwalloe shore.

Shyburriowe lane, leading up to the southern serpentine down-lands, must have been a delight to John Boaden's children. Rough, twisting, in places running like a cavern beneath the gnarled branches of mossy oaks, muddy in winter, dusty in summer, the place where the first primroses and bluebells came in spring, its hedgerows once teeming with rabbits whose burrowings have added to the mud and dust, the lane quickly comes out on the wild open moor. From the top of the lane on the moor a gate on the right was the entrance to Burnoon, farmed by John's brother Will Boaden. To the left there is a rough trackway continuing across the height of the moorland, rutted with cart tracks and pitted with the hooves of cattle and horses.

Alongside this tract are one or two small enclosures, sometimes ploughed, at others covered with a rough herbage hardly worth the name of grass, the evidence of attempts to reclaim the serpentine downs. Going through a thorn brake, the track branches into two, one part leading to the lane connecting the main St. Keverne road to Cury Cross Lanes, the other turning sharply to the left, bordered with blackthorn, heather-brush, furze, and a few willows to a sheltered valley on the further side of which lies Bojorrow, John Boaden's home after his family left Trease, about a mile and a half by this lane and moorland track from Skyburriowe. Along the last part of this track the transition from the infertile serpentine to fertile mixed soils is most marked – almost as sharp as a cut of a knife. Bojorrow is another sheltered site, but the steepness of the valley meant that it was built inconveniently far from the stream although relics of older buildings suggest that the present farmstead, may not be on the site of the original farmhouse on the borders of the 'heath of Arthur'.[1]

Bojorrow Farm might seem to be remote, yet the nearest neighbours were only about a quarter of a mile away down a farm lane at Tregadjack; across the fields in the opposite direction Chygarkye was about the same distance, while up the lane and then turning left back along the St. Keverne road the hamlet of Garras was within a short mile. A ring fence of about two miles would almost enclose the three holdings with which John Boaden and his brother were connected – Skyburriowe, Burnoon and Bojorrow – and have included Trease, Gwealeath, and Tregadjack as well.

John Boaden, however, spent the first three years of his married life on another farm, Gear, in the parish of St. Martin in Meneage, a considerable move to those stay-at-homes who, looked on the next parish as foreign territory, but Gear was part of the Trelowarren estate, and John Boaden went there not as a farmer but as the farm-baliff of Sir Richard Vyvyan. Gear was almost on a hill top – a pleasantly wooded hill which descended steeply down to the Mawgan Creek of the Helford estuary while at the back the Gearhills wood ran up to the grounds of Trelowarren. Before it

[1] Bojorrow may be a corruption of *ros* – *Arthuiu*, which gives this suggested translation.

had become a farmstead it had, as its name indicates, been a prehistoric camp, one of a cluster of three fortified hilltops on the southern side of the upper Helford estuary while on the northern side a fourth looked down from above Merthen Wood.

The times in which he lived, the country he farmed, and Methodism were the predominating influences in the life of John Boaden. There was a sternness and a rigour about all three. The times could almost be summed up as a generation of moderate prosperity between generations of agrarian depression. The countryside bordered on the sterile Goonhilly Downs; parts of it fertile enough, but the climate was uncertain in summer even if winters were mild. The Methodists to which he belonged were those of that sterner breed who adopted total abstinence as a canon of faith, who believed that man must be reformed rather than that reforms should be for the benefit of man. Since Boaden's time the climate has not changed and the countryside comparatively little; vicissitudes have affected the economic fortunes of the Meneage farmers. The religious faith has softened, but it has also declined, yet it was his Methodist faith that dominated Boaden's conduct of life, his response to the environment in which he lived and his dealings with his fellow men, and his account of his own life.

2

Kith and Kindred

On his father's side John Boaden came of farming stock. His great-grandparents, James and Annie Boaden were, in the middle of the eighteenth century, living at Killewarn in Cury parish, about a mile from Trease. Generation succeeded generation, but in those days farming families were nearly as rooted to their native earth as their farms. His grandfather, Edward Boaden, was one of the seven sons of James and Annie, who had had a family of at least eleven. Several of their descendants still live in Cornwall, but other members of this prolific family are to be found in South Africa, Australia and elsewhere.

As a staunch teetotaller John Boaden did not quite approve of his paternal grandfather, who was 'addicted to drinking'. Born towards the end of the reign of George II, Edward Boaden had farmed Lower Treloskan, Trenoweth, and Trease, the last two holdings probably together since they lie adjoining each other on either side of the main Lizard road, whilst Lower Treloskan was just a mile away towards Helston and still nearer Millewarne. John hinted that as a farmer he was not entirely successful, through his partiality to liquor which

> 'caused him to neglect his business, and my father had to work hard to mind the business and the family had great difficulties so that father could scarcely get best clothes, grandfather sometime away in the public houses all night.'

Edward Boaden may have been improvident, and selfish in a thoughtless way, but

> 'he was a very loyal subject of King George the Third, and

7

an enthusiastic supporter of the War against France, being a newspaper reader; and the feats of our army and navy, doubtless well garnished, formed the great subject of pot-house conversation.'

It was characters like Edward Boaden, with all their shortcomings, that give the lie to the myth of narrow rural provincialism, of yokels whose sole topics of conversation in times of international catastrophe were limited to the weather, the crops, the ailments of cattle, occasionally a local death, now and again some 'maid' in trouble.

Ability to read was rare in those days, and Edward Boaden's reading was not confined to the small newsheets of the day, which only arrived in the Meneage once a week. His grandson went on

'He was a staunch churchman, and thought very hardly of those who differed from him on those important subjects, thinking them subjects for divine vengeance, but he had liberality enough to believe in the reality and power of the gospel as preached by the Methodists. I knew him a period of fourteen years. I never knew him to indulge but very moderately in drink. He was a smoker and sat for many an hour on the chimney bench smoking. He was also a great reader of the scriptures from the time I knew him, and he might be heard every night on retiring to his bed repeating several prayers.'

Edward Boaden belonged to that generation when the schism between Wesleyans and the Anglican Church had not become irremediable. He may have been a heavy drinker in his younger days, but the wisdom of moderation may have come with advancing years.

When John Boaden first knew his grandfather the latter was already over seventy years old but still hale and hearty, quite good-looking, and fairly active for he did little odd jobs about the farm such as trapping moles, pruning fruit trees and making skewers for the next pig-killing. His unregenerate days were now but a memory; death had taken most of those boon companions who, over their tankards, had fought and fought again and again the Nile and Copenhagen, Talavera and Waterloo with greater tactical and strategical genius than Nelson and Wellington had ever revealed. His Methodist son may have influenced him towards more temperate ways, but there was no longer a war to talk about in the tap-rooms nor so much money to spend since farm prices slumped after the long wars; advancing years made the walk to the tavern at Cross Lanes increasingly burdensome, and even in those days there were grumbles that neither ale nor spirits were so good as they once had been. So Edward Boaden grew more content to stay at home by the fireside telling his grandchildren yarns of his own early days, tales coloured by the glamour of long-past youth. He and his brothers had always been in the thick of the brawling when the feuds of Cury and Gunwalloe broke out, but he does not seem to have remembered a half-legendary battle by Trease when a wreck at the Lizard brought plungering rival hosts a-wrecking from Breage and St. Keverne, who came to blows over the loot, and one party fled leaving a corpse lying on the ground. He recalled that, since there was not enough work at home for him and his brothers at Millewarne, he had been apprenticed

'when a young man with Uncle Henry Caddy, a mutton butcher, at Toll in Gunwalloe, which furnished him with a field of enterprise and adventure in smuggling, which was congenial to his active daring spirit, and many of his advantures he would tell in his old years – he seemed to have spent much of his nights at this period in this way.'

If John Boaden recalled the tales of his grandfather he did not tell them again. True, it was his own life-story that he was writing and writing was not easy to him; his hands and fingers were gnarled and cramped with long years of heavy physical toil; he was nearly blind. Gunwalloe shore in the early years of the reign of George the Third must have been a smugglers' happy hunting ground. There was no harbour at Porthleven then, merely an open cove in which more than one vessel had been driven to destruction by south-westerly storms. Along the coast from the Loe Bar to Poldhu Cove were many inlets. The Customs men at Falmouth were a dozen miles away and much later than Edward Boaden's youthful days had no reputation for zealous efficiency; those at Penzance, about the same distance away, had their hands more than full with free-traders nearer home. Now and again an exciseman or two might venture down to Gunwalloe Shore, but if they went to the Fishing Cove the smugglers could run their goods in at Pork Bean, Halsferran, Church or Poldhu Coves, or even at the Loe Bar. From every one of these coves there were two or three tracks along which smuggled goods could be taken on pack-horse or donkey, or even on a man's back, to hiding-places inland. In case of crisis, ankers and kegs could be sunk and fished up when zealous officials were well away along the sea coast or in the Loe Pool or Carminowe Creek, or buried in the loose sands round Gunwalloe Church or at the Loe Bar. The laws of the realm and the servants of the crown did not restrict smugglers' activities. The hazards of the sea may have done to some slight degree for parts of the Lizard coast were graveyards of ships. What limited them most was the difficulty of finding markets for undutied wares, for in the late eighteenth century there were less than five thousand souls living in the dozen parishes south of the Helford which covered an area of nearly sixty square miles, while communications to the north save to the country market borough of Helston barely merited the name.[1]

Edward Boaden and his boon companions of youth probably broke the law less frequently than he suggested when yarning to his grandchildren, for an ageing man remembers the more sensational incidents of his youth most clearly, not the humdrum routine of the ordinary working days. It is a pity that John Boaden did not give the details of even one of those nights of illicit adventures and hazard, but he was telling his own life-story not that of a man dead and gone sixty years when he began to write.

He had little to say about his maternal grandmother, Elizabeth Lyne, who had lived at Tregoose in Mawgan before her marriage. Edward Boaden had not gone far for his bride; although in the next parish, Tregoose was about a mile from Millewarne with only two or three farms in between, one of which was Treloskan which was

---

[1] The twelve parishes of the Lizard peninsula, Landewednack, Ruan Minor, Ruan Major, Grade, St. Keverne, St. Anthony, Manaccan, St. Martin, Mawgan, Mullion, Cury and Gunwalloe, according to the Census of 1801 had an aggregate population of 5,076; their total area is 37,306 acres of rather more than 58 square miles. It is unlikely that the population was more han 4,000 when Edward Boaden went smuggling.

to be this newly wedded couple's first home. To marry a neigh-bour's daughter in those days was the rule rather than the exception; it was partly the result of the limited travelling of the people of the time, and it meant that the farmers of any rural district were often closely related by ties of blood or marriage. Such ties were all the more close and complex through families being generally larger than today; they probably strengthened the rural community, but there were times when a family squabble might lead to a bitter feud with practically everyone in the parish taking one side or the other.

In a few brief sentences John Boaden gave another glimpse of Meneage life in those early days of George the Third.

'I have often heard my grandmother tell of her tripping down Tregoose fields of a Sunday, how she enjoyed the services at (Mawgan) Church, especially the singing; the congregations were good. She also took part in the dancing and card parties of the period.'

He might have added that, although the congregations were good, the Rector was, more often than not an absentee, leaving an underpaid curate to care not only for Mawgan but also the adjoining parish of St. Martin.[1] The dancing and card parties can only have been held for the most part in the homes of the farmers themselves; neighbours, relatives, and friends would drop in to 'make a night of it'; inevitably hospitable refreshments would be provided, possibly of a type later temperance extremists would condemn. Cards were not in Elizabeth Lyne's youth the devil's prayer book, nor was dancing thought the easiest way down the path to perdition.

John Boaden's maternal grandfather, John Willer, was more like

---

[1] In his return to Bishop Ross in 1779, the Rector of Mawgan, Cox, stated that he had been instituted to the joint livings of Mawgan and St. Martin in 1753, and that 'My health not permitting me to reside on my living, I have for these many years lived at Crewkerne in Somerset. I have a Curate John Farnham at £50 (per annum).' He estimated the population of Mawgan as 85 families, and stated that 30 participated at Communion which was celebrated four times a year; at St. Martin there were 74 families and 20 communicants.

11

the conventional pattern of Victorian respectability. He also lived nearby at Burnoon, which was later to be the home of John's brother, adjoining Skyburriowe and only a few fields away from Trease. He was a man of property, for he,

'A very sober, industrious, frugal man . . . acquired the leasehold of Polkernan in St. Keverne with the great tithes of the same which is now my brother William's; he also had the leasehold of a part of Burnoon; there were three dwelling houses there at that time. He also purchased two blocks of dwelling houses in Meneage Street, Helston, freehold, one of which is now mine.'

Thus by sober industry, thrift, and careful investments in real property were the private fortunes of a family built up; had he had more capital and, perhaps, one or two lucky windfalls, John Willer might have founded a new county family. He may have been most astute in purchasing town property, but it was significant that in his time John Willer could only buy leasehold interests in farm property – the older landed gentry were not so ready in those times to part with their broader acres save in times of acute family financial troubles. Even when land came into the market a tenant farmer had little hope of buying owing to the keen competition of other squires or that of men who in West Cornwall had made fortunes in mining enterprises. Land was to change hands in St. Keverne but the greatest purchasers were to be the Williams family whose fortunes had already, in John Willer's time, been made in the mines near Redruth. It might, too, be doubted whether the leasehold of Little Burnoon proved a remunerative investment. The three dwelling houses to which John Boaden referred, have vanished leaving scarcely a trace behind; long before 1900 land, which a century before had maintained four families supported but one. John Boaden's laconic sentences suggested that here was an instance of rural decline and depopulation. Census returns show that in Mawgan, a predominantly agricultural parish, the population fell from a maximum of 1,094 in 1831 to 713 in 1901, and probably depopulation was greatest on the poorer lands fringing Goonhilly Downs where Little Burnoon stood. The picture of decay suggested by the disappearance of houses and by census returns however is not so tragic as might be thought. The

12

vanished dwellings were probably small cottages, built in cob and mud and thatched with heather rather than with good wheat reed. Those that lived in them can only have grubbed a miserable living from poor and small fields reclaimed with infinite labour from the sterile downlands. Merged into a single holding they may have made a moderately good farm. Small-holders gained little if anything from the great agricultural improvements of the nineteenth century, whilst frequently, in the Meneage and elsewhere, a set-back to the cottager caused by a poor harvest, or the loss of a horse, a cow, or even a pig left him and his family facing penury, even near starvation and ready to quit. On the other side the more substantial farmers for the greater part of this century wanted more land on which to grow large crops because they felt that was the only way they could counter a progressive decline in prices, aggravated at times by economic depressions; larger farms, too, were generally more economical in labour – either hired or that of a farmer's own family. Furthermore, landowners fostered the merging of the smallholdings into larger farms, since it was easier to deal with a few large tenants, whilst the cottagers were a disturbing element in the social community. Their holdings were not really large enough to keep them fully occupied; in bad times they were only too ready to flout the Game Laws or apply for poor relief. Farmers who also contributed heavily, and with prolonged complaints, to the poor rates for that very reason were glad to see them go. When a cottage leasehold expired a landowner could easily refuse its renewal; sometimes it was possible to get cottagers to surrender a lease that still had long to run by giving them enough money to migrate elsewhere; reports of the opportunities of the growing industrial towns, of prospects in the colonies, and even of boom times in the mines of their own county made some cottagers eager to depart.

If the cottager went away, however, his fields remained. In places they reverted back to downland; generally, however, they were merged into larger and more economical, though not necessarily more productive farms. We do not know if John Willer hastened the departure of the little Burnoon cottagers, but probably the amalgamation of three or four small holdings more than doubled the rental value of the little estate in his grandson's lifetime.

John Boaden hardly mentioned others among his forebears and

more distant relatives. Of one namesake, a second cousin, John Boaden slightingly remarked that he was 'overcome by his besetting sin, of vain glory in the use of his own tongue', and that he went under the nickname of 'Lawyer Boaden'.[1] Another relative, a great uncle of the writer, was an innkeeper; on his career teetotal John Boaden was silent.

There was a more tragic element of weakness on the maternal side of John Boaden's family. John Willer's wife, whom he had married in 1802, had been born Joan Mayne, and

> 'she was of Chygarkey family, where her brother Richard resided. He was blind for some years before his death. He had a family of four sons and three daughters. One of the sons and two daughters were idiots, and another son, John, a gardener, became insane and died in the Bodmin asylum where he had been confined for many years. He had a sister that married a gardener Ceats of Helston, the mother of Joseph and John Ceats. The latter married his cousin Johanna Mayne (Richard's daughter); they had two daughters that grew up, who had weak constitutions and weak minds. I have taken charge of them for the last ten years to save them from want and ruin.'

A painstaking genealogist might trace some connection between the Ceats of Helston and the poet John Keats. The social historian, is however, more likely to be struck by this marked case of congenital mental deficiency. Such tragedies might easily be ascribed to close intermarriages which were inevitable in rural communities whose members rarely went far beyond the boundaries of the parish in which they had been born. Whilst Richard Mayne had no obvious blood relationship with the Boadens, his blindness, like that which afflicted John Boaden himself in his later years, may have been congenital cataract. Rural intermarriage certainly increased the risk of inherited mental and physical disabilities; whilst there were instances in which it led to the transmission to later generations of qualities of strength; there may well, however, have been a tendency to the weaker to come together far more often than the strong.

[1] See p. 18 below

The descriptions John Boaden gave of his own parents were rather brief, and, indeed they said more about religious life in the early nineteenth century than they did about family history. His father, whose name he bore, had been born on January 3, 1796, at Treloskan. He was a good Methodist, though perhaps rather a dull one, for

'he was a very steady, industrious, and well balanced man. Prudent, cautious, and methodical, he very early joined the Methodist society which had not long been established in this district. They first preached in Cury at a Carpenter's shop at Cury Cross Lanes (Jimmy Dale's shop) situate at the left hand corner as you turn up Bonython Lane. Father remained a consistent member of the Society till death. At the time he joined, I should think about 1814, this district was included and formed part of the Hayle Circuit,[1] but for many years after this no Methodist service was held in Church service hours, and all Methodists and their families went to Church. I think this was not the case near towns where the population was greater. Members attended the classes with great regularity; to be absent two weeks in succession would demand a visit from the leader; the little preaching places of a week-night preaching service would be crammed full.'

The old carpenter's shop is still at Cury Cross Lanes, with nothing to show that it once was a chapel. A time came when, blessed with worldy prosperity, Cury Methodists built a new chapel nearer the Churchtown, a building as plain as the old tradesman's shop although ostentatiously rather than naturally austere.

John Boaden's mother, Mary Willer, was some eight years younger than her husband, and did not join the Methodists until converted in the 'Great Revival' of 1838-39, nearly a dozen years after her marriage. Still, before this time and always

'her natural disposition was so even, kind, patient and mild, that the change made scarcely any preceptable change in her

---

[1] A slip by John Boaden; the Helston Circuit had been formed in 1799 and that of Hayle cut from it and other surrounding circuits in 1819.

outward conduct. She took great interest in the affairs of the Society. When a young woman she frequently attended Sabbath afternoon services then held by the Bible Christians at Gaiglon Green; there was often a good congregation and a Society existed for some time, but all – even the village of three dwelling houses – have passed away.'[1]

Before she married in 1827, Mary Willer had kept a school at Trevassack,[2] having acquired a good knowledge of arithmetic, English grammar, and a smattering of algebra from a school in Helston and from the Cury schoolmaster, Gundry. She told her son that she and her younger sister had been taken into Helston, when they attended the school there, every Monday morning 'on a slide', showing that the daughters of tenant farmers were given quite a considerable education in the early nineteenth century, and also the primitive transport of that time in the Meneage. If John Willer had had but one daughter to send to school she, most likely would have been taken by him or by a servant riding pillion on horseback; there were, however, two of them, so the horse was harnessed to the slide, or sledge, which was used to carry fodder and other things around the farm, and dragged into Helston on its iron runners. If the road to the outskirts of the town from the Mawgan farmstead were only a grassy track such a mode of transport may not have been very uncomfortable; possibly the parish way-wardens were not over-energetic and rarely, if ever, called upon their fellow parishioners to strew the trackways, or the rutted sections, with stone. On the other hand, part of the road must have been used fairly often by the Vyvyans of Trelowarren and their household. Furthermore even a grassy or earthen track might be transformed by the hooves of animals into a series of pot-holes, and the conditions when hard frost turned up lumps of mud iron-hard are painful even to imagine. Doubtless the Willer girls lodged in Helston, during the week, and walked

[1]This is further evidence of rural depopulation; even the name Gaiglon Green has vanished from the map unless it can be identified with the farmstead of Gilly Gabben on the road from Mawgan to Helston
[2]The presence of a school, even a small one, at Trevassack seems surprising today, but it emphasises the declining population on the fringes of Goonhilly Downs.

home on Friday evening or Saturday. It was getting education a hard, certainly uncomfortable way, but they may have valued it the more for that.

John Boaden, however, thought his mother knew little of farm work before her marriage, but she then

'became as good a wife as ever a farmer had; she had great strength which she freely used together with great activity; she always kept a servant, but if from any cause the servant was away for a time, the work would be done all the same. She would do anything that a small farmer required, learned to winnow the corn, and for some years in the season sold potatoes out of the cart by the weighed gallon on Saturdays in Meneage Street, Helston.'

Physically she was well built and rather above the average height. A hard-working and true helpmeet to her husband, Mary Boaden lived in her son's memory as a woman who was always up and doing; her days were long and full; she milked the cows, fed the calves and pigs, and made the butter, now and again she would have all the housework to do as well for her husband would not hesitate to call upon the female 'help' to go out and work in the fields, to pick stones, to weed and hoe the crops, to help in haymaking, and to gather potatoes. The lot of a farm-wife or of a female servant on a farm was no more a sinecure in those days than was the work of a female factory hand or one employed about surface work in the mines; nor were their hours much shorter than those of the women in the industrial towns. In summer sunset came long hours after dawn; on long winter evenings there was much work that had to be done although Mary Boaden then found time to knit quilts besides the normal darning and sewing. Moreover she, in her son's gravely sedate phrase, 'did not neglect the moral and religious education of her children'.

Still, Mary Boaden had some help. Her mother and mother-in-law were both living at Trease in John Boaden's boyhood; besides the female servant, Susanna Willey. Grandfather Boaden was there, too, lending a hand if need be and keeping the children out of mischief with his tales of smugglers. The only other member of the household was the servant man, James Williams; judging from his nickname 'Old Jim' he, too, was getting on in years. With three old people, an elderly servant, three persons in their prime, and two young sons, Mary Boaden's life can have been no easy one.

Yet compared with her sister Jane, Mary was fortunate. The younger daughter of John Willer married another John Boaden, her brother- in-law's first cousin, the man to whom our John Boaden had already made a brief but slighting reference.[1] At the time of his marriage this black sheep of the family was still living at the older family holding of Millewarn, and was

'rather a remarkable man . . . gifted with great power and vigour of speech which he very freely used and woe to the man who was his opponent; if there was any personal spleen, he would soon overmatch an ordinary man.'

It was not surprising that he did not get on at all well with his landlord; they quarrelled, and 'Lawyer' Boaden had to look for another farm in 1838. It was not a good time to find another place in Cury parish, where the mining magnate 'Captain Joe' Lyle was buying every farm that came on to the market, and other landowners did not want such an awkward tenant. However, Lawyer Boaden found a vacant farm at Trenessin in Veryan quite a distance away, but it was 'excessively dear'. He made a bad bargain, for with all his bluster Lawyer Boaden was not a very astute man. Competition for land in Cornwall was keen; whenever a farm fell vacant a dozen or a score of men would be after it, tendering higher offers of rent to the landowners than were economic, and often more than they could afford. In fertile Veryan the competition for land was cut-throat indeed, and Trenessin's new tenant came on the ever of the 'Hungry Forties'.

Those were times that tried men sorely. Distress was, of course, greatest in the new industrial towns, but if townspeople were complaining bitterly of the cost of bread, farmers had suffered a succession of bad seasons which left them with little grain to sell and crops of potatoes that were too bad even to be fed to their pigs. The repeal of the Corn Laws may have alleviated the lot of the townfolk fairly quickly, but the harvest of 1846 was calamitously bad, and those that followed but little better. The better

[1] Above page 14.

Meneage Landscape – Croft, Heath and Sky

Smuggler's Coast near Cury

farmers and those who had wisely put a little by against the proverbial and inevitable rainy day struggled through. Lawyer Boaden was not of their number. Now and again he would visit his relatives in the Meneage, generally to try to borrow money; it came as little surprise when he was, late in 1849, 'seized for rent'.

John Boaden's sympathies were all for his Aunt Jane who had a hard and difficult life. She

'rarely if ever left the dwelling, and was constantly working.'

and after this failure worse was in store for her, for

'the family consisting of the parents and four sons, the eldest approaching manhood, who had not been afforded by their father scarcely any education and but little Sunday clothes, left as free emigrants for South Australia, where they arrived about the middle of 1850. My uncle, being a smart man of good abilities if he would only mind his business, was not long in his new home before he got a prosperous road contract on a large scale, in which his sons greatly assisted. This continued for some time, but his evil genius followed him; he disregarded and insulted the colonial officials; he lost the contracts and had to sell his plant and go to Victoria.'

The family broke up; the three eldest sons, John Willer, Nicholas and Alfred went off to New Zealand; the youngest son, James, remained with his parents and more or less supported them by working as a carrier. Carrying had been the most prosperous business in Victoria in the boom days of the gold diggings at Ballarat and Bendigo, but the Boadens had arrived there rather too late to make their fortunes.

This branch of the Boaden family were typical of many farmers who left Cornwall at that time to seek better fortune in the Colonies. John Boaden knew little of their careers in the Antipodes, save that his namesake had died in 1867. They sometimes wrote to their connections and friends in the old country.

'but in consequence of my father's refusal to lend my uncle money as he wanted, he and his family became estranged from my parents and did not communicate with them after emigrating, but Uncle John wrote me twice very cordial messages and sent messages to me through my sweetheart. He was in many respects a fine fellow, could dissect other people's characters, and show very clearly how and why they failed. He was a most interesting controversialist, but failed to know his own weakness and overcome by his besetting sins, of vain glory in the use of his own tongue. I scarcely know when I saw him last. It was a great treat to me to listen to him when he came down.'

John Boaden went on to mention two visits he had paid to Trenessin, once in the spring of 1840, when he found the Cury schoolmaster there engaged in 'setting a sundial' – surely a luxury in a farmstead – and in the fall of 1846, when

'I was sorry to see the plight my cousins were in all steadily working, and my Aunt, quite the reverse to my Uncle, always home working. For some years after the family went to Veryan they came down (home), the children with my Aunt, on Mawgan Feast eve, and stayed at Hugh Lyne's, Tregoose, and at Trease for some days. The last time I saw my Aunt was when she and her eldest son came down in 1849 in a van with the body of her dear little girl, Mary, which Mary was buried in Cury. They stayed overnight and left to see this neighbourhood no more.'

In later years John attempted in vain to find out how his aunt spent her last days after Lawyer Boaden's death.

Jane Boaden's story is one of quiet rural tragedy. Given an unusually good education for those days she had learnt the trade of dressmaking before Lawyer Boaden's beguiling tongue won the heart of a girl barely out of her teens. Times grew worse, and Jane must have realised that her husband was not doing all he could to stave off disaster but she stood loyally by him. First, they were forced to leave Meneage for Veryan; now and again she was able to visit her old friends and familiar childhood surroundings. Then she and her family had to make the bitter choice between emigrating to the other side of the world to attempt a fresh start in life, when she was getting on into middle age, or sinking down into the uncomfortable lot of farm labourers. They chose to emigrate, to risk the unknown. Possibly Lawyer Boaden made the choice and boasted while making it that they would make good in the Antipodes; the change seems to have benefitted the parents little if at all, possibly because, in Australia as in England, Lawyer Boaden was fonder of talk than of work and never could control his unruly tongue.

In Australia and in the old country at that time agitators might command prominence, even notoriety but rarely success. That was the reward of those who, whatever they may have thought of matters made the most they could of them and got on with their daily tasks as did Lawyer Boaden's less voluble but more fortunate relations. As he wrote of his relations John Boaden probably thought of the Scriptural contrast – the luckless man who kicked against the pricks and the man who made the utmost use of his talents. True, there was also the Prodigal Son, but however popular he was in the pulpits of nonconformity he was never a welcome member in the daily life of any respectable Victorian family.

3

The Daily Round

John Boaden did not remember all that went on in his youth; other features of those days he seems to have deliberately omitted from his reminiscences, partly because his religious faith convinced him that there was a goal to life greater than life itself; still he did recall some aspects of farming life at Trease in the eighteen thirties.

The decade of the Great Reform Bill and of early Chartism has been inadequately described by social historians. Some writers stressing parliamentary Reform have implied that the Act of 1832 transferred political power from rural landowning to urban commercial and manufacturing classes. Others dwelling at length on social conditions in the new industrial towns have barely mentioned that English agriculture still, and for years to come, employed a greater number of workers than any other industry. Writers on religious history, too, have neglected developments in rural areas in their preoccupation with the progress religion made in towns or in overseas mission fields.

A keen national interest in agriculture seemed to die when the long reign of 'Farmer George' ended in 1820, the year which also saw the passing of the most famous rural publicist, Arthur Young. Six years earlier the long and bitter Napoleonic seige had ended; the bad English harvest of 1817 had proved that the country's increasing urban masses could be fed by foriegn supplies of grain at quite reasonable prices if politicians refrained from interfering with economic laws at the behest of a small landowning caste whom too many regarded as the entire rural community. William Cobbett, the other great apostle of rural life, was already a spent force, before he was elected to the reformed Parliament as the representative of a Lancashire industrial town. Another decade passed before John Joseph Machi began publishing his ideas about applying the techniques of the new industrial age to farming, although back in 1812 the Cornish engineer, Richard Trevithick, had declared that every farm operation could be performed by steam power. A few farmers were aware of the notions Humphry Davy had published on the application of chemistry to agriculture, but the work of Liebig and Lawes did not begin until the 'thirties. Of lighter books with a 'rural' setting there were many, but it was a countryside at play rather than at work, the Dingley Dell of Pickwick and the, later, Handley Cross of Jorrocks. Neither Thomas Hardy nor Richard Jefferies had yet been born. What John Boaden remembered of farming life in this period, realistic and mundane, can, therefore, be regarded as of value by those who wish to find a detailed picture of the daily existence of the great number of English-folk who still relied on the land for their livelihood. Some farmers fared better than the Boaden family, but many fared worse; if a few wealthy tenant farmers lived 'on the fat of the land', there was a host of smaller men living far from sumptuously. As for the labourers they sometimes employed, they had to endure a lot which today would be regarded as downright privation and near starvation.

John Boaden's account shows the monotonous life and diet with which those who lived in remote rural districts had to be content in the eighteen-thirties. Railways were as yet novelties; sails not steam still spanned the seas; farmers living four or five miles from market towns knew few luxuries and, in the main, lived on produce they themselves raised. More than half a century was to pass before barbed-wire and sheets of galvanised iron were to transform the appearance of English fields and rick-yards, or before the farmers' wives of England began to lay on their tables loaves made of American flour, cheeses from Holland, butter and fruit from 'down-under', bacon and pork from Copenhagen and Chicago, beef and mutton from the pampas of the Argentine and the plains of New Zealand. Life and living was but little varied, at times almost unendurably monotonous, although the craving for change may not have been so acute in those times.

At least there was a sense of security in those boyhood days of John Boaden, when

'Things went on with the greatest regularity and order in the household. We arose at 5 o'clock a.m. in summer and 6 in winter; breakfast was about 7.30 so a tolerable lot of work was done before breakfast; dinner (was) at noon just before which (was) the calling of the people from the fields by the different servant girls (for) very few people had watches in those days making the calling necessary. They generally knew before they came in what the bill of fare would be, and it was the same almost in all well-regulated farmhouses in the district. On Saturdays and Mondays it would be fish and potatoes; (on) two days (it would be) potato pie, with a rind or crust around it and with a piece of salt pork washed on top. On Sundays there would be a piece of fresh meat instead. Another day it would be broth with apple dumplings in season, and hard dumplings otherwise; this with either salt or dried pork formed another day's dinner. Friday was a sort of odd day about which there was some uncertainty; sometimes (we had) peas, at other times fry; when a pig was killed it would be the pig's fry. I should say that after the pork and potatoes there would be tea, and sometimes a piece of apple pie, or a slice of white bread and butter. For breakfast and supper, as the evening meal was called, there was invariably milk and bread with mornal[1] after; the bread used for both meals was barley bread, except on Sunday evenings when it would be either white bread or cake.'

The bread, whether of barley or wheaten flour, was all made at home in the farmhouses, baked under a flat iron or *rotile*, to give it its local name, at the back of the immense open hearths; the oven-range, known in the Meneage and most other districts of Cornwall as the *slab*, was unknown in the cottages and most of the farmhouses at the times Boaden was describing. Still this primitive method of baking produced a loaf which did not quickly

---

[1]This local term seems to be absolutely obsolete and its meaning forgotten at the present time in Cornwall. Whilst it is possible that it may be a form of porridge or even mackerel, it seems more likely that it was some beverage, possibly milk and water, perhaps buttermilk, or a liquid made from oat or barley meal. It certainly was nothing very costly or sumptuous.

become dry and stale, and barley bread in John Boaden's opinion tasted 'very sweet'. The barley field and the orchard, a cow or two, and a few pigs made the farm practically self sufficient, although a local butcher supplied Trease and other farms roundabout with a Sunday joint. The food might have lacked variety, and there was only one really 'substantial' meal a day; since such fare was apparently common throughout farming England, however, doubts creep in whether or not the proverbial 'roast beef of Old England' was something of a myth.

The farmhouse was plainly but practically furnished. When he was writing his memoirs, John Boaden was living in a comparatively new house, furnished with the excessive trappings in which the late Victorians took such pride. But in Trease and the other farmhouses nearly seventy years before

'The furniture was, compared with (that of) the present (day) of the very plainest description. The parlour had an uncovered lime- ash floor; (there was) a table in the centre, of mahogany (sic) in our case; a bureau so called in our case with desk on top and chest of drawers below; a few plain chairs; a table beside; a few very primitive ornaments on (the) mantelpiece, but more commonly cups and saucers. The few books would be found in this room; always the Bible, with the births and deaths of the family recorded in the fly-leaf, amongst the others would be the *Pilgrim's Progress*, Baxter's *Saint's Rest*, Doddridges' *Rise and Progress*, a few Methodist Magazines, the Prayer Book, the Methodist Hymn Book; and the periodical period could scarcely be said to have begun.[1] '(There was) a plain old iron-bound grate, (in which the) fire (was), perhaps, not lit more than two or three times

---

[1] The Evangelical Revival, now profoundly affecting the Church of England as well as the development of Wesleyan Methodism, seems between 1810 and 1830 to have led to several new editions and abridgements of Richard Baxter's *The Saints Everlasting Rest*, first published in 1650, and of Philip Doddridge's *On the Rise and Progress of Religion in the Soul*, first published in 1745; neither, of course, were Anglicans, but it is hard to account for their writings being so popular among the Wesleyans whose Arminian beliefs were very different to the Calvinist doctrines of earlier dissenters.

a year on the average; no fender nor fire irons; (on the walls were) a few very plain pictures, generally scripture subjects.'

Such was the parlour, the best room of the farmhouses. The Boadens did not use their's much, though, perhaps a little more often than those who only opened the parlour door for a family funeral, christenings, or wedding. The books may have been typical of Methodist piety, but not until Victoria had been some years on the throne did novels oust theological and devotional works as 'best sellers'. It is rather strange that Boaden mentioned the works of Bunyan and Richard Baxter but none of the writing of John Wesley; another somewhat strange omission in a farmhouse was that of manuals of farming and farriery.

John Boaden's description of other rooms in the farmhouse was less detailed. It is rather surprising that he wrote a generalised description of the farmhouses of his boyhood days rather than a particular picture of Trease. His dismissed the kitchen, in which the greater part of the indoor waking life of the family was spent as containing a table, a bench, two or three chairs, and an open fireplace with a bench by its side; he also mentioned that in many kitchen chimney-places there was a brick-oven set in the wall, but that at Trease was no longer being used. The dairy also served as a larder, and 'contained the dairy utensils', by which he meant a few earthenware bowls; cream separators and aluminium pans had hardly appeared in farm-dairies by the time he himself retired from farming. There was an eight-day clock on the stairway, and a burnished warming-pan which even then was kept more as an ornament than for use. Neither upstairs nor down was there much in the way of carpets, whilst:

'The iron bedstead was unknown here; they were all wooden (and) many of the four-poster class. As washing upstairs was never thought of, there was a total absence of wash-stands; but the beds were often well-trimmed and the tyes well filled with home-grown goose feathers.'

Home-grown goose feathers! What a hint of comfort is there in that phrase and what pride in the amenities the farm itself produced! Yet one is left wondering where they washed – and how often: probably an earthenware bowl in the kitchen, or a wooden tub or even a granite trough outside the house were the only 'mod-cons' of those days.

A true child of Victorian prudery, John Boaden refrained from any mention of certain other necessary sanitary arrangements and devices which, perhaps, have gained undue prominence in the writings of many later authors. It must have been 'outdoor sanitation', and if somewhat odorous in high summer they made do with it; ordinary tenant farmer's, to say nothing of the humbler cottage folk they employed, had neither the resources nor the amenities of the 'landed gentry' who, before this, had been installing water closets in their mansions.

Food and goose-feather beds did not exhaust the products raised on the Meneage holdings by the farmers for their use and comfort. Perhaps it was just as well that, in those days, families were large and labour cheap for, as Boaden wrote:

'As almost the sole fuel was furze and turf, there would be daily made a quantity of ashes. Raking up the fire would be the last work before going to bed; it consisted in getting all the embers of fire together and covering them over with ashes. Around the fire in the winter season the farmer and family warmed themselves before going to bed, after tending the horses and cattle as they invariably did at eight o'clock. Servants were expected to be home to do this at that hour. The cattle had hay or straw and (were) bedded down for the night.'

He might have written more. There was no electric light in those days, nor flash-lamps to go the rounds of the shippens and stables; for that matter, not even paraffin-burning hurricane lanterns. At best there was only the flickering light of a tallow-dip rushlight candle in a glass jar, at worst – and that more generally – 'feel and fumble around in the dark', with some nights a moon to help a little in stumbling with bundles of hay and straw from rick and barn to linhay and byre. Stormy nights were worst of all, with rain and hail whipping down and winds dashing through the alley ways between ricks and outbuildings like a mill-race. When all was done they were more than glad to come in and dry and warm themselves before the roaring open fire. Getting back by eight was no real hardship on most winter nights; the towns were far off in those times; three or four miles afoot or even on horseback along rough, narrow lanes on a pitch-black night was not worth while to visit a town which usually had few attractions to offer except the taverns. In a practically teetotal household like that of the Boadens servants inclined to frequent inns were hardly likely to find employment. Now and again in a few towns theatrical players sometimes put on a performance. Balls were the recreation of the higher social classes, whilst popular dances were not indoor winter but out-of-door summertime festivities. Lovelorn ones might have had to cut their courting short, to get back in time, but for the rest the only regular 'recreation' was the chapel service, and that, normally, would be over well in time for the farmers and their servants to get back and get the evening work done.

With little to amuse them, and lighting too poor for reading or games of cards, they went to bed early. At any rate they had to be up betimes in the morning, but one thing most of them were spared – a long trudging journey to work. As it was

'The first work of the servant girl in the mornings was to get the barrow in to wheel out the ashes to the ashes pile which amounted to several loads in the year, (and) then to milking. The milk, of course was all scalded on the brandis,[1] and soon after eight she would be ready to go to the fields to work. The wages for a good woman servant was about four pounds yearly. There was no carpet-beating or mat-shaking to be done as farm houses had scarcely any of either. To bring in the fuel, furze and turf there being scarcely any other, and to use them was an item in their work.'

Furze and turf were generally stacked in ricks near to the farmhouses, but women servants were rarely called upon to do the arduous work of cutting and faggotting furze and peat cutting. Furze could be cut at any time, but peat could only be cut after

---

[1]The brandis was a three-legged triangular iron-rack, about a foot or slightly less in height, and its sides perhaps twelve or fourteen inches, which was placed over the open-fire and the pans of milk brought to a temperature just below boiling point on it; it was also used for boiling food in a saucepan, frying and other purposes.

the normally dry weeks of May and early June, just when the early fields of meadow hay were ready for mowing. Even if the women were rarely ordered to go out to the 'pits' on the moors to cut peat, they usually had the task of going out to turn and turn again the rectangular turves laid out to dry on the banks of the swampy peat bogs before it was brought into the farmyards for stacking. Uncertain weather, the rule rather than the exception in Cornwall, meant that every available hand would be employed out of doors when the midsummer sun was shining, and only two or three farming operations seem to have then been regarded as exclusively man's work – ploughing, mowing and sheep-shearing.

Describing the barrenness of the farmhouses of his boyhood, John Boaden wrote that only in the houses of the gentry, was wallpaper known in ordinary farm dwellings and cottages every room, from parlour to cellar, was merely given an occasional coating of lime-wash, perhaps rather more frequently and more carefully than the stables and shippens were 'white-washed'. Often the same wash was applied to the outside walls of the houses.

Inside the houses, hanging from the rafters and ceilings, were bunches of dried herbs for use in times of sickness. Advertisement columns in local papers show that many varieties of patent medicines were already in the market, but blind faith in their efficacy among the 'lower' classes only came apparently when general compulsory elementary education enabled most people to read the preposterous claims made in advertisements. Till then time honoured, sometimes over-honoured, herbal remedies held sway among the afflicted; if they failed to cure the phantom of pagan belief might declare itself in an avowal that a particular herb had not been gathered when the moon was increasing to the full; in other cases there appeared deeply-rooted rural fatalism with the afflicted or bereaved talking of a 'visitation'; whilst many still believed in witchcraft and ill-wishing.

The changes occuring during his life came vividly to John Boaden as he wrote. More bees were kept in his boyhood days, and:

'the honey was brought out to the sick or as an article of luxury as there were scarcely any jams, neither was there cake kept in the house. Apple pies in season were common, and when a visitor was expected a heavy cake was baked under the baker[1]. The consumptions of sugar was very little, (with) brown (sugar costing) about sixpence per pound, and Wathigla tea sparingly used. The old tinder box, with flint and steel, and brimstone matches stood in the place of the modern lucifer match, (and) the country was traversed by match sellers in all directions. There were also a large number of beggars, frequently representing that they were ship-wrecked sailors, generally with fluent tongues.'

Yet it seems unlikely that these wandering hawkers and beggars were always unwelcome on the lonely farms. The coming of a stranger was an event, and if he sometimes spun too glib a tale it broke the monotony of daily life. Some vagrants, too, were genuine shipwrecked mariners, for a dozen ships usually came to grief every year on the Cornish coast. As for the hawkers, they varied their wares with changing fashions, devices, and needs, but it is interesting that in the eighteen-thirties one of their principal stocks in trade was matches.[2] Many other items were brought around by hawkers in those times, and probably the 'Johnny Fortnights' visited the lonely farmhouses just as they did the hamlets of miners' cottages, selling goods that were or were not urgently needed, beguiling womenfolk into buying shoddy articles that they could ill afford by their over-plausible tales – and, sometimes, by half-veiled threats. Cheap and increasingly fast transport to the towns, coinciding with the rise of the chain stores, swept these picturesque, intriguing and sometimes rascally characters into oblivion. They were, however, still wandering about the countryside when John Boaden wrote, so he did not describe them more fully. In boyhood he must have met many of them, whilst in later life as a poor Law Guardian he came into

[1]i.e. 'Under the hob.'
[2]The value of matches in those days is amusingly shown by the anecdote told by a Cornish Australian in 1889. He had left St. Agnes in 1856 after selling his goods and chattels. At the end of the sale:
> 'there was a box of matches, and we said in a careless way, 'Oh let them go', but an old lady friend of ours, said, 'Oh, chiel take them, for thee's might never get another box out there.'
(*West Briton*, 9 May, 1889.)

contact with the many hawkers who used the Union Workhouses as their 'Commercial Hotels'. Sentimentalists sometimes now look upon the passing of these rugged and generally extremely ragged individualists with regret.

A respectable Victorian tenant farmer saw them in a very different light. John Boaden dismissed them in a few lines. Then, feeling perhaps that he had depicted a rather monotonous and even somewhat sombre way of life he sententiously closed this section of his narrative with words that seem to echo from a nonconformist pulpit:

'I have no reason to complain but much to be thankful for that a kind providence with such an environment surrounding me, endowed with healthy body and mind, and placed in a favourable position to grow up a healthy, industrious, thrifty, intelligent, religious person, and consequently useful and happy man. Of course, the training and example of my parents largely contributed to help me in that direction.'

4

The World Was Young and Not So Gay

A man over seventy could hardly be expected to recall events of his early days clearly or in chronological order, and Boaden's memoirs mentioned happenings which he could only have heard from others, for he wrote at some length of events occurring in 1832, whcn he was hardly four years old, besides repeating some of the favourite tales of his elders.

In the Meneage, as in Hardy's Wessex, the memory of the war against Napoleon was often recalled. Mischievous youngsters were warned by their elders that 'Boney' would get them if they did not behave themselves. John's uncle, Edward Boaden, was often reminded that when he was a child

'during the great French War, when fear of invasions and its rumour terrified the people, news came to Trease either in earnest or in frolic that the French had landed. The boy ran down to the bottom of the orchard and bolted over the hedge, was caught in falling in the highway and suspended by his legs over a catchpool which I well remember by the side of the hedge just above the present shoot (water chute) above Trease field, his head downwards in danger of falling in; he was quickly released.'

This trivial affair, and its memory, shows how the ambitions of Bonaparte affected the lives of all who lived near the shores threatened with invasion, whilst veterans of Nelson's navies and Wellington's armies talked to their dying days of the Nile and Badajoz, of Copenhagen and Waterloo.

Another story John Boaden must have heard many times was that of the murder of Hancock, a Mullion farmer, about a mile from Trease by the young Goonhilly desperadoes, John Barnicott and the Thompson brothers, in 1820. The tale usually ended with someone remarking that 'Old Mall', the mother of one of the men hanged for the crime was a witch.

In those days a murder was something more than a seven-day wonder in the press. Only two papers, weeklies, then circulated through Cornwall, four-paged sheets costing sevenpence a copy, a sum beyond the means of labouring classes whilst even farmers combined in subscribing to them, each reading the papers in turn and then passing them on. With many people hardly able to read or illiterate and with the sheer physical discomfort of reading blurred type by candle-light after a hard day's work, newspapers were not very important in social life, while any man who could tell a story was welcomed to the hearthside on winter nights or the barns or outbuildings where men were waiting for the rain to stop to get on with ploughing or harvesting. And the tale of Hancock's murder was not merely sensational but the people involved were well known in Cury, one of them, Hugh Johns, who had helped apprehend the murderers being a relative of the Boadens.

It was a tale of highway robbery and violence. The victim was a humble farmer returning home from Helston market late on a summer night; the criminals were young ne'er-do-wells who lived in hovel-like cottages in the heart of Goonhyilly Downs. All John Boaden wrote, besides the reference to 'Old Mall's' suspected relations with the powers of darkness, was that:

'Thompson lived at the Dry Tree, and Barnicott at a cottage not far off; I think it is still standing; the Dry Tree cottage has been down many years, but I can remember it occupied.'

thus hinting that the very dwellings of the ungodly shall vanish. As Hugh Johns, who was one of the main witnesses at the Assizes trial, began the story young John Boaden hung on his words, saw again the tragic events which had happened barely half a mile from his home some years before he had been born. He knew Bray's Corner where on the night of August 12, 1820, three or four robbers leapt out of the deeper shadows and called on William Hancock, quietly jogging home from Helston market on his old grey horse, to stand and deliver. Hancock spurred his horse, but one of the robbers leapt at its head, grabbing at the reins; the horse reared, plunged down on the man's foot, and he stumbled back, shots rang out, and Hancock fell from his saddle. His assailants leapt on him, kicked and beat him as he lay on the road, robbed him of a few coins and a new hat he had bought that day, and then vanished quickly into the darkness.

A little later the silence of the starlit night was broken by the cloppetting hoof-beats of two horses, one ridden by William Jose, another Mullion farmer, the second by his wife. Before they rounded the corner the scene of violence was repeated – dark figures leaping out into the roadway, cries and shouts, frightened horses rearing and plunging, one or two musket shots, the thundering hooves of the horses as they galloped away into the night with their riders somehow keeping in their saddles.

The shots alarmed the district; although the road was lonely there were half a dozen isolated farms within a half-mile, and others were about that night who found Hancock lying in the road, and carried him to the inn at Cury Cross Lanes.

Suspicion immediately fell on John Barnicott, the three Thompson brothers, and on a fifth youth, William Daw. Early the next morning Hugh Johns and some others had gone to the cottages of the Barnicotts and of the Thompsons. They must have been persons of ill repute in the district, perhaps suspected of being implicated not only in poaching or smuggling but of cattle-reaving which had, recently, reached 'rustling' proportions on the downs of the Meneage. Barnicott was limping and they felt certain he was the man who had been injured by Hancock's plunging horse. At the Thompson cottage they found a gun-lock on John Thompson's person, a gun which had obviously been fired recently, shot, and an old scythe-handle with grey horse hair sticking to it. Perhaps there were few grey horses in the district; Hancock had been riding one, and someone had struck it with a stave when the robbers had attacked the luckless farmer. It clinched the suspicions of the men, and they thereupon took Barnicott and the two older Thompson boys – John aged seventeen and Thomas a year his junior – to the inn where, in the presence of a magistrate, the dying Hancock identified Barnicott and John Thompson as among the gang that had attacked him but was not certain that Thomas Thompson was the other, for he thought that only three had waylaid him.

The Assizes trial at Launceston took place the following March. Bills were presented against Barnicott, a young man of twenty-four, the three Thompsons, and William Daw, a sixteen year old lad whom the Thompsons had apparently tried to blame for the actual murder. It was not clear how many had actually taken part in the attacks on Hancock and the Joses, and the bills against fourteen year old William Thompson and Daw were thrown out, probably because the dying Hancock had sworn that only three men had attacked him. The three accused youths were first tried for the attempt to rob the Joses. William Jose swore that Barnicott and John Thompson were among the gang that attacked them, but would not swear that Thomas Thompson had participated in the crime. To this charge Barnicott pleaded not guilty, but John Thompson wrecked his own defence by first entering a plea of being guilty of being with the other accused but of not being guilty of the attack on Jose; this being inadmissable was changed to a plea of not guilty. Although the identification of Barnicott and John Thompson by the statement the dying Hancock had given to the magistrate was ruled out as evidence, Barnicott's defence collapsed when one of his witnesses swore that he had lamed himself by cutting his foot with a turf-knife a week before the crime and a second witness, a child of twelve, first said that he had seen a horse step on Barnicott's foot when he was taking it to water and then naively admitted that he had been told to tell this story by the accused man's parents. In half an hour following a hearing lasting ten hours the jury found Thomas Thompson not guilty, and the other two guilty, which almost automatically decided what the verdict would be when, on the next day, they stood trial for Hancock's murder. At this second trial an alibi for Thomas Thompson was sworn by his father and sister, but the other two were again found guilty.

So on Friday March 36, 1821, the Judge passed sentences of death on Barnicott and John Thompson. Three days later before 'a great concourse of spectators' they were hanged at Launceston. Hugh Johns and the other local witnesses had probably stayed in the Assize town over the weekend to see the execution. To the end Barnicott protested his innocence, but John Thompson went to the scaffold swearing that the real culprits were his younger brothers and Thomas Daw. The youth of the criminals evoked little pity in those days and there was no chance of an appeal;

once passed the capital sentences were quickly carried out. No-one in the Meneage doubted the guilt of Barnicott and John Thompson, and their crimes and fate became a story told often by Hugh Johns and others to wile away an hour of leisure and to serve as a warning to irresponsible youth.

One of John Boaden's early personal memories strikes a morbid note. What he saw looking back, however, must have been very different from his feelings at the time. In his memoirs he wrote

'My earliest recollection, and that is rather shadowy, is that I once saw Uncle Joseph Boaden at Transingove, and as he died in November, 1830, I could not have been much over two years old; but I have a very clear recollection of being taken by our servant girl Susannah Willey up to see the funeral of my Aunt at Treloskan move off from the house while we stopped at the gate of the meadow at the bottom of the townplace.[1] This was about July 20, 1831, about the time of my brother William's birth. I think my mother came down for the first time after the confinement that day. I was not three years old till August 29th following.'

Seventy years later John Boaden saw no reason to wonder why at such a tender age he had been taken to see an aunt's funeral. Many Methodists dwelt overmuch on human mortality, saw nothing wrong in taking infants to burials, never dreamt of possible psychological injuries to infant minds, thought that the lesson of 'ashes to ashes, dust to dust' should be early learnt. Possibly both the latter and modern psychologists had little real notion of what a child's impressions were. Some children might have been terrified by the funeral trappings of mortality, but others regarded it as just another interesting sight in the world and in the society in which they had just come utter strangers to live. If John had started asking questions why his aunt was in 'thiccy there box' after somebody had told him she had gone to heaven, as like as not before the harrassed Susannah Willey had time to think of a reply his attention would have been lured right away by the flight of a butterfly or a flower in the hedge.

[1] i.e. the group of farmbuildings, 'town' being used in the original sense of dwelling place or steading.

A year later in 1832 when cholera ravaged the land and the conflict over Parliamentary Reform threatened to wreck the state, John became aware that the world extended far beyond Trease farm and Cury parish. For, about that Easter a group of families left the district for Canada including Hugh Johns, and his son, Joseph Gilbert and James Boddinner, who were close friends of the Boadens and the Bullears and Masons. Ever since the end of 'Boney's War' Cornishmen had been going off to North America mostly farmers and farm labourers, driven, by falling grain prices and a succession of indifferent harvests. This, however, seems to have been the first considerable migration overseas from the Mcneage. Upper Canada attracted these men and their families, but when they arrived some of them found it far from their liking and quickly returned home again, bringing with them tales of the hazards of their voyages and of the lands they had seen, mighty rivers, vast lakes, and miles on miles of forest utterly different from their familiar Meneage. So John Boaden seventy years later recalled

'When Hugh Johns and his son came back. It was the year of the cholera visitation, when many died at St. John's near Helston. Many died of it at Newlyn and other places. Among its victims was the well-known Wesleyan minister, Dr. Adam Clarke. I remember that father purchased a lot of young trees for re-planting Trease orchard (most of them have matured in the interval and are now down); the nurseryman he bought them off, who lived near Newlyn, died of Cholera. I remember the trees planted.'

The cholera epidemic, which began on Tyneside late in 1831, reached Cornwall in the summer of 1832, but apart from the outbreak at Newlyn, which took a toll of thirty-two lives, its incidence was slight in the south-west, and it was its swift fatality rather than its wide prevalence which caused most fear and dread. Many references to Adam Clarke in Cornish Methodist services only increased such fears, and his death showed that cholera was no respecter of persons.[1] The farming population may have drawn

[1] Clarke was well-known in Cornish Methodist circles since he had first come to St. Austell as an itinerant minister in 1788.

reassurance from the fact that local outbreaks, in Cornwall, were practically confined to the fishing ports and mining towns and villages. Nevertheless, every case of sudden illness roused tenfold alarm in those days, and Boaden wrote that he remembered as if it were but yesterday that

> 'in January 1833 that my grandmother Willer was taken ill one evening, and my father and mother pulling her to the door for air. It proved to be a seizure, which was the cause of her death after a few days illness. She was buried at Mawgan.'

The older people were passing away, and possibly his own burden of years led Boaden to mention them seventy years later. John Dale, whose funeral he attended in 1833, may have been related to the Boadens. Boaden also recalled that

> 'About this time I used to see old Mr. John Thomas, then living at Nantithet, down looking over the premises at Trenoweth, then occupied by his son who had married Mr. Henry Dale's daughter of Gilly; he used a long stick which he held about a foot from the top. I recollect seeing his coffin making in 1834 in Cousin Hugh's carpenter's shop at Cross Lanes.'

Nothing then or ever could keep an old farmer while he could walk from wandering over the farms occupied by his sons or by his relatives, often criticising and finding fault, saying that things had been different when he had been a young man, now and again offering useful advice. Old John Thomas could remember the early seventeen-seventies when grain prices were lower than they were ever to be for a century thereafter. He could recall times when far more people lived on the land; even at this time on this very farm, Trenoweth, two cottages which had long been uninhabited were demolished – a certain sign that farmers were reducing their labour bills.

The greatest excitement of the year 1832, however, was the political struggle over Parliamentary Reform, and the Meneage farmers were keenly interested because their local landlord, Sir Richard Vyvyan of Trelowarren was a diehard defender of the old system. When the issue was referred to the old unreformed electorate for the last time he and Lord Valletort:

'contested the county as Tories against Mr. Pendarves and Sir Charles Lemon and were defeated . . . Sir Richard had sat previously for the City of Bristol, but on another contest he was defeated. The contests cost him an enormous sum of money and explain how the Trelowarren property is embarrassed with a heavy debt. The election of the county was much talked of in my early years. It took place at Lostwithiel, and most of the electors from this neighbourhood were never up country so far before; a great many from the west were put up in a boat drawn on wheels. All the public houses in the country were open houses for three weeks previous to the poll'.

The landowners went down; their pockets were not so deep as those of the mineowners Lemon and Pendarves. The fantastically ingenious mode of transportation to get the western voters up to Lostwithiel failed to save Vyvyan's set in Parliament. In a five-day polling at the hustings, Pendarves received 1,619 votes to Vyvyans 901. Only the bitterness of the contest seems to have led Vyvyan to persist beyond the third day.[1] Rejected by own county he found a seat elsewhere, and went on defending the outworn and discredited institutions of the past in Westminster.

Sir Richard Vyvyan was undoubtedly the most prominent man in the district. Even those who opposed his politics took pride in his fame. His home at Trelowarren was the focal point of the Lizard Peninsula, and great interest was taken in the new road constructed just after this time from Trelowarren out to the main

---

[1]The state of the poll at the end of each day for the leading Whig and Tory Candidates was

May 10	Pendarves	213	Vyvyan	100
May 11	Pendarves	711	Vyvyan	395
May 12	Pendarves	1,156	Vyvyan	604
May 13	Pendarves	1,542	Vyvyan	794
May 14	Pendarves	1,819	Vyvyan	901

Lemon, the other Whig, who was elected, got 1,804 votes and Valletort, the other unsuccessful Tory 811.

Helston-St. Keverne road to Carrabane. Vyvyan might have made this road in any case, but he used it to strengthen his political interest not only in Cornwall but also at Bristol. John Boaden recollected

'The new iron railings in Park Sladdis purchases by Sir Richard of a Bristol ironfounder when he sat for that city cost ten shillings each. My wife clearly recollects the making and opening of the new road to Trelowarren. The old roads for carriages were by the Double Lodges or (by) a now disused road through Lower Halligy Downs, the ordinary farm road by Carrabane to Carleen at the time referred to. We visited Halligy Mount, then in course of making, it was made up to within a few feet of its present height, the scaffoldings from which the earth was thrown from one to the next above were up, and a party of boys were there jumping from one to the next below. The earth to build it was being brought from the excavation by the side of the garden wall for the new road to be made from the Tregenna to the Mansion.'

The day had not yet come when local gentry could no longer afford to lavish money and labour on their estates. If his electioneering exploits had straitened Sir Richard's means yet labour was still cheap enough; possibly the work he provided at Trelowarren delayed the migration from the Meneage which became so pronounced later.

The 'common folk' talked about the activities of the squire but they were more concerned with their own particular interests. These were the epic but stormy years of Cornish Methodism. John Boaden himself could remember Methodist morning services being held at an early hour so that those attending could then go on to the services at the parish church. In November, 1934, the new Wesleyan Chapel at Garras was opened, and the servant girl, Susannah Willey took young John to the first afternoon service.

He then described the 1835 schism in Cornish Methodism which was another manifestation of the democratic tendencies of the age stimulated by the Parliamentary Reform Bill. Writing of the 'separation', John Boaden stated that there had long been:

'much dissatisfaction felt by a section of the members of

these societies[1] with the power invested in the (Annual) Conference and exercised over the Societies by the Superintendent Minister as the Agent of the Conference. Local self-government was then only in its infancy stage in civil life and its correlative in Methodism was weaker still, and the Superintendents in many instances very unfit persons to be entrusted. The government erected by Mr Wesley recognised to a slight extent the rights of the people. The dissatisfaction was fanned by what was deemed by many as despotic acts by the preachers, which was collected and made the most of by a newspaper called *The Christian Advocate* while the conservative side was represented by the *Watchman*. The storm burst in this year (1835). It appears to me that no event which occurred in my lifetime caused such deep feeling. Scarcely anywhere in the Kingdom were its effects felt so much as in the Helston Circuit. About half of the local preachers, and those often of the best abilities and the most influential, seceded in this circuit, with a large number of members of the same character. The old connexion here found it difficult to supply the pulpits, the number of preaching places remaining the same, so help was had by obtaining the services of local preachers from the adjoining circuits; and though the numbers were less, the Circuit soon had a young additional minister. The secession was confined pretty much to the south side of the circuit; it was especially severe in Cury, Ruan, Gunwalloe, and Mullion. In this latter place an old local (preacher), a very intelligent man, and family called Foxwell, exerted great influence in promoting the principals (sic) which caused disruption. The new party had influence enough to take with them the chapels in Cury, Gunwalloe, and Mullion. This movement scarcely affected the societies in Mawgan, St. Martin and St. Keverne district. This rupture caused the greatest activity to build chapels in most cases where a separation had occurred. Preachers and sympathizers from a distance helped each party, and a spirit of rivalry and prejudice that has happily for many past years considerably decreased.'

[1] i.e. by the rank and file membership of the Methodist 'persuasion'.

41

Boaden, a staunch orthodox Methodist himself may have exaggerated the schism in the Cury district. Following the 'Great Revival' of 1833 the total membership of the Methodist societies in the Helston Circuit had reached 1,598 in 1834; there had been a slight decline the following year, but in 1836 membership was down to 1,203 and sixty more were lost by the autumn of 1837; thereafter lost ground was regained by 1842. This was nothing like the catastrophe which struck membership down from 696 in 1834 to a mere 59 the following year in the Camelford Circuit in North Cornwall.[1] Nevertheless the losses to Methodism in that sparsely populated agricultural district of the Meneage were severe. If the Wesleyans recovered the ground they had lost, in a few years the groups which broke away gained more. The schism revealed active popular religious zeal and life but left bitter and long-lasting local rivalries. As late as 1902, Boaden wrote

'After nearly seventy years of experience the effects of divided Methodist churches could still be plainly seen. The spirit of party rivalry had led to lavish expenditures on the decoration of chapels, the provision of musical instruments, and so forth, that in too many cases could be considered as wasteful extravagence; many parishes had twice the chapel accommodation they needed and there was consequently much wasted spiritual labour.'

Strife and bickering were perpetuated discrediting the faithful and provoking the derision of scoffers and unbelievers, yet in his old age John Boaden admitted frankly that

'such was the condition of Methodist ecclesiasticism that most people now would hardly condemn those who considered it their duty to secede in 1835. It would seem to me,

[1] These figures are taken from the Methodist *Minutes of Conference*; the figures given represent the members in the Circuits on the eve of the yearly Conference. It may be added that there was another revival in the Helston Circuit early in 1843 which sent membership over two thousand; it was declining badly again towards the end of 1845 and by 1847 was down to 1,622.

if the Methodist bodies are to be reunited, the initiative will have to be taken by the people; the ministers seem the least likely (persons) to promote it.'

He briefly mentioned the local circuit steward who had been so active in promoting secession, a lawyer's clerk called Richards, who, after he had gone to live at Penryn quickly left 'the new party he so actively helped to establish.' Apparently the man was a natural rebel, unable to brook any authority; yet the secession he promoted was stronger than he.

Nothing may seem so dead as forgotten religious controversies, but the schism in Methodism had profound social significance. The revolt against ministerial domination may be traced to the introduction of local lay preachers – 'amateurs' who filled, often with outstanding ability, the chapel pulpits when regular salaried ministers were unable to officiate. Boaden's remarks suggest that many ministers had their faults. They had a role to perform but among the Methodist rank and file the opinion grew that the burden of organisation, even the task of spreading the faith, besides the financial cost were borne mainly by the laity. More and more the sentiment was voiced that the ministers were servants and not masters. What happened in the Meneage and in the Camelford Circuit was repeated elsewhere; indeed, the secession of the Bible Christians led by the Cornishman William O'Bryan had occurred twenty years before, and subsequently O'Bryan and his new 'connexion' had parted company through this very antagonism of minister and congregation. Such developments were inevitable once John Wesley had abandoned older Calvanistic tenets and started preaching salvation by conversion, opening the floodgates to individualism. By the time that Victoria came to the throne Methodists believed that they were the masters of their own spiritual fates and the captains of their own souls.

It was rugged religious individualism. They did not subcribe to the radical belief that Jack was as good as his master; the nearest they came to a notion of equality was the assertion that Jack could, maybe with a little encouragement, prove himself as good by the rightful use of the inborn talents which were the spiritual birthright of all men. In this climate of belief it is a little hard to see where some of the ministers fitted. Almost the same outcry was now being made against the men prominent in 'Conference Politics' as that against the more prominent disciples of John Wesley who, after his death, had attempted to set up a Methodist episcopacy in Britain. And it has often seemed only too clear to outsiders that those who were most ready to denounce others for their arrogant assumptions of ecclesiastical leadership were only too often themselves tainted by the same moral flaws.

The way in which chapels were built in sparsely-peopled rural districts, in particular in places like Cury and Mawgan where the population was declining, was not merely extravagent; it set up lasting memorials of spiritual vanity and internecine bickerings among 'the people called Methodists'. Cury Parish, it is true, escaped; a new chapel was built nearer to the parish church. Up at Garras, however, the United Methodists secured a site within a couple of hundred yards of the chapel opened in 1834, and built a chapel larger than that frequented by those whom they denounced as 'Stiff-necked Wesleyans' in 1864. Newness and sheer size counted for much, and in John Boaden's lifetime the Wesleyans at both Garras and Cury built new chapels alongside their older ones which were then used as Sunday Schools.

If Methodism was an assertion of democratic individualism, other influences affected rural social life in those times. Interest in politics was slight and spasmodic. The farmers of Cury and Mawgan would have taken little interest in the Reform Bill had not their landlord been so bitterly opposed to it, although one or two may have hoped that a reformed Parliament might reduce the burdens of tithes and poor rates. Some years passed before they realised that there might be something in arguments that the transfer of political power to the new industrial magnates would only lead to attempts to cut the price of corn in order to stave off demands for higher wages – although such arguments were not best or most effectively put by landowners who were reluctant to reduce rents. As for the more immediate sequels of the Reform Act, the Poor Law Amendment Act was desirable if it reduced the rates which had fallen heavily upon a depressed farming industry, although there had never been many paupers in Cury or in Mawgan. Another new 'reform' which John Boaden recalled was the act prescribing the registration of births and deaths, the local registry office being in Helston. Some at the time grumbled that it was merely another dodge to put money into the pockets of lawyers, a profession whom farmers ever suspected and distrusted.

Boaden remembered this measure because a notice about it was posted up on Trenoweth Tree, just across the road from Trease. A little later posters of the Anti-Corn Law League were put up on the trunk of this gigantic ash tree, known more generally as Cury Great Tree, and which was a well-known landmark; Boaden recalled that:

'it was of immense circumference, its stock firmly set in a maze of convolitious roots which surrounded it. It rose to the height of about twenty feet to a sort of crown, from which huge branches stretched in all directions. They were of immense size, and used to stretch over the hedge for some distance into Trease premises. The trunk was very hollow, and how it bore its great top was a mystery. Some huge limbs had fallen before we left Trease, but after successfully bearing the gales probably of hundreds of years, one fine summer night the neighbours went to bed with the old tree looking just as they had ever seen it, but in the morning it was a complete wreck; the huge limbs had broken down and carried with them splinters of the hollow trunk. It was completely destroyed; this great natural curiosity was no more.[1] This great tree, called Trenoweth Great Tree, standing in the triangle between the roads, attracted the attention of every stranger for hundreds of years, when the coast scenery of Mullion and Lizard had scarcely a single visitor. People told

[1]A. H. Cummings in his *Churches and Antiquities of Cury and Gunwalloe*, (1877) devoted a chapter to this tree, writing (p. 111):
'It spread its giant arms over the greater part of the open space (nearly 70 feet in diameter) between the hedgerows, and its girth immediately above the ground was 27 feet. The hollow trunk, 5 feet up was 14 feet in circumference, and its internal cavity 5 feet, tapering away to 3 feet.

It once had six spreading limbs spring from the trunk, at about 15 feet from the base; some of these, however, were broken off close to the trunk before the tree came down.'

me, when a child, that its roots ran in under Helston Market House.'

Little wonder that such a gigantic tree was an object of local pride till it collapsed in 1857; in the next few years every vestige of it had been removed. In its hoar antiquity it may have been an object of awe, rather than of beauty and the fact that so many came to see it made it the natural place to put up notices of farm sales, public meetings, lost property, stray cattle, new laws and regulations, and 'wanted' criminals.

Whilst the Reform Bill led to many changes affecting the country generally, local changes took place in the years when John Boaden was enquiring the rudiments of education from a rather unusual collection of teachers, and becoming acquainted with persons outside his own family circle. About half a mile from Trease stood the old manor house of Bonython. In bygone times such a dwelling normally remained with a single family for generations. But there seemed to have been a curse on the place since the last two members of the Bonython family had committed suicide. In a century half a dozen different families had owned the house and estate, and, in 1837, Sir Richard Vyvyan, who had bought it not many years before, sold it to Captain Joseph Lyle, a 'newly-rich' mining magnate for £8,000.

5

Schoolteachers, Shopkeepers and Smugglers

John Boaden's first school was kept by Miss Susan Trouson at Cury White Cross. He was about five at the time, probably not a very big boy since in later life he was rather a short, thickset man. Every day Mary Northmoor of Tregadra, a girl six years older than he, called for him; she remained a lifelong friend; in his memoirs he mentioned her marriage to William Lugg, a Lizard man, and her death from cancer. By footpath the school was nearly a mile from Trease, a fair distance for a small child. After a short time he went to another school to be taught reading by 'old Mrs. Polkinghorne', who kept

> 'a good specimen of an old Dame's school. We sat in her small kitchen while she taught us and did her ordinary work at the same time. We read our lessons by her side while she washed her clothes. She kept good order, had kept schools for many years, and was considered a good teacher.'

Then, to learn to write, John was sent to Miss Dale who kept a grocer's shop at White Cross.

He was Miss Dale's first and, for a time, only pupil. He wrote that she was rather clever and rather peculiar, widely read, and 'a very bold good writer'. Lessons were frequently interrupted while she served a customer, a prolonged, gossippy business in a village shop, so discipline was lax and at times it was a school for scandal. The shop kept a variety of goods, and there John first saw a lucifer match, but 'the grocery trade here did not include the sale of flour and very little bread. People were supplied almost entirely by grists from the farmers, and the miller's leading boy was a very familiar figure on the roads.'[1]

If miller's men dusty with meal, still made regular rounds collecting grain to be milled and delivering flour, black-faced coalmen were almost unknown then in Meneage, for Miss Dale was the only Cury householder who burnt coal.

Some things John learnt there were unusual. Since paper was scarce Miss Dale gave him some 'old assorted Tax schedules' on which to practise writing. When a customer came in and lingered schooling came to a full stop, but

'then I learnt the news. Miss Dale's shop was a centre at which all the educated and refined of the neighbourhood visited. Mrs. Dunstone of Skyburriowe, Mr. Gundry when home from Breage[2], the Foxwell family, and the family of Mr. Joe Thomas of Trevithoe, and others of that class would occasionally stop there, and I had the benefit of the chat, and I think sometimes understood what they did not intend for me to do.'

Often these local worthies had much to talk about, paying no need to the small boy who was supposed to be learning his letters, talk of mining concerns by Gundry, of farming matters by the Thomases, of the short-comings of 'Methody' ministers by the Foxwells.[2] The reluctance of a certain owl to pay his debts, the brawl between a swallow and a gull in Helston tavern last market-day, the squabbles of a most respectable family of kites

[1]Grists were rough grains, often obtained by the cottagers gleaning in the fields before the time of the self-binding reaping machines in the eighteen-eighties, or grain given by farmers to their men.
[2]Possibly a connection of the Goldsithney family who then owned Wheal Vor, the fabulously rich tin mine in Breage. The Thomases were prominent Meneage farmers, Boaden had already mentioned the part played by the Foxwells in local Methodist schisms.

over a grandfather's will,[1] the likelihood that a certain girl would have a child in the cradle ere she brought a husband to church, all provided an excuse to mind someone else's business and kept the gossips' tongues from rusting.

Still John learnt more at that school then the facts of village life. Miss Dale gave him stories and 'pretty riddles' to copy. If he did not understand any word he had to write it down, look it up in a dictionary and then write down its meanings. Miss Dale, too, had artistic leanings, her walls being covered with pictures 'of a comic character' unlike those religious prints so favoured by the methodists. After a time her

'scholars began to increase, and I think it was on Good Friday, 1838, having had a box of paints and brush the previous Saturday, I went with three or four other boys to Miss Dale's to learn to draw pictures, by means of pinning a paper against the picture to be taken and tracing it with blacklead pencil against a window. From this time to my leaving Cury I indulged in this freely. I suppose many scores if not hundreds were painted. This would not make us artists, but it gave me a taste for pictures, some of which are still in my possession, also an increased love of beauty and a better appreciation of nature.'

A modern art school might despise such methods, but this old-time untrained teacher knew how to develop the aptitudes of her pupils, and made good use of the limited 'scholastic apparatus' at hand – a few picture books, some pencils, and the blank sides of official forms which local and national bureaucracies were already scattering with a prodigal hand.

If he made no claim to be an artist, John Boaden had a gift of shrewd observation, going on to write that Miss Dale

'had a literary taste, was a great stickler for pronunciation, used to stay up late with a few others reading fiction, had

[1]These birds' names were nicknames applied to Meneage parishes. Thus the inhabitants of Mawgan were known as owls, those of Gunwalloe, Mullion and St. Martin as swallows, gulls, and kites respectively; Cury folk were called crows, and the unfortunate St. Anthony people pigs.

most of the fidgets attributed to old maids, was rather stout, took snuff, and died at the age of sixty in 1856 . . . I am indebted to Miss Dale for fostering in me a love of books, but she rather weaned me from boyish games which was a loss.'

Taking snuff is hardly a feminine accomplishment, and the pronunciation Miss Dale stressed was probably only clearness of speech; years after his death many remembered John Boaden's own deliberate slow speech.

John did not say what the boyish games of the day were. There were few ball games except hurling in remote Cornish villages, but boys had plenty of other pastimes. The sea was a little too distant for paddling and swimming excursions, but the Cury lads probably took a few tumbles in the nearby streams when they went fishing for minnows. Armed with sticks they hunted adders on Goonhilly and Boscawen moors. Late summer saw them blackberrying and nutting in the lanes and in Trelowarren woods, and spring searching for birds' nests and climbing trees at the risk of limbs and necks and the destruction of their garments. On Sunday evenings when they managed to give their parents the slip after chapel they wandered in gangs in the wake of courting couples who had not the least desire for their company. They wrestled and sometimes fought among themselves, got into mischief, but often their elders frustrated this by giving them some work – scaring rooks from the corn-fields, picking stones in the meadows, fetching the cattle, and helping about the milking, and many other jobs.

There were annual village feasts, usually with sports and sometimes with free teas, but Cury does not seem to have held any special celebration when the Queen was crowned on June 28, 1838. Possibly the Boadens were getting on with the hay-saving that fine Thursday afternoon lest the fine weather break, and hardly stopped to listen to the church bells echoing across the vales and hills from Cury to Mawgan. Doubtless a neighbour called in that evening or the next day to tell them of the coronation celebrations in Helston, which had included the grand old dance from the time immemorial and evermore associated with that 'quaint old Cornish town', processions of civic dignitaries, bands playing, free teas, and fireworks at night.

Later in 1838 John Boaden left Miss Dale's school for that kept

Trease, the birthplace of John Boaden photographed in 1995

Ploughing with oxen in West Cornwall

by the versatile Hugh Johns, having acquired from the 'fidgety' old maid the rudiments of learning and probably a politer culture than otherwise he might have done. Miss Dale had her faults, but 'Cousin Hugh' had his weaknesses, and his establishment

'was the third school I attended in Cross Lanes and (they) were for some years open together, the three houses adjoining each other, and then the principal school (in Cury) was being carried on by Edward Dale at Cury Church Town, so let no one think that education was being neglected at Cury in the thirties.'[1]

Three schools alongside each other was, perhaps, undesirable, and one day when John had been at Miss Dale's

'a scuffle took place between Miss Dale and old Mistress[2] in the highway . . . arising from old Mistress striking one of Miss Dale's scholars on the road for some offence with her cane, which Miss Dale seeing went out and tried to wrest from her. It became a regular scuffle while Hannibal Johns, a notorious son of Cousin Hugh, stood by and prevented the women from parting (them), while the children of both schools looked on. But let no one harshly judge of these women; it was done on the spur of the moment.'

Still it gave the village something to talk about, and scapegoats like Hannibal Johns rejoiced to see the prim and proper Miss Dale attacking a women nearly twice her age, for if Miss Dale was then on 'the wrong side of forty', Miss Polkinghorne was nearly eighty.

Hugh Johns started a school apparently in the belief that it would be an easy way of making a living. His qualifications as a teacher were not outstanding. His part in arresting Hancock's murderers may have made it hard for him to settle down to the

[1]The population of Cury was 523 in 1831 and 541 in 1841; only a fifth of this number could at most have been attending school. Four schools for about a hundred pupils was rather excessive. Both boys and girls attended at Miss Polkinghorne's and Hugh Johns', but Boaden does not say whether the other two were 'mixed' schools.
[2]Miss Polkinghorne: she died, aged 94, 1849.

monotony of daily life, and he had then, in 1832, emigrated to Canada, quickly returning because it was no place for elderly men,[1] particularly for those with a weakness for drink. Of him Boaden wrote

'He was generally called Cousin Hugh. He frequently used the word 'dear' in conversation, so by many was called 'Cousin Hugh dear'. He had been a carpenter, and did our work at Trease, but the gout had rendered him unable to attend to that work. So after trying to get (the mastership of) the national school (at Cury Church Town) and failing, he started one independently in the room called the hall in his own house, which became pretty well filled with scholars.'

He may have been patronised mostly by Methodists who objected to the 'Church school' on sectarian grounds, or perhaps he charged lower fees. He turned his 'hall' into a schoolroom with his carpenter's equipment, for

'in the middle of the room there stood a large tool chest and carpenter's bench which served for desk, and around the room on one side were other desks opposite the fire-place.'

Other things which would now be regarded as primitive make-shifts were used in this school, for

'quills alone were used for writing, and to make and mend them occupied a not inconsiderable part of the master's time: no steel pens then. The slate pencils were found by the boys, and taken out of the soil and scraped and pointed for the use for which purpose two knives were kept just inside the school room door. A large jug well supplied with water was kept in the kitchen, for the use of the scholars that might be thirsty, which as it afforded an opportunity to leave the school room was well patronised.'

The master himself

[1] Hugh Johns was over fifty when he went to Canada; he died in 1858 at the age of 77.

'was a good arithmetician, so that was the strong point in the school. He stood before his desk opposite to the window, spectacled, with a double rope hung by his side with which we were flogged if necessary . . . The master was lenient up to a certain point, but when that was passed and his temper aroused woe to the scholar – it was a mixed school – that offended; the double rope would be hastily snatched and a very severe use made of it. We soon got and continued as quiet as mice until the storm abated. We might be told on these occasions to pick up our kit and be gone, but these storms did not often arise. We generally had a plenty of latitude.'

Cury teachers in those days did not believe in sparing the rod and spoiling the child. Johns had his rope to hand whilst Mrs. Polkinghorne always had her cane by her, probably a switch cut from the hedgerow, to keep discipline, to emphasise lessons some pupils were slow to grasp, and to 'correct' spelling and 'figuring' slips.

Worse than the makeshift school equipment was the limited knowledge of the teachers and their personal shortcomings. Old Mrs. Polkinghorne was short-tempered, Miss Dale loved gossiping, and as for Hugh Johns, though he started school with morning prayers often he was in no fit state to conduct either school or prayers, for

'he used to kill pigs for the neighbouring farmers before school hours, and I have known him to return under the influence of drink; indeed, this was his great failing, which explained his gout and his poverty, by which he was pinched. He was a character and no mistake. He also cleaned clocks, measured land and castrated cattle which afforded him his principal means of support after he gave up his school – which must have taken place at the latter end of the forties. He (was) also a cattle doctor.'

Truly a man of parts, perhaps even of talents, but few would be as charitable as his old pupil, John Boaden, who summed him up as a genius.

Something of a ne'er-do-well, who lived and died poor, Hugh

Johns was afflicted with a bitter-tongued scold of a wife, Grace, who often berated him hammer and tongs to the doubtful edification of his pupils. He had

> 'very warm sympathies which would be aroused by any act of injustice, or pain, or loss. While at his school occasionally a waggon would pass before the windows, at which Hugh stood, laden with anchors of brandy which the coastguard had seized from the smugglers with several coastguardsmen with it. This touched Hugh hardly – the loss of the smugglers and of the brandy he loved so well.'

Much smuggling was still going on in the Meneage in those times. Often at nightfall men galloped furiously through White Cross that none might recognise them though all could guess the errand that took them to Poldhu Cove or Gunwalloe Strand. There were then no less than three gin shops in the tiny hamlet of Nantithet, a group of perhaps half a dozen cottages a mile down from Trease on the stream running into Gunwallow Church Cove, where anyone 'in the know' could get brandy any time they wished. Hugh Johns probably often strolled that way after school hours, and the refreshments provided by local farmers at pig-killings and harvest times must have come, untainted by duty, through the hands of these Nantithet shopkeepers – Richard Dudley, 'Little Jimmy' Shewis, and 'Old Fooley' Skewis. The last may have gained his nickname through his astuteness in deceiving excisemen, whilst Little Jimmy had gained local fame by falling into a quarry near Helston carrying an anker of brandy one night and escaping unhurt.

Many tales were told about these smugglers. John Boaden's wife told him that when her father lived at nearby Burnoon he used to get up in the night to make sure that the smugglers had not left any gates open for cattle to stray in the growing corn. Boaden recalled that James Williams who died in 1901 had done

> 'some smuggling in his youth. It was only last year that he was recalling that he was with a party at Praa Sands for ankers when Tobias Johns fired a pistol at a man supposing him to be an (excise) officer, shooting off the finger. It was a mistake, the man being one of his own party. The people

generally could see no harm in smuggling, the smuggler being regarded as a public benefactor, and those few that condemned it as strainers at gnats and swallowers of camels. But smuggling, which had prevailed to such an extent in the Meneage and afforded such scope for the speculative and enterprizing man with the love of luck and adventure, had mostly died out soon after the century just gone.'

One by one they slipped into the past, the 'amateur' schoolmaster, the miller's man, the smuggler, and the very much unlicensed victualler. They had played their part in the life of rural Meneage, enjoying some local fame and notoriety. It would have been a duller place without them and without the local gossips. Good old days or bad old times – anyone can form his own opinion, but the wise may, like John Boaden, look on them with tolerance, forebearance, charity, and friendship. For good or ill these were John's 'ain folk', with whom he lived over three score years and ten.

6

Changes and Uprootings

It was nothing new in Cornwall for successful mining speculators like Captain Joseph Lyle to buy estates like Bonython. Landowning conferred social prestige, but over the years many with money have forced their way into 'county' society by buying estates. In 1825 the Daveys of Gwennap Consolidated Mines had bought the manor of Bochym in Cury, while the Williams family were buying estates in different parts of Cornwall with mining profits just as, in early times, the Godolphins and Robartes had done. Lyle, a self-made man, who had started work in a tin-stamping mill in St. Mewan at the age of twelve was essentially practical. He certainly had social ambitions, but he believed a lavish investment of capital and labour would pay handsome dividends in farming as it had done in mining, that new methods and new devices should be adopted, and that unprofitable small estates would pay if they were amalgamated just as merging small losing mines into 'consolidated' mining ventures had proved successful.

Soon after buying Bonython Lyle came down to inspect it, with his farm-baliff, Tamblyn, whom he put in charge of all his estate improvements. Tamblyn, according to Boaden, could hardly read or write, and was tactless in dealings with older Bonython tenants. He made a new farmyard by sweeping away the little tenement of Cots, till then occupied by John Boaden's father's cousin, a butcher, whose son, James Boaden, was one of John's lifelong friends; to him eviction was bitter, though it was the prelude to a career as a schoolmaster, railway clerk, study at Cambridge, ordination, and a living in Wales. James Boaden's life might have been different had not Lyle bought Bonython.

At first the enterprising mine captain had some success in his new sphere. With a gang of two hundred navvies, the entrance to Bonython from Cury Cross Lanes was reconstructed, trees were planted, and the whole estate improved after the rackings of the succession of short-term owners. Lyle then attempted to reclaim two-hundred acres of Goonhilly Downs, thinking its serpentine soils much the same as the granite of growan tracts he had seen bought under cultivation round the mines of St. Mewan, Gwennap, Illogan and St. Agnes. Parts of Goonhilly were reclaimable, but Captain Joe might well have listened to the old adage which reflected the relative fertility of soils – gold under furze, silver under bracken, and copper under heather, and left them as a hunting ground for the pack of harriers he bought to set himself up as a sporting squire. He could, too, have given more attention to grassland and leys at a time when corn prices were so unreliable and for the most part, declining; but any man who desires to see golden corn whitening unto harvest on barren looking heathlands can be forgiven, and if Lyle was throwing money away, it was his own and no-one else's.

The district too, benefited. Labour was cheap, and often underemployed; neighbouring small farmers hired their horses, carts and wagons, not by the day but by the year, to help Lyle carry out his schemes of reclamation. John Boaden wrote

'All this appeared to be very wonderful to me. Father had a draught employed there for a considerable time. I sometimes carried the dinner to the driver, and I well recollect being driving a pair of oxen in ploughing a croft there at Mawgan feast, 1839, for when my cousins from Veryan, then home with their mother on their annual visit, came up with my brother William with our dinner finding they were going to Mawgan Teetotal Festival I grew restive with the plough and went to Mawgan.'

He did not add if this truancy meant a whipping from his father, but the eleven-years old boy was probably only leading the oxen and the ploughman made a shift to get along without a 'driver'.

Most of the Goonhilly reclamation was done by ox-drawn ploughs, nor did it stop with the first ploughing, for

'several years afterwards the improved crofts were all broken
through by hand, drained, and the rocks removed. I recollect
being in the hundred acres with my grandfather when the
first crop – wheat – and being carried; patches where
the wheat had failed was sown to pasture turnips which
grew very large. The crofts were reclaimed by a party of
men with spades so-called which they pushed before them
and cut the turf by a series of jerks. This (i.e. the turf) was
burnt.'

This shows that land-reclamation proved more difficult and far
more costly than Lyle anticipated, but he had money to spare.
Bonython and its vast moors did not satisfy his ambitions of
landownership, and he started buying farms like so many mine
shares. There was Polglaze

'a small farm which consisted of the land now one field lying
against Skewis and four small fields now forming part of
Cross Lanes Field: this was purchased from Parson Stabback
for £1,200. Higher Tregadra from Mr. Thomas Tregideon for
I think £1,600. Afterwards Trease for £2,100 – about £100
per acre – and Trenoweth for I think £1,600. He also
purchased the part of Skewis which lay before the Lizard road
the lease from Mr. Grose who lived (at) and owned Nan-
plough and he purchased from Sir Charles Lemon. As these
farms became annexed a great deal was done in levelling
hedges and stone-fencing others. He also kept a good stock
of hackneys, built a kennel, and kept a pack of harriers.'

What with road-making, moorland reclamation, and land
purchases, Lyle made a stir in Cury. The Boadens had probably
regarded the purchase of Bonython with indifferent interest at the
time, not thinking it would affect them at Trease.

Many years before Trease had been part of the Bonython estate,
but the Boadens had occupied it for generations, John's grandfather
taking it over in 1796, the previous tenant being his brother who
had just died. It was only a smallholding of twenty- four acres,
and the Boadens had held it by a succession of fourteen year leases,
paying £42 a year, a rather high rent which reflected the keen
tenant competition for small family farms in West Cornwall and

the high corn prices of the French war years. Still this rent roughly represented the annual wages of a man and a boy in those days, or the produce of six or seven acres of wheat in a moderately good season. The landlord was a Devon parson who had inherited the farm and had never set foot in the place. With agents taking commission from the rent for their services, with the lease due to expire in 1838 or 1839, and with Lyle eager to buy land near Bonython, the parson was ready to sell the farm.

The legal firm who acted as the parson's agents, however, precipitated the sale. Despite some sort of verbal promise that Boaden's lease should be renewed

'as the time came he could not get the deed . . . He was suspicious that there was something wrong, and feared what afterwards turned out to be true. Mr. Grylls was withholding the deed that Mr. Lyle might purchase the farm and hence have immediate possession. Not being able to get any satisfactory assurance about the deed at the Great Office Father and James Hodge, who was in similar circumstances determined to go and see their landlord who had never seen the property. True he resided and was the Rector of the parish of Clayhanger . . . near Wivelscombe . . . For anyone except an independent gentleman to go such a distance as that (in those days) fell to the lot of extremely few, but the two tenants left by coach.'

The lawyer acted in the best interests of his client, but a promise had been given and should have been kept. In those days, however, stewards and agents took little account of tenants, rarely giving an old tenant first consideration for the renewal of a lease, or compensation for improvements he had made during his occupancy.

Neither Boaden nor Hodge could easily afford the time or the money to go to East Devonshire, and they were too worried to enjoy the trip. The return coach fair between Falmouth and Exeter was just over two guineas, and that travelling outside – still one could see more of the country that way, although night fell before they reached Exeter. To men whose longest journeys had been jaunts to markets at Truro and Penzance, Exeter was a strange city in a strange land. They put up at an inn for the night, and there the Rev. Walter Long, who had been stationed in the Helston Circuit four years before, dropped in to see them and spent the evening talking of old times and old friends.

The following day they went on to Clayhanger and saw their landlord Harrison, who treated them with kindness and consideration, indeed entertained them for some days. They had a look around the farms of the district but were struck most by the work in progress in constructing the railway line from Bristol to Exeter, and there were many tales to be told of their experiences and impressions when they got back to Cury.

Parson Harrison was hospitable, but when it got down to business merely promised to come down to Cury himself in the spring and see matters. When he came he looked at the farms and told his tenants the verbal promises made by his agents were worthless, that he was going to sell but they could remain in occupation for a further six months. Bitterly, sixty years later, Boaden wrote.

This business had been engineered by the Great Office. My father's interest and his father regarded as nothing in spite of agreements, so that Mr. Lyle in whose interest they worked might get the farm. An auction was held. Mr. Lyle became the purchaser, and my father and his aged father and mother and children had to leave. But the whirl-i-gig of time works its revenges. The last of the Lyles had to leave Bonython unable to keep it in their possession and go to New Zealand. It has been managed by the mortgages (sic) ever since, and the Great Office, that did the dirty work, is the Great Office no longer save only in name. Mr. Frederick Hill, however, the present head of the firm is an amiable gentleman, and I believe incapable of acting as his father did if he had the power.'

It amounted to eviction, and revealed the antagonisms in rural society between landowners and tenants which contributed much to the decline of the so-called landed interest in Victorian times. True, time brought its revenges; Lyle's heirs ran through his fortune; one of them fled to New Zealand after a breach of promise action, another was sued for debt by the local piano-tuner and aggravated local bad-feeling by a libel action against another 'evicted' tenant who, in his wrath, had not refrained from referring to the Lyles and their morals in terms luridly reminiscent of the most forceful Old Testament prophets.

The Boadens resented having to leave the farm which had long been their home, but money talked louder to landowners than any consideration for old tenants who had farmed well and paid their rent on the nail. Uncertainty about the renewal of tenures made the Boadens, like many other farmers, ambitious to own their farms. There may have been more good and considerate landlords than bad, but few tenants could count on fairness at all times; the only chance of security was to buy freehold land, to do so they had to save money, and if many farmers did so by ruthlessly racking rented farms, the landowning classes as a whole had only themselves to blame.

In 1839, however, the Boadens could not buy Trease when it was sold by auction. Parson Harrison naturally wanted and was entitled to make the best price he could, and his agents, with first-hand knowledge of local conditions knew that, in the open market no-one could stand against Lyle. The Boadens had to find another farm, for Lyle's schemes of large-scale farming meant they could not stay at Trease as his tenants. When Michaelmas came the Boadens still had no place to go. Lyle, having got his Naboth's vineyard, was generous enough and allowed Boaden to keep his stock in one of the Trease fields for a time. Then, rather unexpectedly, Bojorrow Farm, about a mile away in Mawgan parish, was advertised to be let on a twelve-year lease. In desperation the elder John Boaden offered £85 a year for it, more than twice his rent at Trease, but about twenty others wanted it; Boaden's tender was accepted, and he moved his family as quickly as possible.

'The family included Father, Mother, Grandfather and Grandmother, two sons, servant man – William Skewis – and servant maid, old Mr. Bartlett putting the old people down in his singular market cart. We carried about a hundred loads of various things from Trease to Bojorrow.'

Boaden may have exaggerated the amount of good they moved, although the capacity of a farm cart was limited and the amount of 'lumber' that can be accumulated on a smallholding in fifty years or more is phenomenal, especially bits and pieces hoarded in the belief that they might come in handy some day. The old folks must have had an uncomfortable journey jolting over the rough lanes in Bartlett's cart, but why John described it as singular is a mystery.

The move had its compensations, the farm and dwelling house being larger than Trease, and the Boadens had risen in the rural social scale from smallholders to farmers. There was a pleasant garden with evergreen ornamental shrubs, which

'with a well-stocked orchard gave it a most respectable appearance. We kept a young servant man to work horses and an occasional labourer, twice as many (hands) as would be kept now.'

Young John, too, now thought that he had entered upon man's estate and that he had now left school for good and all.

Though only eleven years old he had already been to four schools, for he had recently left Cousin Hugh's school

'where I had advanced pretty well through common authorities. I then went to Church Town National School kept by Hugh Lyne a cousin of father's . . . The moral and religious teaching here was greatly in advance of what I had been accustomed to, and the presence of teaching of the clergymen Rev, John Stevenson and Way contributed to it. There was a large number of scholars here for the district. School always opened and closed with singing and prayer, and the children were well grounded in scriptural knowledge. Together with Will and Dale we had a box of mathematical instruments and began geometry.'

This stress on mathematics in what must be regarded as an elementary rural school is surprising, but it seems to have been taught for very practical purposes. Hugh John's ability as a land-surveyor may have forced the National School to challenge his mathematical prowess, but it is possible that Lyne, too, had a flair for mathematics, and in those days there were no very rigid standards prescribing what teachers in rural schools should teach their pupils.

The churches and chapels also made their contribution to local education, and in the late eighteen-thirties the latter entered a new phase in their history – the teetotal movement which, in a decade, probably did more to eliminate smuggling in the Meneage than exisemen had done in the preceding century.

Total abstainers had caused a stir in many Methodist societies before they appeared in the Meneage in 1839. In 1833 it was stated at a 'Temperance Society' meeting in Bodmin that 'signing the pledge' had originated in America, and that outside London where sixteen thousand had taken the pledge it was strongest in Yorkshire and then in Cornwall.[1]

The movement was associated with the rebirth of puritan asceticism which came in the wake of the Wesleyan and Evangelical movement. The sensational feuds and schisms in the Methodist Connexion obscured the growth of teetotalism, but rebels against Conference domination used the teetotal agitation as a weapon against the 'tyranny of ministers'. In 1840 a schismatic Teetotal Wesleyan Methodist Connexion was set up at St. Ives, after Conference had refused to follow the practice of the Primitive Methodists of using unfermented wine in the celebration of the sacraments and had, moreover, attempted to ban the use of Methodist chapels for total abstinence meetings. Teetotallers had already made considerable progress in Cornwall, and John Boaden remembered a crowded meeting at the Cury Chapel in 1839, presided over by Thomas Mullion and addressed by John Sims and a preacher called Patterson. At Garras Chapel on Friday April 9, 1839, advocacy of total abstinence attained revivalist fervour

'The hearts of the people wre like molten wax, and at the close of the epoch-making meeting over a hundred signed the pledge, including all the officers of the society and most of its members. Thus was laid the foundations of that sobriety here which has distinguished the parish ever since. It was not long before the nine beer and cider shops in the parish (of Mawgan) were closed, not by any authorities but for want of

[1]The figures given were 5,000 for Yorkshire and 2,400 for Cornwall, the total for Britain being 45,000. It was vaguely stated that the movement began in America 'five or six years since'.
(*West Briton*: March 1, 1833)

custom. The (Methodist) Church has not yet put forth anything like its full power in abstaining from drink and faithfully proclaiming the fearful responsibility of those who stood on the other side.'

Possibly there had been too much drunkenness in Mawgan and other Meneage parishes before this time but there was a dark side to the new crusade. What John Boaden called 'very warm' temperance feeling was a rebirth of intolerance attended by 'witch hunts'. Revealingly Boaden wrote that he remembered

'Alex Wicks going out of a prayer meeting when my father engaged in prayer because at that time (i.e. the elder Boaden) was not a teetotaller. There soon began to be agitation on this question in consequence of some of the preachers not being abstainers. I signed the pledge in the fall of 1841 at a meeting addressed by Mr. Jennings an agent in the Baptist Chapel. Teetotal prayer meetings were held alternately in the various chapels.'

The total abstinence movement thus brought people together besides dividing them. It did much good in the country but it is impossible to assess the decline of tolerance and of Christian charity against an improvement in general social and individual welfare brought about by the reduction of drunkenness, whilst the emotional religious revival techniques used by so many teetotal advocates were not the best or most desirable methods of achieving a lasting social reform.

Mawgan parish was more populous and in some ways more progressive than Cury. At the time which John Boaden was now writing the Garras chapel had a larger membership than that of Cury, and many of its services were crowded. There were, however, already signs that people were leaving the Meneage; the exodus from Mawgan had already begun although it is hardly likely that the fact that ten souls less were returned in the parish census in 1841 than the 1,094 in 1831 caused any comment, but in 1861 it was down to 895 and by the time John Boaden wrote was barely seven hundred. In Cury the population was nearly stationary, rising only from 505 in 1821 to 549 in 1851 and then progressively declining to 325 by 1001[1]. Emigration from these parishes was more considerable than these census returns would suggest, for generally there were a considerably larger number of births than deaths. From rural parishes, too, those that departed tended to go for good, whereas in Cornish mining regions many men went abroad for a few years sending remittances back to support wives and families they left behind at home.

Many Mawgan parishioners found employment at Trelowarren where Sir Richard Vyvyan had just started building a new lodge at Carrabane, and enclosing and bringing Garras Common under cultivation. In short, when the Boadens moved to Bojarrow prospects looked good even with the high rent they now had to find and certain unhealthy tendencies in the grain markets despite the protection of the Corn Laws. Although controversy was arousesd by the total abstinence movement, hardly anyone apparently suggested that teetotalism would have disastrous effects on barley prices or alleged that the agitation was promoted by East Indian tea merchants. The Boadens and many other farmers did not hesitate to take the pledge and tried to get their friends and servants to do likewise. Mawgan parish 'went dry'; in other parts of Cornwall there was slightly more resistance. In certain places there may have been a slight increase in secret drinking which profited the few surviving 'free-traders' more than the regular inn-keepers. One of the strangest results of the teetotal movement to occur in Cornwall took place in the mining parish of St. Agnes. A vestry meeting was convened there at Michaelmas, 1842, to appoint twenty-five parish constables. The extent to which intolerance had been fostered by the movement among both its adherents and opponents alike was revealed when

'it was moved by a maltster and seconded by an innkeeper that no teetotaller should be eligible for that office. The reason assigned for the motion was, that such is the antipathy of teetotallers to drunkenness, that should one of them be

[1]The census returns, of course, do not reveal the years in which the population of these parishes reached their maximum. Probably Mawgan reached its highest populations sometime between 1831 and 1841, and Gury just before 1851.

invested with the authority of a constable he would not hesitate to knock a poor drunkard's brains out.'[1]

Today that motion seems facetious, but the vestry passed it, thereby annoying the more extreme advocates of total abstinence, although it is likely that some who had taken the pledge were only too glad to escape public duties which were inconvenient rather than onerous and carried no remuneration.

[1]*West Briton*: October 7, 1842

7

To Be a Farmer's Boy

Agricultural changes since 1800 have been as great as those in urban manufacturing industries. The only unchanging features of British farming have been the seasonal cycle of seed-time and harvest and utterly unpredictable climate. At the mercy of the weather, dealing with animals and crops which cannot be absolutely brought under mechanical routine, farmers had to be innovators, improvisers, and often inventors. Jibes about using binder twine and baling wire to repair harness, carts, and even implements, about old wheels and bedsteads being used to stop gaps in hedges or as gates, and about countless other makeshifts being seen on so many farms, did, in fact, prove the resourceful- ness of the rural population. They were untidy ,but they were effective, and if often they became permanencies it was because the farmers had too many other urgent tasks to do anything more about them.

Urgent tasks, even crises, a working day sometimes four and twenty hours long, made up the farmer's life. After a long day's ploughing or harvesting a farmer often had to stay up all night looking after a sick animal. Shepherds declared that lambing always began on the coldest and stormiest night of the year. A 'catchy' harvest could take weeks to 'save', and then there was a rush to put a covering of sorts over a rick before a thunderstorm broke with torrential rain.[1] Sometimes things went smoothly, but hardly a day passed without some worry, a week without trouble, or a year without some crisis or loss. Often something had to be done straightaway which demanded every available hand and often extra hands as well.

[1]Thomas Hardy's *Far From the Madding Crowd*, Chapters xxxvi and xxxvii describes such a crisis in farming life.

During John Boaden's life farming problems increased. Besides falling markets and vanishing profits, the exodus of labour from rural parishes meant labour problems, only partly solved by machinery, especially as the men who left were usually the younger and the stronger and more enterprising.[1] Women almost vanished from the fields, but juvenile labour was still common in 1900. No humanitarian legislation or compulsory school attendance laws stopped farmers from sending their children to milk, feed cattle, or work in the fields both before and after school hours; farmers on rural School Boards often fixed holidays and minimum attendance regulations to suit the demand for extra hands for potato-planting and harvesting.

In the late eighteen-thirties, before he was ten years old, John Boaden was kept home from school moreoften than not at potato-lifting and corn-planting time. In his memoirs he stressed the great changes since those days. Potatoes were then the main root crop in the Meneage. Turnips were sown broadcast, not with drills, which meant tedious hoeing with cumbersome, long-handled hoes. Still more arduous was manuring, for

'there were no artifical manures used till Mr. Lyle introduced bone dust by having a cargo from Exeter about 1838. It was a matter of surprise to see what turnips were grown with it on improved crofts. He was also the first to sow turnips in rows, and this very quickly became generally done

[1]The extent of rural depopulation in the norther Meneage is shown to some extent by comparing the census returns of 1901 with those of the highest population returned at any previous census, though this does not show how the excess of births over deaths in these parishes meant a still greater exodus.

Parish	Highest Census return	Year of Highest Census Return	Population in 1901
Manaccan	654	1831	372
Mawgan	1,054	1831	713
Gunwalloe	298	1841	135
Mullion	808	1841	673
St. Keverne	2,469	1841	1,675
St. Anthony	313	1841	173
St. Martin	565	1841	322
Cury	549	1851	325

throughout the district, and the quality tilled began to increase. Manuring was generally done by the wheeling of four or five bottoms – which was a man's day's work – called wheeling voars, per acre; then after earth was carried from the ditches frequently on the piles; this with any scrapings and sometimes sand were levelled and about two loads of dung from the yard were turned up together and wheeled out abroad. Sometimes the piles were turned twice.'

The term *wheeling voars* and many others then used to describe tools and practices now long obsolete have been forgotten. Farmyard manure was then taken out into the fields in wheelbarrows. 'Bottom' seems to have been a descriptive term arising from the practice of leaving heaps of manure at the bottom of fields where less would be leached away by rain, a practice that was natural enough when carts were rarely used. Such practices and such heavy demands on manual labour were partly responsible for the many small fields which made up west-country farms in those days.

When there was an hour to spare a farmer or his man would load up a barrow of dung in the farmyard, wheel it out to the field, tip it up by the bottom hedge, cover it with old straw, bracken, or hedge-parings, and leave it until the time came to 'dress' the field. Dirt and mud from the road, especially plentiful after rainy spells, was also collected on the barrows and taken to the fields. Sea-sand was often used to remedy lime deficiencies. A Cornish contemporary of Boaden's wrote in 1889

'Only a few decades ago, and the number can be counted on the fingers of my right hand, wheat vanquished all opponents in the struggle for first position in the commerce of Cornwall. Every stretch of sand along the coast which was available to the public, and to which access could be obtained, was then the scene of great activity. From 'early morn to dewy eve' boys could be counted by dozens and donkeys by scores, on the beaches during the summer months, all employed in loading sand, and conveying it inland for the purpose of mixing with dung and other dressing preparatory to its being scattered over the lands to be tilled to wheat in the autumn . . . Every farmer in those days – forty or fifty years ago –

kept so many teams of donkeys the number being pro-
portionate to the size of the farm. Each 'team' was managed
by one boy, and the number of donkeys in each team
depended on the size and age of the boy in command. The
numbers of donkeys in a team ranged from three or seven.
Each donkey carried two bags of sand, and the bags were
made with only one seam in them, and were placed on the
donkey's back with the seam upwards, so as that it might
not cause injury (to the animal). There were a number of men
and women employed at the beaches in helping to fill the
bags with sand, placing the same on the backs of the donkeys,
and driving the donkeys up, over the beaches and directing
the boys homeward. These were called 'sand leaders'. Each
boy had to go so many turns daily, and when he had finished
he could spend his time in what way he chose. Of course,
every day the boys found time to take their 'dip in the briny'
during the summer, and if a dispute arose among them about
anything – and this was often the case – the question was
decided by a pugilistic encounter.'[1]

Scenes like this could be seen at Gunwalloe Sanding Cove and
elsewhere on the coasts of the Meneage, although the writer of
this account lived in North Cornwall.[2] He added that these lads
were not those described as 'happy as a sand boy', for they were
parish apprentices who

'were "bought at the lady-day ventry in this kind of way; they
were offered to the farmers by the parish officials, and the
farmer who would take a boy and maintain him during his
apprenticeship for the least premium got him. The boys are
apprenticed until they were twenty one years of age, and

---

[1]*West Briton*: November 21, 1889.
[2]The passages quoted are from one of a series in the *West Briton* in 1889
by 'Our Agricultural Correspondent'; frequent allusions to places in the
Stratton area suggest that he had lived and farmed in that district for
many years. The sand on this coast tends to be calcareous. Much of the
sand on the south Cornish coast was non-calcareous and Plymouth
limestone was burnt in lime kilns on this coast including the Helford
area.

many of them commenced their apprenticeship as early as six years old. During the whole of this time they would receive no money at all for their services, and in case they ran away from their masters the latter, accompanied by the parish constable who was equipped with a staff and a pair of handcuffs, were soon on their tracks to demand that they retrace their steps or otherwise suffer the consequences – spend the remainder of their apprenticeship at Bodmin (jail). The parish apprentices were often cruelly served, and had to subsist on the coarsest food, which consisted of pork, barley bread, and potatoes, or as an electioneering poet put it –

> Barley bread as black as your hat,
> Taties fried without any fat,
> Pudding made without any suet,
> That's the way the Tories do it." '

At Trease the Boadens had only employed one 'servant man', William Skewis, who went to Bojarrow with them, and may have been a youthful apprentice, for John did not say if he was the 'young servant man to work horses' they kept at the latter farm. Both John and his younger brother had to work at Bojarrow, and the fare on which the Boadens themselves lived was little better than that denounced by the 'electioneering poet'.

Boys could help spread dung, carry corn to the men who sowed it broadcast and other lighter and less skilled jobs. The crop rotations were simple for

leys of two or three years old were broken for wheat. Arishes[1] were ploughed in the fall, mostly for barley. After the voars had been wheeled in the spring it was ploughed across (an operation) called threarting; then when the land would work[2] it was got down; then the piles of manure were wheeled out, three hundred barrows being a day's work; these were scattered; then the land was again ploughed – called ploughing for barley – then the crop was tilled . . . My father used to begin his crop rotation by preparing a lea field for potatoes with a little turnips. He let out a good part for others

[1]Stubbles
[2]That is when the ground was not too heavy or frozen.

to have potato ground at a shilling per lace[1]. Two butchers from Helston regularly tilled with the rest at Trease in twenty and forty lace plots measured out by Cousin Hugh. This after went to wheat and then barley, and then left to ley.'

The practice of letting out potato-ground by the season, not only to neighbouring cottagers but to townspeople living some distance away, was not a survival of an older system of communal husbandry but simply a matter of mutual convenience. Potatoes were an ideal 'cleaning' first crop, but small farmers did not want the toil and expense of cultivating so many acres now that turnips and mangel wurzels had proved a better and cheaper 'green' crop for cattle-feeding; the cost of harvesting and sending maincrop field potatoes to market too, was often unprofitable. Even till recent times Cornish farmers allowed men to plant a 'row of taters' in a field in return for a helping hand at harvest, but in John Boaden's youth when labour was cheap and fairly abundant, a rent of four pounds per acre was charged for potato ground.[2]

At Trease the Boadens had kept a few cattle, which were fed mainly on straw during the winter. Pigs were important in the farm economy, Boaden recalling that a pig of fourteen score and upwards live weight would be given half a bushel of barley to fatten it off;[3] nowadays pigs of eight or nine scores are reckoned as more than ready for the butcher whose customers would reject the coarse and extremely fat pork formerly almost a staple diet on farms which raised most of the flesh their folk consumed. Farmers then generally killed their own pigs, or employed the services of a village 'professional' pig-killer like Hugh Johns.

The corn mow paid the rent, Boaden remarking that 'the returns from the farm were mostly from corn sold of which there was the greatest care taken.' The last remark could not be applied to the draught animals Cornish farmers kept, for

---

[1]The lace was an old Cornish measure of about six yards square, and seems to be related to the old Cornish rather than to the English statutory acre.
[2]About sevenpence, or half a day's farm wage, per lace.
[3]Fourteen score or 280 pounds, approximately 127 kilos; eight or nine score roughly 75 kilos.

'horses had little oats. Our horses were put in the orchard to graze, In the middle of the day during spring tillage hay (for them) was pulled frequently out of the rick by a crook. The horses were smaller and being badly fed much weaker than at present; used to hear of farmers obliged sometimes to stop their teams before leaving work time, the horses being run down, but oxen did a large part of the work everywhere, and were often shod and worked on the roads to draw sand and ox-wains.'[1]

Improvements in the care and management of horses in Cornwall only came slowly, and then through trying to check the declining farm profits by economising in labour. Horses replaced oxen because they were quicker which meant that a single ploughman got through more work. In 1845 it was stated that a pair of horses could do a third more work in a day than four oxen and were cheaper to keep than a double ox-team.[2] Horses were needed to draw the mowing and reaping machines that came into fairly general use after 1850. The horse, too, was far better than the ox for carrying produce to market; long after the repeal of the Corn Laws British corngrowers got good prices if they managed to harvest and thresh their grain quickly and into the markets before supplies were brought to England by sailing ships from Odessa and the Baltic ports. An early harvest, too, depended partly on getting seed-time over early; it was the horse rather than the plodding ox that 'sped the plough'.

Farm implements at Trease were primitive. Till John's father turned an ox into a horse wain he had used a wheel-draw, that is a sledge with two small wheels, to carry hay and corn. Furthermore

'The harness was of a cheap sort; not many of the farm horses, as I remember them first, had leather back bands, the chain had simply a rope belly band as it was called under the horse's

---

[1] The poor quality and management of Cornish horses were mentioned by Worgan in 1808 (*General View of the Agriculture of the County of Cornwall*, p. 154), and in 1845 by the Truro Veterinary surgeon, W. F. Karkeek (*Journal Royal Agricultural Society*, Vol. VI, pp. 453-455.)
[2] W. F. Karkeek: *Journal Royal Agricultural Society*, Vol. VI, p. 456.

belly. When in field traces horses scarcely had anything but rope halters, and mongers made of spinned straw, a pair of wood hames tied at each end with rope yarn – these frequently broke; the traces were almost invariably rope instead of chains as at present. The ploughman had almost invariably a driver (a lead boy); This gave the boys their introduction to farm work to which they often went soon after they were eight years of age. The implements were very light and poor. The ploughs had a wood ground called the chip; the share having a shoe was slipped in it. All the plough was wood except the share and coulter. There was a halter and pin at the end of the beam to pull it by. The harrows were all made of wood, tines excepted, very inefficient compared to those of the present, but the (poor) horses (of those days) could not pull the present implements. All the threshing was done by the flail and winnowing out on the sheets with sieves by the servant maids. It was quite a job to carry out the unwinnowed corn and winnowing things from the barn and bring it back again.'

On some farms, especially those of the gentry, implements were better than these, and included iron ploughs and horse-driven threshing machines.

A few economical farmers had already dispensed with the driver in ploughing, but labour was still cheap, for, as John wrote

'wages for labourers was eight shillings per week; a few, principally gentlemen, gave nine shillings. Women, who were numerous in the fields, had sixpence a day, in harvest a shilling and dinners. Many labourers had their corn where they worked at the uniform price of ten shillings and twenty shillings for barley and wheat per Cornish bushel which was considered an advantage by the labourers.[1] Sometimes there was a glut of labourers, when work at quor had to be paid for

[1]The Cornish was three Imperial or Winchester bushels, so these labourers got barley and wheat for £1.33 and £2.63 per quarter respectively; the market prices in the 'forties rarely fell below £1.50 and £3.00.

by the parish vestries at a shilling per day[1]. I can also remember several young persons of both sexes who were serving as parish apprentices. The best wages for boarded men servants was about ten pounds per year and for maids four pounds. Money was scarce and labour cheap and a great deal used to little purpose.

In short, before migration from rural parishes became general in the 'hungry forties', places in the Meneage felt the consequence of an increase in population which had become marked by the eighteen-thirties.[2] At the same time declining farm prices limited the amount of labour a farmer could afford to hire, while the very scarcity of money sometimes made it almost impossible to find cash to pay even the cheapest labour.

Still changes for the better had and were taking place. John wrote

'very shortly, before my remembrance the furze was carried on horses' backs to the ricks; a large lot of furze was laid down called a tross and found at each end by ropes called tross ropes; this was set on end and tipped over on the horse's back; a man then stuck a pole into the tross by which he balanced it as he led the horse. This was how the people got their fuel. We always had ours from Treloskan crofts, (which are) mostly cultivated now. The poor would pick any fuel they could from the hedges and also, in summer, the dried droppings of the cattle, which they called picking glows. I

---

[1]'Letting out at Quor', was a local term referring to the practice of drafting the unemployed on to the ratepayers in proportion to their rate assessments by the Parish Vestries. The Vestry at Ludgvan, near Penzance, in the harvest of 1822 hired out able-bodied unemployed at twopence and fourpence per day. (*West Briton*: August 16, 1822)

[2]The increase in population revealed in early British census returns may have been due more to a reduction of infant mortality than to an increased birth rate. This meant that more females survived to child-bearing age. If more children survived, too, these included the children of farmers as well as those of labourers, and meant that in time the amount of outside labour employed on farms was drastically reduced; most of the smaller holdings in Cornwall became 'family farms'.

remember to have seen women weeding corn with reap hooks; this used to be the common tool for the purpose.'

Very truly was a horse a beast of burden, and some Cornish ones must have been superbly docile or extremely dispirited indeed to stand heavy faggots of prickly furze being put on their backs in this way, for there is no hint that a protective pack-saddle was used. With such low wages it was little wonder that the coalman was unknown, and furze so widely used in the Meneage, though in Boaden's day many crofts were brought under tillage.

Not only was rural life primitive, but many superstitious beliefs were prevalent. Tales John Boaden heard of evil spirits, witches, death tokens and the like, in his boyhood, almost he admitted, made him afraid of the dark. He recalled that

'Mr. James Dale, not long since dead, was driving a sow belonging to his father, who farmed Gilly, to Bonython, when near Grygler Green she fell dead; they had also lost some cattle previously. Mr. Dale in returning by way of Bojorrow was advised by Mr. John Thomas, a Baptist local preacher, to go back, take out the sow's heart, stick it over with thorn pricles, then roast it in a fire: while this was proceeding a blue cock would emerge from some hedge or thicket and while the cock was in sight the person who had ill-wished Mr. Dale would be out of his mind. But though it was carried out to the letter, no blue cock appeared. I was an eye witness. This happened in the early forties.'

This was strange advice from a local preacher, and the episode suggests a fantastic amalgam of primitive beliefs and folk lore. Still Meneage farmers were no worse than others. In the Scilly Isles, in 1836, a man who, like Dale, had lost several cattle, attributed it to witchcraft, and on the advice of a neighbour, tried to break the spell by burning a living calf.[1]

Only slowly and far from surely did old superstitions die. The religious revivalism of the period did not stamp them out, and some even alleged that the unleashing of wild emotional forces by irregular preachers actually reprieved dying superstitious

[1]*West Briton*: April 15, 1836.

beliefs. The lurid contrasts so often drawn in 'Chapel' pulpits between salvation and damnation certainly played up the dark, deep-rooted subconscious terrors in the minds of uneducated people. Evil was real, and too many preachers and congregations personified it into tangible 'powers of darkness'. Some preachers welcomed any ally, no matter if born in deepest paganism, to make the 'stony-hearted' more aware of their awful latter end. Most preachers, however, were less concerned with comparatively harmless superstitious rites and beliefs than they were with great and pressing social evils. Religious extremists were directing their main energies against drunkenness, and John Boaden rightly called this period that of the 'Temperance reformation'.

Boaden alluded to other contemporary evils, but made little of the poaching to which underpaid labourers were driven to stave off starvation from their families, nor did he mention that, in the early forties Cornish men and women were transported to Australia for fifteen years for sheep-stealing. Even when bitterly condemning the 'Great office' he did not enlarge on the general ill-feeling prevalent between landlords and tenants. As for the wages of labourers he did not question their justice, but another farmer of his generation declared

'The farm labourer, who worked like a slave, received seven shillings a week. I have interviewed several old men now living (in 1889) as to whether they could really manage to exist and maintain a family with seven shillings per week and pay twenty-eight shillings per bag[1] for wheat, and the answer has invariably been no. "It was no living in it", said one. They ransacked ships which had been driven ashore, poaching was general, and all kinds of plunder had to be resorted to in many cases. Who benefited by the privations of the poor? The farmers? Not often. The people who were the main cause of this state of existence . . . and who mainly benefited thereby were the landlords. During the first half of the present (nineteenth) century landlordism was probably responsible for more crimes than all the other isms put together in Cornwall.'[2]

[1] Probably the Cornish bushel bag of 24 gallons.
[2] *West Briton*: November 21, 1889.

This can hardly be reconciled to John Boaden's remark that 'hunting and shooting were favourite pastimes and many of the labourers devoted most of their leisure to it.' When working the labourers had very little leisure, and when they were unemployed their main concern was to find something to eat.

Other changes took place since Boaden was a boy. Briefly he noted that

> 'A number of provincialisms then in use are now almost forgotten; pronounciation was very broad; the people not so well-informed as at present, but quite as shrewd and knew their own districts rather better. There were more 'characters' then. Unfortunately there were a great many drunkards, several of whom were reclaimed by the advent of Teetotallism.'

If a little inclined to regret the passing of local provincialisms he believed that great moral progress had been made in his time, but viewed a vanishing race of unconvential 'rugged individualists' with less regret. He welcomed the appearance of the cheap newspaper, mentioning that his father and two neighbours had clubbed together to buy the *Cornwall Gazette*, then costing fourpence a week, between them, each taking turns to read it first; what John recalled, most vividly, were 'vials of wrath' its ultra-Tory editorials poured on the head of the Irish Nationalist Daniel O'Connell.

8

Methodists and Others

When the Boadens moved to Bojorrow farming life went on in much the same way as it had done at Trease. The main business was still the harvest; that of 1841 was almost ruined by bad weather, but Sir Richard Vyvyan helped his tenants by hiring them to cart stone from Chygarky Quarry to hedge the reclaimed Garras Downs. There were new neighbours, and young John Boaden became friends with the Dales of Gilly, a mile away, and through them, with the Lorry family at Trebarvath Farm in St. Keverne, nearly seven miles from Bojorrow. That distance, however, was not regarded as much by a sturdy farm lad of thirteen or fourteen summers although John and the young Dales went mainly in summer in the lull between hay and corn harvests, or on Sundays when a special service at one of the St. Keverne chapels gave the youngsters an excuse to visit their friends. Their father sometimes probably encouraged them to go and see what the crops were looking like in the district known as the garden of Cornwall. Occasionally curiosity about the latest wreck on the Manacles, which could be seen from Trevarbath fields, drew them. Doubtless the Lorry children returned the visit, and the way the boys of three farmers 'chummed together' rather than seeking their closest friends among boys born in different stations and walks of life nearer home is significant.

Garras, however, was the main centre of local social life for the Bojorrow family. There in November, 1842, a Methodist Sunday School was opened

'This was done almost entirely through the activity of Edward Oates Orchard who was learning the printing business in Helston but (who) remained on Sundays with his parents in

Carrabane. The congregation at (Mawgan parish) church was good; There was a large, good Sunday School; Mrs. Mann, the Rector's wife, and his large family being very active. There was no public service at the Garras (Methodist Chapel) save only on Sunday evenings and fortnightly on Monday nights. The Church had no Sunday evening services. The Methodists attended the church services. There was a Sunday afternoon service held at the Baptist Chapel at Roseveare . . . I think it was in the latter end of 1844 I became a Sunday School teacher which I have continued to the present time, with the exception of only a few years in the early 'fifties when the Garras school was closed.'

Whilst there was a variety of religious denominations in Mawgan parish there was little if any sectarian prejudice or jealousy. Anglican, Wesleyan Methodist, and Baptist not only lived side by side but attended each other's services. The Rector apparently conducted Sunday evening services at St. Martin, which had long been held with the living at Mawgan. Neither Anglican nor Methodist services were held at the same time as the Baptist Sunday afternoon meeting. One or two Anglicans may have tended to look somewhat askance at the Methodists, but the latter still regarded the parish church and its clergy with respect, and both Anglicans and Wesleyans tolerated the Baptists. The over-worked Rector was not perhaps altogether sorry that the Methodists were helping to keep religious life active in the parish.

Outstanding among the many zealous Methodists of those days was the father of the youth who started the Sunday School, William Orchard, one day to be John Boaden's father-in-law. Will Orchard was a dynamic personality, with great natural ability and talents, a born leader of men. Unfortunately lesser men were jealous of him, and for that very reason he became the cause of a local schisms in Wesleyan Methodism. Concisely Boaden told his story

'Will Orchard when a lad went to sea for a voyage or two, but his mother could not rest from the danger, and he was apprenticed as a shoemaker to Ben Tonkin at St. Martin, where he got acquainted with his future wife and both went to class meeting together about the year 1833. In ten years after they were married he had bought the leasehold of Carrabane from Edward Dale. He settled there and began a shoemaking business which grew to be a prosperous one; he usually had two apprentices, so he learnt (i.e. taught) a great many, and they generally turned out well. He also had the five meadows and two cows. He began to preach about 1820 and to lead a class about five years after. But his active mind and superior intelligence drew upon him the opposition of those who envied him, which was strikingly manifested. Just after the great revival of 1839 he was a member of Mawgan Sick Club which met at the public house; it was large and prosperous and had about £400 in stock; a revision of its rules was deemed necessary. Will Orchard was entrusted with getting this done; he employed L. H. Edwards a conveyancer to do it, but at a meeting of the club about this matter a very stormy discussion arose; among others Mr. Peter Andrew spoke excitedly. It ended in a trial before the Helston magistrates, when Will Orchard gave evidence. The opposite party said he had taken a false oath because he said he did not hear Mr. Andrew say certain words. (My wife, his daugher) Eleanor Jane says that she remembers that word came to Carrabane before her father arrived home from Helston that he had taken a false oath. The calumny grew; the Wesleyan Society which had just been so largely augmented was greatly agitated, and Will Orchard was pained to see what he had worked so hard to accomplish to a large extent destroyed. John Carlyon who had been recently appointed a leader left the chapel with most of his class, and joined the Baptists who had built a chapel at Roseveare about (the year) 1820; for the above reason they (the Baptists) wre flourishing when we came to Mawgan in 1840.'

Looking back this seems a storm in a teacup, but it created much ill-feeling in Mawgan. Regrettably John Boaden was so concerned with the wrong done his father-in-law that he did not give more details of the village sick club.

Clubs of this type were formed in many villages early in the nineteenth century. Some had developed from burial clubs to local friendly societies which provided small pensions to bereaved widows and orphans besides sick benefits to their members. The funds accumulated by the Mawgan club seem very large indeed for those times, adequate if wisely invested to provide benefits equal to half their weekly wage to five or six of its members without drawing upon current contributions. Significantly in Mawgan this club was managed by the parishioners themselves; perhaps the guidance of Rector or squire might have averted the disputes, but even so their betters could not have compelled the men of Mawgan to contribute and maintain such a club set up by those who, having no liking for parish relief or the sour bread of charity, believed that by mutual help it was possible to look after themselves and their families in sickness.

John Boaden naturally told the story from his father-in-law's viewpoint. He recalled that

'one beautiful Sunday evening in 1846 I walked home from Helston with Will Orchard . . . he then told me the whole tale. The separation of 1833 scarcely affected the Mawgan (Methodist) Society. Hugh Lyne only leaving the new chapel, of which Will Orchard had been the most active promoter and which was opened in June 1834 . . . But more trouble was in store for Mawgan Wesleyans and (for) Will Orchard in particular. The teetotal zeal in Mawgan was rather opposed than helped by most of the ministers who frequently were not abstainers. This had increased for sometime and culminated early in 1845 by a large number of members leaving the Garras Society; they were joined by several who had a few years before seceded to the Baptists, and joined a new church under the title of Teetotal Wesleyans. The difficulty of managing a new connexion was so great that in a few years they joined the Wesleyan Methodist Association, now the free Church; they stipulated in doing so that no preacher who was not an abstainer should occupy their pulpit or any non-abstainer be a member of their society. The foremost man in this Temperence crusade was Tobias Johns of St. Martins, a very zealous, devoted, and determined man, a converted smuggler. But as Will Orchard was the principal man in the Wesleyan Society, and tried to take a middle course, he could not expect to pass through these times of reproach, and strife, and excited feeling unscathed. Though

Cornish Mow made up of about 100 sheaves

there is no manifestation of injury in his manner and spirit, these wars somewhat affected his business, and probably were one of the causes and perhaps an important one of his leaving the country in 1849. He often when not away preaching on Sunday would take his children to his bedroom and give religious instruction to them. He was a force for good anywhere, especially at home.'

Men like Orchard were natural leaders of Methodist non-conformity and the backbone of the local chapels and societies: ministers came and went but these staunch laymen were there all the time. But jealousy, next oldest sin to disobedeience, crept in, and was as much the mainspring of new 'connexions' as genuine uncompromising religious principle. Will Orchard was, perhaps, a little too ready to compromise to preserve unity and brotherhood. Ministers coming from other districts could not grasp the strength of the total abstinence movement and emotional prejudices against strong drink. Tobias Johns with the zeal of the proselyte who had seen the error of his ways was utterly determined that he would do all in his power to deny others any chance to fall into similar temptations. Others thought that if the local shoemaker could run a chapel so could they.

Methodist quarrels at Mawgan were unpleasant and they were repeated in many another local community in those times, revealing why those outside the Connexion often looked at it with derision. If there was an outstanding local leader too often his associates would combine to drag him down for no real reason save petty spite and jealousy. John Boaden was lenient in his brief description of the zealous converted smuggler but showed Tobias Johns to be an intolerant fanatic. The slanders against Orchard were spread without any consideration of what had actually happened at the Helston court; it is unlikely that he had lied to the magistrates when he said he had not caught the words the excited Peter Andrew had spoken in a tumultuous meeting, and the importance of those words may have been very slight. The incident, stimulated the temperance movement and led to the organisation of a local teetotal Rechabite friendly society replacing the old sick club which, to the disgust of teetotallers, had held its meetings in the public house. Will Orchard, at least, took a truly temperate line; he did not regard a person's partiality to strong liquour, either in moderation or even in excess, a test of salvation or damnation.

Still the main issues in the 'forties were not theological controversies but these disputes showed that a really alive social life existed in the rural parish of Mawgan. The provision of a second Sunday School in that parish helped to educate the young. John Boaden's connection with that school at Garras was life-long, for he was in it the day before he died in 1904.[1] Just how much such schools were needed in rural districts is revealed by the anecdote a well-known Cornish farmer told to refute the claims made by some that the old dame schools provided all that was necessary in the way of education. Writing in March, 1870, John Penhallow Peters said that in the old days

'An education was given to the child of the labourer in a dame school, where the teaching was much after this model: Scholar: G missus, O missus, D missus: GOD, God missus. I missus, S missus: IS, is missus. L missus, O missus, V missus, E missus: LOVE, Love missus. God is love, missus. Which would meet with the approval of the mistress dame in 'Well said, my little opticock.'[2]

John Boaden's other life-long interest was temperance, and his family were among the first Rechabites in the district. Sixty years later he vividly recalled that

'On Mawgan feast Monday Edward Oats Orchard and myself spent most of the night at Joseph Gilbert's painting letters on a Rechabite flag for the next day's procession'.

Formerly parish feasts had been most intemperately convivial: the teetotallers determined to put an end to that, and in many places the parish feast died out altogether, elsewhere it became little more than a name. There were villages, although apparently not Mawgan, where there was considerable opposition to the blue-ribbon 'spoil-sports' and 'kill-joys' but, for good or for ill, old days

[1]*West Briton:* April 14, 1904
[2]*West Briton:* March 31, 1870

and old ways were dying; the Victorian age of respectability and conventional seemliness had dawned.

Yet life was far from dull. There were many opportunities for harmless amusement and many high-spirited individuals who could bring gaiety to even the most sober circle. Thus John Boaden did not hesitate to declare that

'All through my early years and up to the 'seventies no visitor so interested me and perhaps insensibly educated me as Father's cousin Joseph, called Josey. He came tolerably often (to Bojorrow) was a shrewd man, knew well what was going on, could estimate men very well, was a humourist and a capital mimic. I was always glad to see him come in; it was a treat to me, and I occasionally went to his house.'

It is a pity John Boaden said no more about this relative, but by the time this was first written Cousin Josey was dead and gone, those he had mimicked long forgotten; but from him John Boaden may have got the knack of shrewdly appraising men and learnt to be more tolerant of human weakness than many who shared his religious faith.

It was the Orchard family at Carrabane which influenced John Boaden most in his youth. He recalled one Sunday he spent with them when some of Edward Orchard's Helston friends were present. Among them was Thomas Hosking, who was

'the best phonographer (shorthand writer) in the district. E. O. Orchard soon after learnt it and in the spring of the following year was engaged by the inventor Mr. Isaac Pitman, afterwards knighted, to go to his offices at Bath, where he printed various books, including Paradise Lost, part of the Bible, and published the organ of the movement; but he was not robust and I think had come home to be nursed before he was there much over a year. My contact with the Orchard family induced me to learn the new system which I did in 1845; an apprentice (shoemaker) at Carrabane named Nicholas Keverne, who had been instructed by E. O. Orchard being my teacher. I afterwards taught a class at the Garras, but few of them derived much permanent good from it.'

Perhaps John was not a good instructor in shorthand, but this interest in a remote rural district in this new 'invention' is rather surprising.

Those meetings of young people at Carrabane brought young John into contact with persons who had more to talk about than the crops and the weather. Edward Orchard's Helston friends brought him in touch with the wider world, for Helston was then the centre of an extremely busy mining district, with many prosperous tradespeople and professional men whose young sons and daughters thought that the world was one of infinite prospects. Edward Oates Orchard brought several of them out to Carrabane, and his younger farmer friend recalled that

> 'We met, I think, for three successive years at Carrabane the last day of the Old Year. Bryan Dale, then a clerk in Mr. Plomer's Office, now a retired congregational minister in Bradford, used to attend. These meetings were also managed and attended to by my future wife.'

But when he wrote these days were long gone. Those that met at Carrabane were dead or far away.

There was regret in looking back to those happy days of John Boaden and his youthful friends. Work on the farms was hard, but they had some leisure now and then to engage in social activities at Garras Chapel and in attempts to 'self-improvement'. Novelties from the progressive outside world reached them, and they were eager to spend time and effort on the acquisition of knowledge. Friends and relations came and went, bringing news and information, sometimes staying for a night or, at least, for a leisurely meal. Day followed day, and season followed season.

Yet, despite the hopes of youth, all was not well in those times. There were years when the whole cycle of the weather went wrong, and farmers' troubles meant troubles for other people too, for spoilt grain meant less and dearer bread and blighted crops meant scarcity, sometimes famine, for man and beast. In a brief paragraph John Boaden referred to the unhappy 'hungry forties'

> 'there was a great agitation going on held by Cobden and Bright for the abolition of the Corn Laws. This movement was very materially helped by failure of the potato crop in

1845 and the Irish famine. When in 1846 the price of corn was very high at its very extreme, which only lasted for a short time, the price for barley and wheat was nearly 20s. and 40s. per Cornish bushel.[1] I recollect being put by my father one Saturday to sell some barley in Helston market, he being almost afraid to go, and selling in consequence. The miners came in on Saturday, the town was full of people, and the excitement was intense. It was feared that the corn would be taken from the farmers, or the shops attacked. The Riot Act was read by the Mayor, and a detachment of military arrived, and the peace so seriously threatened was not broken, but from that time the price began to fall. It was in this year that the Corn Laws were repealed by Sir Robert Peel, who had been moving in that direction for some years, but the repeal did not come into force till 1849 when the price was only moderate.'

Boaden's memory, however, served him false. The Helston troubles he mentioned occurred in May, 1847, a year after the repeal of the Corn Laws. Nor was he in Helston that market day when the miners 'invaded' the town.

The harvest of 1846 had been bad, and was followed by a long, bitter winter; even before Christmas there were special collections in many parts to provide relief in kind to the labouring poor. Distress was acute in the Cornish mining districts, and Boaden rightly attributed the Helston disturbances to the miners although many were goaded on by their womenfolk. Towards the end of January miners in mid-Cornwall had attempted to stop cargoes of grain from being 'exported' from Par and Pentewan; a similar demonstration by miners and quarry workers at Wadebridge on May 12th seemed to be the signal for disturbances throughout the county from Tamar Valley to Land's End. John Boaden's own trip to Helston market was probably on Saturday, May 15th, when some women threatened a corn dealer who, was, apparently, unjustly, accused of attempting to 'corner' all available supplies of grain and flour. He quickly made himself scarce.

Before the next weekly market the town authorities took steps

---

[1] The Cornish bushel being three imperial bushels this meant barley at 53/4d. and wheat at 106/8d. per quarter.

to prevent further disturbances. The unpopular corn merchant's accounts were audited and a statement issued over the signature of the mayor to the effect that, far from attempting to establish a great monopoly, he had actually imported large quantities of grain in a praiseworthy and public spirited endeavour to keep down local prices. Men and women feeling the pinch of hunger were sceptical of such a declaration: probably many of them could hardly read let alone understand a financial statement. The local authorities, however, had no illusion that a 'scrap of paper' would keep the peace. Fifty Royal Fusiliers were brought to Helston from Falmouth the following evening, no less than sixty special constables were sworn in, and the local coastguard force, two dozen strong, were marched into Helston on Saturday morning.

About noon, that Saturday, word came that a formidable force of miners were coming in from the west. The mayor and corporation attended by the special constables went out to meet them; it is not certain that the Riot Act was read as John Boaden stated, for there is no reference to it in the contemporary local newspapers; at all events they did disperse, but later came into the town by twos and threes; only one trivial passage of words and nothing but words took place between a group of miners and a constable. The market day, in fact, passed without trouble, although many farmers, fearful of disturbances, had stayed at home, and as a result the limited supplies of wheat in the market fetched about 111s. per quarter whilst barley soared to 61s.[1]

Famine, however, was threatening the mining districts. It was all very well for the 'principal inhabitants' of Helston to meet and issue a declaration pledging themselves to the utmost economy in the consumption of food in their households: that was no comfort to the families poor labourers and miners and doubtless grumbles went about that the deep pocketed and fat-bellied tradespeople and lawyers would not go short. Miners who had thronged to Helston that market-day had to bear the jibes of their bitter-tongued, half-starved womenfolk during the days that followed, and there were a few hot-headed youths who boasted that they would have done more than their over-cautious elders. Lads like the seventeen year old John Williams of Ashton in Breage

[1] i.e. 38s. and 23s. per Cornish bushel respectively. (*West Briton*: May 28, 1847.)

were breathing blood and thunder against corn merchants and profiteering farmers. Hunger knows no reason, and thoughtless trouble-makers did not realise there was little grain left in the district after the long winter. Even more foolish were the Helston authorities who apparently thought that since that last Saturday market had passed off without conflict there would be no further trouble. The troops went back to Falmouth, because there was some difficulty in providing them with rations and because trouble was feared in that port. Furthermore, the rising discontent in the mining towns of Redruth and Camborne meant that all available troops in West Cornwall were being drafted into that district.

Many farmers, however, decided that they had no urgent business in Helston the following Saturday, May 28th, and by nightfall probably thought that they had been wise. Rumour doubtless exaggerated what actually took place in Helston that afternoon, when

'about twenty noisy and discontented women . . . came into the market, backed by some hundreds of miners armed with bludgeons, with the full determination to have the corn sold at their price. In the early part of the market, 36s. was asked for wheat and 21s. for barley, but the farmers soon found to their great annoyance that the prices fixed by the mob were 30s. for wheat and 16s. for barley. A scuffle ensued, but for want of firmness on the part of the farmers, the mob soon had the ascendancy, and protested against any corn being carried out of the market at a higher price than they had fixed. A farmer of the name of Lawrence was the first to give way, and others followed in his steps, notwithstanding the authorities of the town, backed by about seventy special constables, together with the police force, were ready to protect the farmers in the sale of their corn. There were about two hundred bushels of corn in the market at the time . . . About seven O'clock the miners began to leave the town, which at ten had assumed its unusually quiet state.'[1]

[1] *West Briton*: June 4, 1847

The 'maximum' prices fixed by the miners were not unduly low, amounting as they did to 80s. the quarter for wheat and 42/8d. for barley; on the other hand the farmers were not particularly grasping when they had asked for 96s. and 56s. respectively. Two years earlier, however, at the same 'scarce time of the year', wheat had only been fetching about 49s. and barley 33s. per quarter. But there were only seventy-five quarters in a market which served a population of some 17,500 living in Helston town and the neighbouring mining parishes of Sithney, Wendron, Breage, and Germoe.[1]

The next market-day troops were back in Helston, more special constables had been sworn in, no-one was allowed in the market carrying a stick, and a close watch was kept on known trouble-makers and firebrands. The day before, June 4th, there had been riots in Redruth and Camborne. In Redruth a corn-store had been broken into and looted, but only fifteen sacks of flour had been removed; for this the two ringleaders, mere youths in their early twenties were transported to Van Dieman's Land[2] for seven year terms, and others imprisoned. Up at St. Austell many miners attempted to pull down the market building, and in Torquay a starving mob set fire to shops and stores. Compared to these places, Helston was quiet, for the labourers there had attempted to control prices in the interests of the consumer, following an example set a few weeks earlier by the Caradon miners in Callington market. Such an attempt should have been a graver warning to the authorities of the town and the corn dealers than

[1]Fluctuations in the census returns in this district makes it impossible to give more than a rough estimate of the population at this time. The successive returns were as follows:

	1841	1851	1861
Helston	3,584	3,355	3,843
Sithney	3,362	2,768	3,306
Wendron	5,576	5,321	6,008
Breage	6,166	4,543	5,173
Germoe	1,336	970	1,015
TOTAL	19,924	16,957	19,345

[1]Tasmania.

the violent excesses of an entirely unorganised mob. Yet had the authorities not been so prompt in taking steps to check disturbances, worse might easily have occurred in Helston and there is no doubt that the crisis was alleviated by bringing corn and flour in from outside and from foreign sources.

9

Rustic Romance

John Boaden dismissed some of the more significant events of his early days briefly, assuming, perhaps, that they were too well known to insert in his brief autobiography. When he wrote there were still many living who remembered the Helston disturbances of 'forty-seven; yet he might have stated what exactly contemporary farmers thought of the repeal of the Corn Laws. Accounts of meetings in those days show that there was acute controversy, but since there was no secret ballot those tenant farmers who voiced an opinion usually only echoed the views of their landlords. The Wadebridge Farmers' Club, most of whose members were tenants of the Radical squire of Pencarrow, was an assembly of free traders with few dissesntients; tenants of Port Eliot and Menabilly estates in south-east Cornwall, when they spoke, uttered very different sentiments.

Most tenant farmers were indifferent, although many thought that protection had been simply a device to safeguard the interests of land-owners. In any case the Corn Laws had failed to keep grain prices from fluctuating in local and wider markets, and it was possible that free trade might stabilize prices and give farmers a better idea where they stood financially. Under protection when prices were low, they generally had had a glut of grain in their barns and ricks, and when high they often had had scarcely enough for their own use. As for the local miners who had set the hearts of the Helston shopkeepers and professional men fluttering, it was obvious that they looked upon 'engrossing' middlemen and dealers as their foes, and were unlikely to swarm south to ransack the granaries and barns of the Meneage farmers – although, driven by hunger, they might have done so had not supplies of flour and grain been brought into the districts from outside. There had been many similar incidents in the past when, in times of famine-prices, riotous mobs of hungry miners and their families had demonstrated; rarely had they resorted to more violent measures; nevertheless in 1847, with the Corn Laws already practically gone, the demonstrations which occurred in practically every considerable market town in Cornwall,[1] might easily have developed into bloody riots and even insurrections.

John Boaden, however, was more concerned with his personal affairs. At this point his reminiscences have a 'chapter heading' entitled 'The Romance of My Life'. Like many other country lads he started courting young, his romance being a somewhat prosaic rural idyll, set in a background of chapel life. Many a Cornish love story started that way in those days. Fidgetting in a far from comfortable seat during a tedious sermon, a lad would stare around, spy a pretty face, or catch the eye of a girl like him uninterested in anecdotes of the misdeeds and failings of dead and gone Israelite Kings. So it was that young John

'sat in the gallery of the Garras Chapel opposite the seat of the Orchard family of Carrabane, which consisted of three girls approaching womanhood and two smaller ones and two brothers. A. Wicks also sat in the same seat. Their father (William Orchard) was a local preacher, a man of great energy, and one of the most intelligent men in the parish, and took great pride in his family. He had given them, for those days, a good education. They were always neatly dressed, and would be called a good looking and interesting lot of girls. It is not to be wondered at that they attracted my notice, but the second daughter, Eleanor Jane, made by far the deepest impression on my mind. Indeed her bright eyes, cheerful countenance, and sweet voice, and a something undefinable something else soon won my affection without any efforts on my part. I succeeded occasionally in getting in her company.'

[1] Incidents and riots also occurred in May, 1847, at Wadebridge, Callington, Redruth, Camborne, Penzance, and St. Austell in Cornwall; there were disturbances elsewhere in England at the same time and caused by the same 'famine prices', *vide my Cornwall in the Age of the Industrial Revolution*, pp. 158-162.

The affair had become 'serious' by the time of the Helston disturbances, and John thought more of the romantic flutterings of his own heart than of politics and social unrest.

With naive sincerity he wrote that one evening in the spring of 1843 he heard that Eleanor Jane

'and her little sister had gone to Trevassack; I went there and escorted them there across the fields a nearer way home.'

Maybe the nearer way took the longer time, and possibly little sister was encouraged to linger behind to search for spring flowers. At all events nigh sixty years on John had cause to write

'may I be forgiven if I stole the first kiss of love. On her way to Travassack she passed through a muddy gateway to Bojorrow Croft. Their footprints wre firmly imprinted and the dry weather rendered them firmly stamped for some time. I looked on those footprints almost as if they were sacred. The same year I went after a Sunday evening service to Trelowarren Lodge by Relowas Gate, then occupied by R. Kevern, with Eleanor Jane, her aunt Mary, Uncle Hannibal and his affianced (Miss Blewitt) and their cousin Betsy Pentecost.'

If three is a crowd, the two young men doubtless felt that evening that they were in a thronging multitude. Still John described these as

'enchanting times. I also went to meet Elizabeth Janes and Eleanor Jane returning from St. Martin one Sunday evening; we met at Trelowarren and I accompanied Eleanor Jane home, but did not impart to her the feelings of my heart.'

John probably had to put up with some teasing from his elders though others started courting as young as he: Sunday evenings after chapel services were courting times, and lads and lasses drifted away together whilst their elders lingered at the chapel doors talking perhaps about the sermon they had just heard, more likely about the weather, sometimes with malice and uncharitableness about the failings of some of their neighbours. It was easy enough to linger in the lanes on the pleasantly long springtide evenings, stroll over to Mawgan, come back through the Trelowarren drives, or wander off towards Cury and return by lanes and downland tracks – provided one did not walk alone.

Soon, however, John and Eleanor were to be parted for

'in the early part of 1844, Eleanor Jane not being much wanted at home took a situation as nursery maid at Captain Passingham's near Falmouth. The master died very soon after she went there. She used to take the children almost daily to Swanpool. Her father coming down and not liking her situation took her home with him, forfeiting some wages. She was there eleven weeks.'

Eleven weeks seemed an age to young John. Falmouth and Swanpool were too far away those days for any visiting. He doubtless rejoiced that Will Orchard did not like his daughter's place and brought her home so quickly. It is significant, too, that the Orchards could leave a situation without notice whatever the cause, that they were not bound by supercillious feelings of being 'beholden' to local gentry, their so-called social betters, even in those times.

At a loose end during Eleanor Jane's absence, John Boaden managed to pass the time away profitably by persuading his father to allow him to attend another school this spring, one kept by Mr. Odgers in Helston where he improved his grammar and writing, and gained a smattering of a few other subjects. His education seems to have been rather various and most haphazard, and it seems strange that a lad, who to all intents and purposes ended 'regular schooling' at the age of eleven to work on his father's farm attended yet another school when seventeen. There is no hint, however, that this school imparted 'technical knowledge' of especial value to farmers, nor did John ever indicate that he regarded specialist theoretical studies of much account. Already in farming circles there was talk about scientific drainage and chemical fertilizers, but tenants and landowners alike were prone to regard nitrates, phosphates, sulphates, and micro-phosphates as 'crack-jaw names to make we farmers stare!'[1]

At this school John Boaden made a number of new friends, including the two Rows brothers. Kit Rows died in Australia some years before Boaden wrote his memoirs, having emigrated like so many from the Helston and Meneage districts. John G. Rows, in later life Boaden's associate in the first Cornwall County Council, and one of the best known public figures in the Helston district, had 'superior abilities which he industriously cultivated', and was a man of 'great benevolence'.

It is hardly likely that John Boaden got to this school for its early morning sessions which began at seven o'clock, for the journey in from Bojorrow must have taken him a full hour. This early period of the day was devoted to 'respect lessons', whilst the normal day school began at nine and ended at half-past four. William Charles Odgers, the master, possessed considerable talents as an artist and engraver and musician. His strong line was penmanship, and he also emphasised grammar, besides giving the sixty or seventy boys and girls attending his school a smattering of history and geography. He charged a fee of two guineas a year for each pupil besides a shilling extra for the quill pens with which he provided them. This school would today be ranked as a primary one, but in the days before compulsory education the pupils in such a school wre of all ages from five to seventeen or even nineteen.

John Boaden reckoned that this belated return to school did him good, but he was often daydreaming of his love and when Eleanor Jane returned to Carrabane her home meant more to John than all Bojorrow. In rather quaint and stilted fashion he wrote

'The whole place had a charm for me, everything about the family was tasty and respectable, and situated near the principal gateway to Trelowarren it seemed to have a share in its aristocratic importance, and at that time Sir Richard was indisputably king of the district.'

[1]Speech of Edward Archer at the meeting of the East Cornwall Agricultural Society on May 30th, 1849. (*West Briton*: June 6th, 1849)

Even when he wrote this Boaden did not realise that the days of the local squire-kings would soon be with those of the proud emperors of Ninevah and Tyre, although in his lifetime their glory had somewhat faded.

He was not much concerned with the Vyvyans, with their legendary descent from a fugitive of sea-engulfed Lyonesse. He was only concerned with the relatives of the girl he hoped to marry. His account of this family is somewhat confused – there were so many of them. Will Orchard, her father, was the son of William and Betsy Orchard, and one of a family of seven, there being three more brothers and three sisters. One of the brothers, Hannibal, was 'a successful seafaring man who resided at Falmouth and sailed in a pack ship, Eleanor Jane spent some holidays there', the second, Philip, farmed County Bridge, about a mile from Bojorrow towards Dry Tree, and was a skilled thatcher whose services were widely called upon by neighbouring farmers, the other brother, Joseph, was a highway labourer. The Orchards, in short, were a respectable family although rather lower in the rural social scale than tenant farmers. Way back, though John Boaden mentioned it not, there was gipsy blood, and the seafaring career of Hannibal Orchard and the earlier voyages of a young Will Orchard was but a natural consequence of this. Betsy Orchard, Eleanor Jane's grandmother, who

'kept the grocer's shop where Mrs. Pearse lives now, was the daughter of old Tom Cooke who came down a young man as a wheel-wright to Trelowarren. She had three brothers, Ned, John, and Tom, all fond of drink and all carpenters; and three sisters, one married to Allen at Traboe, another to a Pentecost in St. Keverne, and the other, the youngest, Jane, to a Trelowarren servant called Green – I think two of her sons and one of the daughters still survive. Eleanor Jane's mother was the eldest daughter to John and Eleanor Oates; the father came down as a smith to Trelowarren and settled in St. Martin's Green; he (later) bought a freehold property, now three fields, near Newtown. Mrs. Oates was a Williams from Gwealeath; they had one son called Edward Oates, who died when he was about twenty-one, and five daughters. The elder, Jane, married William Orchard, Mary married Richard Charles a miller who once had Skyburriowe Mill and lived in the old mill-house at Gwealdrinkas. Rosa married John Carlyon who farmed Trelease. Clara married Thomas Eva a Helston builder, and Eleanor married John Tresise who remained at home with the old people. The old man (i.e. John Oates), who had been blind for years died about 1845, and the old woman, Aunt Eleanor, died triumphantly about 1858.'

Such a host of relations was inevitable at a time when large families were the rule rather than the exception. Their trades and callings were a fair sample of rural occupations of the times, and it is noteworthy that three of them were employed by the 'big house' – the old wheelwright Tom Cooke and the blacksmith John Oates as well as the 'servant' Green. Such 'long' families, too, contributed to that notorious rural phenomenon of most of the inhabitants of a district being related by blood or marriage to nearly everyone else in the neighbourhood. The term 'aunt' applied to a grandmother seems strange, but it was the custom in West Cornwall to call one's older friends, whether relatives or not, 'uncle' or 'aunt', the term 'granny' being a local title given to the oldest woman in the district irrespective whether or not she had 'chick or child' of her own. The phrase 'died triumphantly' shows that Eleanor Oates was every whit as staunch a Methodist as her son-in-law, Will Orchard, long the mainstay of Garras Chapel.

The troubles of Garras Chapel probably worried the elders far more than it did the younger people, and when John Boaden and Eleanor Jane Orchard wandered along the lanes and across the downs they had other things to talk about. The departure of Edward Oates Orchard for employment in Bath left the organisation of the Garras Sunday School anniversary in John Boaden's hands, and it gave him an excuse to go up to Carrabane to consult Will Orchard about arrangements. Older than any Sunday School Anniversary, older even than the parish feast itself, was another of his activities in 1845, for he on 'Feast Monday'

'went to Carrabane about five o'clock in the morning to lay down laurel leaves on the fence for the girl I had long loved to sew on; no work on earth could suit me better; we accomplished the work much to our own satisfaction; but

I was too young as yet even to divulge to her the affection I felt for her, but ever and anon I tried to get in her company.'

It is obvious that the gaiety of the parish feast had not yet departed, that good Methodists were not yet denouncing pleasant old rural rites as heathenish and that village life gave the young many chances to enjoy themselves and speed their courtships.

True, outside chapel services and parish feast there were little opportunities in those times for young people to go off or meet together unless they unblushingly declared to the world that they were 'going courting'. If boy was attracted to a girl he had to seize any and every chance to meet her. John Boaden recalled that on Good Friday, 1846, he had

'an intimation that Eleanor Jane along with Selina Curnow, Henry Dale, and some others were going over to Tremayne to see a fleet of Colchester oyster snacks that had come down and bulgariously (sic) entered the oyster beds in Helford River, the private property of Sir Richard Vyvyan. This they did with impunity, and carried off a rich booty in the shape of a very large quantity of oysters. Someone soon after for taking a small quantity was convicted at Bodmin Assizes, and the judge warned the public that the taking of the oysters was a crime like that of any other property.'

News of this episode stirred the Meneage. A little sly poaching at Trelowarren was possibly nothing unusual, but the wholesale raid by 'foreign' oyster-fishermen on the preserves of the most prominent landowner in the district was a local sensation.

There had already been trouble over the Helford oyster beds and many still remembered that a few years before the 'land-owners' Parliament' had enacted that the taking of oysters from 'private' reaches was larceny punishable by imprisonment or even transportation. The squire might have spent some money in improving the Helford oyster beds, but lawyers had been wrangling since the first appearance of the notion of outright private right to land about the title to foreshores and to strands that were only above water at low tide. Men ignorant of the law, more than distrustful of lawyers, were only too ready to suspect attempts to deprive them of their share of nature's bounty, and were prepared to flout laws which they regarded as robbery wrapped up in fine parliamentary phrases. When the 'up-country' raiders managed on this spring day to get off with a catch worth something like £5,000, some 'locals' felt that they might do likewise; and that autumn a group of men attempted to dredge an oyster bed at Treveder. They came to blows with the employees of John Tyacke, who had leased the beds from Vyvyan and at the Spring Assizes in 1847, eight of them were sent to jail for terms varying from one to six months. Two years later sentences of six and four months' imprisonment were inflicted at the Assizes on two men who had helped themselves to a few oysters which they had not taken away but had actually eaten on the spot.[1]

Whatever Meneage people thought of the law and of Assize justice on these issues, to John Boaden in 1846 the raid on the oyster beds was an opportunity to see Eleanor Jane. It was a pleasant walk by footpaths along the side of Mawgan Creek, and then through the woods to the waterside below Tremayne Farm. Possibly Eleanor Jane had been responsible for the 'intimation' John Boaden received about her intended jaunt. At that time she was living in Helston to learn the trade of dressmaking, and, by some mischance

'had run a needle into the bottom of her foot, which had broken and left a piece in the foot, but still having her foot in that condition did not deter her from undertaking and accomplishing the journey and I had her company whenever I well could on the journey.'

An injured foot was good reason to linger on the way that Good Friday; doubtless their companions went on ahead, whilst young Boaden and the lame girl dawdled behind watching the sunlight and shadows dancing on the waters of the creek.

The love affair then became 'serious'. Hitherto it had been little more on Eleanor Jane's side than a liking for John Boaden's companionship, a slow-spoken youth, one of her brothers closest friends, perhaps too serious in his outlook on life to modern eyes, but she, too, had been brought up in a strict Methodist home. It

[1] Based on accounts of the Cornish Spring Assizes of 1847 and 1849 in the *West Briton* of April 2nd, 1847 and of March 30th, 1849.

was not an irresponsible rural flirtation, and Eleanor Jane, well aware that her elder sister, Elizabeth, then already, in country phrase, was 'courting strong' thought she might as well follow suit. In a year she would be twenty; John was a little younger, but youth ever feels that a few, very few years ahead, it will be old. Maybe had they been able to look into the future they would have been more than ever convinced that they were right, for within two years Elizabeth's love, Daniel Edwards died on his way to America. Mercifully they could not see ahead, and now, Boaden wrote, that if the two Orchard sisters

> 'went anywhere of a Sunday evening somehow I knew it and was found with them, but it mostly took place under the cover of darkness. I recollect going to Cury Chapel and returning with Eleanor Jane through Tregoose.'

Of a truth this was a longer way around for both of them, but it was along footpaths that were more pleasant than the rough roads and lanes connecting Cury and Garras. Then, on another occasion John and Daniel Edwards went

> 'to meet the sisters returning from Traboe – this was on a Sunday evening, after I had attended the Garras Chapel. I had cause to be careful for (my) father's suspicions were awakened, and he was opposed on account of my youth and also to my having a dressmaker (who was) not accustomed to farm work.'

There is a hint of the hard parent, but John's father believed that marriage was a more serious than romantic business; and that a man as the years pass by values a helpmeet more than girlhood's swift fading charms. His son thought otherwise if he did not dare suggest, that a girl who could diligently and successfully learn one trade had all the qualities necessary to make an ideal farmer's wife, and that it was not necessary to restrict one's choice of a mate to a farmer's daughter although that was what the majority of young farmers did.

Still John felt that his father did not approve of Eleanor Jane, and so 'my interviews with my girl were the reverse of public, but as time went on became more frequent. Saturday and Sunday evening we walked the new road together; this would be in 1847, and often have we seen the moon in its brightness rising over the firs behind the pond cottage, and gazed together on the pond as we leant against the parapet. Eleanor Jane succeeded in getting a business and had an apprentice. I did not go in but came to her workroom window; she came out and we repaired to our walk in the new road, an almost ideal place for lovers.

In the spring of 1848 the Rechabite Club was broken up;[1] being a member I was chosen with James Curnow and A. Wicks to divide the moneys. We went to make up the accounts at A. Wicks' on two evenings, but at that time Eleanor Jane was sleeping with Mrs. W. Harry (Selina Curnow) for company just before she went to (join) her husband in London. I choose to be in Selina's – which adjoined A. Wicks' – more than attend to the accounts, and Mrs. Harry very kindly going early to bed left us in possession downstairs. If anyone reads these pages he will wonder at my reciting such trivialities, but they were not small matters to me and still as Robert Burns says –

> "still on those scenes my memory wakes
> And fondly broods with miser care,
> Time but the impression deeper makes
> As streams their channels deeper wears." '

John Boaden's courtship may have been precocious, but in his twentieth year he realised that life was something more than the friendly circle around Garras Chapel and the pleasant Meneage. Even to that remote district came the news of the fall of the monarchy in France in February, 1848, and that spring and summer scarcely a week passed without tidings from the Continent of a government overthrown, of statesmen fleeing into exile, of despotic monarchies collapsing. There were signs too,

---

[1]Boaden does not say why this club was abandoned: the first flush of teetotal zeal may have vanished, but it was more likely on account of bad times in rural Mawgan and emigration of many members from the district.

that the comfortable world Cornish farmers knew was passing away, for in the spring of 1849

'The ports (of Britain) were open to the importation of foreign corn with only a shilling per quarter duty. The price of corn fell, and the prospects of farming became very gloomy, without any apparent chance of improving. Up to this time corn had been looked upon as the source of the farmer's income, and cattle as quite a minor matter, and it required many years for cattle to be uppermost, but the balance in the latter's favour has been increasing from that time to the present.'

Although the repeal of the Corn Laws did not immediately bring ruin to many British farmers it deprived them of a sense of economic security, made some of them more cautious and less enterprising, led many of them to hold back money they should have invested.

Still they could enjoy life, and in the fall of 1848 John Boaden, Simon Lugg, and Henry Andrew made a most praiseworthy attempt at local 'self improvement' when they

'Established a subscription library, of about twenty members with entrance fees of five shillings and half a crown, and a quarterly subscription of a shilling. I was the Secretary, and attended to receive and deliver books every Monday evening at Mrs. Lobb's at Garras – Mrs. Hubbard's now. I spent much time about this venture, James Boaden, who was then a schoolmaster at Cury, assisting, but subscribers dropped off and after about five year's existence we closed the books. My dear Eleanor Jane was a member paying her five shillings.'

This venture deserved better success, yet it was something that it lasted as long as it did – besides giving John another chance to carry on his courtship. Books were hard to obtain in remote country districts although the reading public was small; there was much else to do on long summer evenings, whilst on Winter nights, after a hard day's work, many might pick up a book or paper and then quickly drop it to go to bed, for reading by flickering candlelight was a physical strain as well as mental toll to many whose formal schooling – had they had any – ended when they were ten or eleven years old.

With a capital of scarcely four pounds and a diminishing income of never more than that amount yearly the Mawgan Suscription Library cannot have had many books, although the stock may have been increased by gifts from its members. John Boaden does not give any indication of the titles of the books circulated; possibly it was through this that he read some of Burns' poems, possibly some of the novels of Scott and the earlier works of Dickens passed from hand to hand. Among the books may have been the work of a local author, the Rev. C. A. Johns, who, before going to London, had taught at the Helston Grammar School. If so his pleasant *A Week at the Lizard* may have prompted a local trip for

> 'Just after harvest this year – 1848 – I went with a party that filled A. Tripconey's van on an excursion to the Lizard. The party consisted of the Andrews, Warrens, Elizabeth Dunstone, Orchards (Eleanor Jane and Clara), Richard Nancarrow, and three from Manaccan. Very few went to the Lizard then, and a small low public house was all there was to accommodate visitors. Eleanor Jane was my partner on this excursion.'

Times have changed since then, but many living in remote rural areas can recall the next village or hamlet referred to as 'foreign parts'. The Lizard was not far from mawgan, but Tripconey's horse-van must have taken nearly three hours for a ten-mile journey over roads that were little better than rough cart tracks. It was then, as always, better to ride than walk, but there were many jolts and jars riding in unsprung vehicles with iron-tired wheels. Still, if John Boaden could hold Eleanor Jane's hand he probably forgot the discomforts of the trip.

But the springtime of romance was passing. Contrived meetings, stolen kisses, walks in the Trelowarren drives and lanes were all part of the joy of heedless youth. A puritanical Methodist upbringing meant that neither Boaden nor his girl were gay and feckless, and early in 1849 John began to think seriously of the future, writing that he had

'searchings of my heart or not it was prudent or right for me
to continue my attentions to Eleanor Jane in consequence of
my father's hostility and (my) being unable to get married for
several years. I told my dear Eleanor Jane of my difficulties:
We almost agree to part, and for a short time I did remain
away but the instincts of the heart were too powerful to be
resisted. I found that no other could fill the place of my
affections occasioned by Eleanor Jane, so it was not long
before we met as often or perhaps more so than ever.'

It was not youth taking itself over-seriously that caused these
doubts and heart-burnings. The opposition of John's father and
hints that he was too young to marry must have made matters
rather uncomfortable for him at home. Furthermore, the depression in farming made it impossible for John's father to provide
him with the capital or stock to set up even as a small tenant
farmer, nor was there any room at Bojorrow for a second family.

John, however, could not give up Eleanor Jane, but then still
another thing had to be taken into account, for

'Eleanor Jane's eldest brother had been obliged to return from
Bath two or three times, and it was feared that he through
his health would not be able to stand a return to his old
employment. This was a great disappointment to the family.
He had received an expensive education for those times and
seemed to be destined for success, but his repeated failures
of health clouded the hopes. He thought the Australian
climate would suit him. Added to this his father's business
had somewhat failed, and the girls especially were a fine
family for emigration. The father's eldest brother Joe – who
had married a Bolitho – who had emigrated from Ponsanooth
to South Australia, had commenced to send home very good
accounts. All this made Will Orchard and his family turn
their eyes to South Australia. Eleanor Jane when she thought
we had parted was anxious as either to go but the father being
over fifty and so firmly rooted and so useful and such a figure
in the parish it was scarcely possible it was thought for him
to go. But times here grew very depressed and many were
leaving.'

The two lovers may have felt that everything was against them. The consumptive Edward Oates Orchard had 'small chance of making old bones' if he stayed in England. Village tradesmen, dependent on local farmers were suffering from the agricultural depression which, throughout the 'hungry forties' had been growing in severity.

It was not only labourers and tradespeople who studied the prospects of emigration in those days. Many farmers read accounts of land overseas which could be bought outright for less than the rents they were paying in England, land not burdened with rates and tithes. A succession of bad and indifferent harvests had swallowed up the capital reserves of many farmers whom at best, had only just been paying their way; they were now in debt and had no idea where to look for relief. They complained of rates, tithes, and rents, but it was useless hoping that Parliament would lighten those burdens. Indeed, since the Reform Bill, local rates had been reduced by the Poor Law Amendment Act of 1834 and tithes, perhaps, by the Tithe Commutation Act of 1836; it was hopeless expecting a Parliament dominated by industrial interests to transfer the cost of poverty and of the Established Church elsewhere, but there was some agitation that mining royalties be rated and that the Church be supported by the whole nation. As for rents, no-one thought of subjecting the relations of landlords and tenant to legislative restraints in the age when the doctrines of *laissez faire* had gained their greatest victory by the alliance of the Anti-Corn Law League and Irish potato blight. Several farmers naturally turned their eyes to places where they were assured

> 'The landlord's steward ceases from troubling,
> And the tithe proctor is unknown.'

Many landlords made fairly substantial remissions of rents in those hard times, but with too many tenants on the look-out for too few farms permanent reductions wre not to be expected. The landed gentry, too, wanted to maintain their social standing and prestige in competition with the new plutocratic industrial magnates. In the Meneage Sir Richard Vyvyan, who had impaired his fortunes by his electioneering activities, had to 'keep up' with his neighbours, and those neighbours were Richard Davey of Bochym, who had the profits of the great Gwennap Consolidated

Mines behind him, and Captain Joseph Lyle who was still getting rich dividends from a dozen or more mines in the Redruth and St. Agnes districts. Vyvyan's estates included some mining properties, but he did not have the direct and more profitable connections with mining ventures these new county gentry possessed. Yet to keep his local position and prestige he had to emulate their lavish expenditures on his estates; if Lyle enclosed part of Goonhilly Down, Sir Richard had to do likewise with Garras Common; if Davey rebuilt lodges, farmhouses, and cottages at Bochym, Vivyan had to do the same on the Trelowarren estate.

The end of the Corn Laws seemed nearly the last straw to many tenant farmers. They realised that the competition for land through the increasing rural population made it likely that rents would go up rather than down – indeed, they had been increasing throughout their own lifetimes for that very reason; and the prospects of younger sons becoming successful farmers were rapidly lessening. Moreover, there had actually been a decline in the numbers of farms in the 'old country'; Lyle of Bonython was not the only landlord who had amalgamated small-holdings into larger farms, while farmers believing that the corn mow would no longer pay the rest were seeking more and more acres for pastoral farming which, many believed, was the only way to avoid ruin. Thus, although agriculture was very depressed, competition for land was keener than it had ever been.

The only solution was the drastic one of emigration, and at that time South Australia seemed to be the Promised Land. For some years it had been the most widely propagandized of all British overseas possessions as a field for emigration. Many Cornish people, although mainly miners, had already gone thither, and, like Joe Orchard, pressed their relations to join them, to come to a colony now flourishing on an economic basis of copper and wheat, while in Cornwall farmers were struggling along with the help of mines which provided local markets for farm produce.[1] After a succession of wet, or, at best, 'catchy' harvest, too, Cornish farmers were longing for a country where the sun was far more likely to shine than the rain to fall; to them drought was less than

---

[1]Mines & Clayworks, too, provided farmers and small-holders living in their vicinity with lucrative work carting ore-stuffs and materials.

a myth. There were persuasive emigration agents publishing propaganda lauding South Australia but still more persuasive were letters sent home by relatives and friends who had already gone.

Yet it was hard to decide to emigrate. Few people living in the rural Meneage had ever travelled much more than a dozen miles or so from the place where they had been born; many families had been living in the same parish for generations. Yet if they had to leave to find a living, they might as well go ten thousand miles as twenty, forty, or even a hundred. Friends and relations, too, had shown the way; it would be good to see them again, and their assured welcome would assuage the pain of uprooting, would greet them in no strange land, for where-ever kith and kindred are there is home.

Older people, however, who had spent the greater part of their lives in one place, found the decision hard to make, but Will Orchard's brief seafaring youth perhaps made him less averse to emigrating. Some of the younger members of the Orchard family were eager to go, but the question was doubly difficult for the love-lorn Eleanor Jane and John Boaden. In one respect the position of the Orchard and Boaden families was very different. Will Orchard was a tradesman and it was generally believed that a tradesman could easily find work and prosper in South Australia; his little small-holding at Carrabane was a mere 'side line'. The Boadens, however, since coming to Bojorrow, were substantial farmers; they were a small family able to live in modest and frugal comfort on that farm, and if the elder son went his father would have to pay a labourer in his place. In short, unless conditions worsened very much, the Boadens would be well advised to stay; for them or for any one of them emigration for the love-light in a girl's eyes, would have been an utterly unwarrantable gamble.

The feelings of young John Boaden when he was told the Orchards had finally determined to go can be imagined; he can have had but little heart for work those days, although in his memoirs he prosaically wrote

'My dear Nelly and myself had to consider our position and arrived at the conclusion that if the Orchard family went, she had better go with them and return to me in a few years. This we thought might afford a solution of our matrimonial difficulties, as then the objections to age would be gone and the effects of time and other possible circumstances might open the way easily to our union. True we ran a greater risk than we were aware of, especially on my part in leaving an attractive young woman to go to Australia at that time and laying on her the burden of the tenderest separation and the burden of her return; but, under a kind providence and the sterling qualities rarely unequalled in Eleanor Jane, everything would assuredly turn out just as we wished.'

Busied with preparations for departure the Orchards had little time for regretful repining. There were farewell parties to bid the emigrants good fortune, and John Boaden took every opportunity to be with his girl, with her hoping against hope that, somehow or other, the plans of migration would fall through. Years later he wrote

'On St. Martin's Feast Sunday I went over in the evening, as I had done on feast times previously, to chapel and to accompany Eleanor Jane home. I met Mrs. Orchard with her little lanthorn near the Garras. Sandy Boaden and I met at St. Martin's Green and accompanied Eleanor Jane and (her sister) Clarinda to chapel and of course back through (the grounds of) Trelowarren house. The girls surrounded by friends from St. Martin's; they always went there to (their) grandmother's to (the parish) feast with other cousins. Sandy and Clara had an inclination to each other.

'The question of emigration was an exciting one at this time and because much more so after the gold discoveries in Australia in 1851. Times were bad, corn ruinously low without any prospects of improvement, and accounts from Australia very good. There was free and assisted emigration to South Australia. Will Orchard had made an application for his family and had been accepted. Sailing orders might soon be expected, but we scarcely thought they would really go; their hearts would fail or something prevent (them). It was too serious an affair really to be carried out, but Eleanor Jane and myself had given ourselves to each other unreservedly in heart, often met, and were prepared for anything. One evening, I think (in) the first week of December, (1849), I accompanied Eleanor Jane to Trelowarren; she was getting orders of (dressmaking) work from the servants, when Clara hastily came up to tell her sister not to undertake anything; sailing orders had just come and their family would be leaving in a fortnight. We went hastily back, but I did not put in an appearance at their home even then. They had much to do in a short time.'

It did not take Will Orchard long to dispose of the property he could not or did not wish to take to Australia. The unexpired part of the lease of the Carrabane smallholding was sold by auction, being bought, significantly enough, by Sir Richard Vyvyan – the first step towards merging yet another cottage holding into a bigger farm. The time came to say the last farewells. One evening there was a 'singing meeting', presumably at Garras Chapel, attended by 'some singers from a distance'. News travelled fast that the Orchards were leaving. Nearly every night John Boaden contrived to see his girl, then

'The night of leaving came. A great many people from far and near to say farewell, parties from St. Martin, St. Keverne, Helston, etc . . . The ceaseless activity of the past fortnight had resulted in all the baggage being packed and ready. Edward Oates (Orchard) had started in the morning for Falmouth with a carriage and the heavier baggage. Elizabeth only arrived from Bath – she had been there in service after leaving Trelowarren – after dark, and soon proceeded to Trelowarren to see some of the maids – (her) old acquaintances. We went with her, but from there Eleanor Jane and I took a walk to Regoose grotto; the night was beautiful, starlit, the moon was almost full, still and frosty. Ours was a long walk: it was to be the last for years, and what was before us we knew not, but we knew our own minds.'

When they got back to Carrabane, home for the Orchards so long but after the morrow to be home no more, they

'found a large number of people, with a prayer meeting being held in the kitchen, where those leaving and those remaining were commending to each other to the care of their Heavenly Father. Just after midnight Mr. Dunstone's wain of

Skyburriowe and A. Tripp's van were loaded, the one with boxes and the other with members of the family, and with the warmest good wishes and sorrow of their friends they left Carrabane for ever, but they kept their spirits up well, especially Mrs. Orchard who was leaving her mother and a large circle of near relations. I went with Eleanor Jane to past Stony Gate on the way to Nanswarne, where she got on the van. I wished them all farewell, Mrs. Orchard saying, "John, I will get a leg of mutton for you when you come out to us." I hope to see them all again in the eternal day. I met Will Orchard and his brother Hannibal walking just behind and bade them both farewell, though the latter did not emigrate for some months after.'

Many have described the long voyages of emigrants in sailing-ship days, but the brief account of the stay-at-home John Boaden depicts with a rare poignancy the actual uprooting of a Cornish emigrant family. Many left west-country homes in similar fashion, departing at night so as to reach a port betimes for a tide. The Orchards left apparently at the very last moment, saving the trouble and cost of lodgings while waiting for a ship. They had only to get to Falmouth, a dozen miles away, take a ship to Plymouth, and there embark on the vessel that was to take them to Australia. So one family left the Meneage on the longest night of the year, helped by a full moon, their belongings packed on a farm wain, themselves cramped in a carrier's van, and the father walking behind for some distance, walking for the last time along a road he had often travelled to preach at some little chapel or Sunday School. They did not know what lay ahead of them, but at least they were together.

Slowly walking the opposite direction to his home went John Boaden – alone. The moon now sinking to the west could fall no lower than his spirits. The longest night of the year, the saddest night of his life.

A steamer took the Orchards from Falmouth to Plymouth next day; it was a cold passage and they had little to do to keep their minds from brooding on the irrevocable step they had taken. In Plymouth, there were some formalities to comply with before they left on the *Trafalgar* on Boxing Day. It must have been a cheerless Christmas for them and the two hundred others who sailed with them, most of whom were Irish. They reached Adelaide on April 2, 1850, but a fourteen-week passage was comparatively swift at that time. Some 'teens' of those who sailed from Plymouth died on the passage, mostly infant children.

Not until August did John Boaden hear from Eleanor Jane; her letter told him that they had arrived safely and found a house in Adelaide; she had been able to start a dressmaking business almost immediately. It was a long time for John to wait for a letter which he, doubtless, read and read again, but it was never re-written into his memoirs. Instead, rather laconically he wrote

'This may be regarded as the close of the second chapter of my history. During the 'forties events of great importance had taken place, while locally there had been social fermentation. On the subject of emigration there must have been upwards of fifty persons left this parish for Australia. About the close of the 'forties and beginnings of the 'fifties the price of corn had fluctuated violently, but seemed to have settled down permanently to a remarkably low level. The emigration of the Orchard family seemed to give a melancholy tinge to everything; they had been active (in the chapel at Garras), Eleanor Jane and Clara in the choir and school and their father the perfect worker.'

The Orchards and the others who left Mawgan were missed, but life still went on in the parish and on the farms. There were changes, and despite grumbles about the weather, which was rarely right, the price of corn, which certainly was low though not ruinously so, and the government which, in the eyes of some, was always wrong, the farmers of Mawgan were not, and could not afford to be idle. Small farmers began to follow the example of Captain Joe Lyle and other landowner in applying 'artificials' to their fields. By 'high farming' methods heavier crops wer raised, especially on the poorest soils which a few years before had been under heath, bracken and furze. Grain prices might be low, but if bigger crops were harvested the rents could be paid and living standards maintained. Many thought, with the wide waste of Goonhilly within a couple of miles, there was no point in going thousands of miles to reclaim wilderness. Experience, rather dearly bought, was to show that most of the Goonhilly Downs was irreclaimable, but early Victorian farmers in the Meneage knew that their immediate forebears had brought its fringes under cultivation. Farmers as well as industrialists in those times could see no limits to human progress; they expected too much from the application of chemistry to agriculture; scientific researchers were hopeful that chemical analysis would reveal the deficiencies of moorland and heath soils and suggest remedies. And so young John Boaden, keenly interested in 'the spread of knowledge and the march of intellect', despite the departure of the girl he held most dear to Australia, hardly considered emigrating himself. The only hint that he ever did so was Mrs. Orchard's jovial remark that she would have a good meal ready for him in the distant southern land. But the Meneage was his home and was good enough for him. As times slowly improved Boaden and other Cornish farmers regained confidence that, despite the end of the Corn laws, despite the weather, despite squire, parson, pauper, and everything else, agriculture would pull through and they would enjoy good times again.

10

Holidays and Working Days

Till Eleanor Jane's letter arrived young John Boaden probably at times wished he had gone to Australia as well. The revival in farming fortunes was slow. Some landowners had remitted rents considerably, but had made no permanent reductions. Some agriculturists and landowners admitted that the Corn Laws would never return, and advised tenant farmers to cut their losses by spending less on labour and on manure. A strike of farm-hands near Looe, in south-east Cornwall, showed that it was almost impossible to cut wages, and the few farmers who economised on manure soon found their crops down by twenty per cent, their rent the same, and wheat still only making fifty shillings per quarter. At that price wheat paid if twenty-eight bushels were raised on every acre sown, but the average yield was two bushels less, falling below that in 1850, when, too, potato blight again appeared. Still prophecies of doom had not been fulfilled; few farmers had gone bankrupt and none had starved; some had given up farming or emigrated, but that had made a few landlords and tithe-owners a little more accommodating about rents and tithes. There were signs of a revival in trade, and many believed that industry could not flourish without helping to bring agriculture out of the depths of depression.

Although times were not as good as they might have been, the early Victorians were optimistic. The grumbling farmer was already a popular joke. Faith in progress was a marked characteristic of the Methodists and other evangelicals. Occasional doubts and misgivings were quickly dispelled. Potato blight, turnip fly, the rust in wheat were trials to prove a man's ability to endure and rise above misfortune; the weather was the affair of an inscrutable but well-designing Providence which always

Trelowarren in 1823

Trelowarren in 1995

John and Eleanor Boaden, c. 1880

worked for good, though its ways passed human understanding. Man, however, could save himself, by sheer hard work and determination, and surmount these petty trials. That was progress.

So, in 1850, optimism re-asserted itself. In London preparations for the Great Exhibition, to be held the following year to commemorate 'the march of progress', were under way, quickly arousing widespread interest. Even in the Meneage there was talk of it, and John Boaden recalled how he and his friend, James Boaden, determined to see if it possible, although

'for persons like us to go to London then was an unprecedented event in local history. I was then taking in *Cassell's Magazine, The Working Man's Friend*,[1] which devoted much of its columns to this great event, the first invitation ever given to the whole world for a competition in the arms and manufactures which minister to man's happiness and well-being, and many were sanguine enough to hope that its influential tendency would go far to promote and usher in the reign of universal peace. We prepared and looked forward to our visit with eagerness. The Exhibition was opened on May 9, 1851; everything seemed to promise a great success.'

So, on a June morning, the two young men set forth on their journey, in a spirit of high adventure.

The quickest way to London from West Cornwall was by taking a steamship at Hayle for Bristol, thence by train. Not until 1859 was there to be a direct railway line between Paddington and Penzance, and long after that there were no through trains since part of that line was standard or narrow gauge and the rest wide, or broad gauge. So John Boaden's brother Will drove the two travellers in a market trap to Fraddam whence they walked down to Hayle, and dined with a relation before embarking on the steamer which sailed that afternoon.

[1] *The Working Man's Friend and Family Instructor* first appeared as a penny weekly periodical in January, 1850, with the avowed aim of instruction rather than amusement, including everything from 'potted biographies to gardening hints': it ceased publication in March, 1853.

Steamship travel, however, had its disadvantages, for

'After being out about two hours I got seasick, a new and not pleasant experience; we were deck passengers and took the berth of a sailor.[1] I got better when we neared Bristol, and the scenery on the shores of a fine summer morning was delightful. We landed soon after 4 a.m. and proceeded to Berkeley Square where Cousin Hugh's son, Nicholas, was a butler and valet. After waiting for their rising, the front door of a fine mansion was thrown open for our admittance; we were sumptuously treated. Nicholas then took us to the railway station.'

Boaden then wrote briefly of the railway journey, the first time he ever travelled by such a conveyance

'Crowds were going. Our carriage had no backs to the seats, simply rows of wide forms, but all seemed glad to go anyhow as long as it was to London. We were occupied all the way in looking at the country, a new one to us. We arrived at Paddington and took a bus for the Bank; thence we walked to Messrs. Rotherhams of Shoreditch, to see John Boaden who belonged to the shop. He took us to lodgings in Ludgate Hill in a Coffee House. We were rather surprised to be charged twopence-halfpenny for a cup of tea.'

Obviously the excursion had been well planned beforehand, and relations contacted to get their help for the two young travellers. They may have been fortunate in having so many relations, but the way in which they were widely scattered over the country shows how rural people had already migrated to the towns.

John Boaden wrote a long letter to Eleanor Jane describing all their wanderings about London, but although it was still in existence when he wrote his reminiscences – he did not copy it into his account of his life. Instead he wrote, and might

---

[1] The Steamship fare from Hayle to Bristol at this time for a deck passenger was five shillings, a cabin passenger was nine shillings, and the 'saloon' passage sixteen. (Advert of the Hayle and Bristol original Steam Company in the *West Briton* of April 6, 1849.)

well have written more, that

'The visit taught us many lessons. The enormous population, the immense wealth, the trade and traffic were amazing; most things seemed to be done regardless of expense. Then on the moral and religious side, the vice which would withdraw itself in shame at home flaunted itself openly and elbowed the best people of the world here, and according to our Cornish ideas there seemed to be a lack of earnestness in places of worship; services were cold and intellectual generally; religion did not take the place, which, if it is real, its professors and ministers had a right to claim for it. We felt, too, that the business in the House of Commons was lacking in the decorum and order that we expected but we had the good fortune to hear the best debate I have ever had the good fortune to be present at, on the Third reading of the Ecclesiastic Titles Bill. This was in the charge of Lord John Russell, and was supported as a very necessary and urgent measure by both parties in the House, the objectors mainly being Peelites and Irish with a few Radicals. It passed with very large majorities. It was not once used, and several years ago it was quietly repealed. I saw Russell, Palmerston, Grey, Sir J. Graham, Gladstone who had just returned from Italy, Joe Hume, and Roebuck who made a smart speech. We left the House early in the morning, found ourselves locked out, and had to get lodgings in Fleet Street.'

This debate took place on July 4, 1851 – the issue having arisen from the decree of Pope Pius I setting up a Catholic heirarchy in England. It seems a dead controversy now, but in the sultry Protestant atmosphere of early Victorian England, coming as it did in the wake of Tractarian Movement, of Newman's secession to Rome, and numerous local squabbles over the conduct of ritualistic 'High' clergymen, it roused a storm. Strained by internal personal rivalries, and conscious that its hold on the electorate was weakening, the Russell administration brought in this measure which, as Boaden remarked, was never enforced to penalize Catholics who assumed English 'ecclesiastic' titles. The Radical opposition to the Bill was led by Roebuck, who had been a thorn in the side of practically every administration since the passing of the First Reform Act. The fourteen members of Cornish constitutencies were far from prominent in this affair; four or five of them voted for the measure; the radical member of East Cornwall, T. J. A. Robartes and one other supported Roebuck; Sir Richard Vyvyan, was absent but a 'diehard', who had before now and was again to represent Penryn, though at this time representing Boston, J. W. Freshfield wanted to banish any Catholic bishop who chanced to set foot in England. There was no support for this extreme proposal, but Russell's bill was passed by 263 votes to 46, and it was nearly midnight when the House rose from a debate which had enabled too many Members to display to the world that in Victorian England there was rampant religious prejudice and sectarian intolerance.

Still, John Boaden, from the Visitor's Gallery, had seen the most prominent political figures of the day – or night. He probably sympathized with the Bill, judging by the epithet 'smart' which he applied to Roebuck's speech, and once again, his memoirs show his concern with religious matters. One is, however, left wondering whether this young Cornish farmer missed the exhibit at the Crystal Palace which *The Times* said justified the entire cost of the Exhibition, the reaping machine sent from America by Cyrus McCormick.

The visit to the House of Commons was the high light of John Boaden's visit to London. Doubtless in the letter to Eleanor Jane he dwelt more on the glories of the Crystal Palace and the wonders of the Great Exhibition. Assuredly in his own way he made the best use of the time he spent in the bustling metropolis, and saw enough of it to prefer the quiet and sedate life in Mawgan in Meneage.

The holiday quickly passed, and after about a week the two young men started on their homeward way. They stopped at Bath where they called upon Ira Miller who a year or so back had been an assistant minister in the Helston Circuit. As in the case of his father a dozen years before John Boaden found that the Methodist system of itinerant ministers made it easy to find friends and kindred spirits on his travels. Ira Miller took his two friends

'to some beautiful spots in the vicinity of the city. I also visited Mrs. Tucker's where Edward Oates Orchard and Elizabeth had lodged for a time; Eleanor Jane's father and mother and her Aunt Mary had also stopped there. We attended Argyle Chapel Service in the evening; a student preached; we saw the venerable Will Jay[1] at this service. On the following day we came to Bristol, took steamer, and arrived at Hayle next morning, and then walked home. We had seen all the principal sights of London, and many great personages, the Queen, the Duke of Wellington, etc. The trip cost me just over five pounds; we spent our money carefully. I also heard Drs. Canning, Hamilton, and Beaumont preach, the two latter in Exeter Hall. I also called on our relations at St. Dunstan's Villas, then occupied by Sir R. R. Vyvyan, Cousin Joe, Simon Bolitho, Miss Lugg of Trezise, and Christiana Lawrence then formed part of his household staff.'

Boaden rejoiced in the opportunity of hearing the most famed preachers of that day. More interesting now is the indication that the drift of men and women to the towns was being furthered by the gentry taking staff from their rural estates to their town houses. Many such retainers never returned to their old homes again even if they sought other masters and work; often, too, they advised friends and relations of chances to get better livelihoods when times were bad at home.

Home again, Boaden had much to tell, but there was work to be done – roots to be hoed, sheep to be shorn, hay to be saved, and soon it was harvest again, rather a better harvest than that of the previous year; wheat crops were quite good that season in Cornwall, but the barley indifferent and oat-crops very light and inferior; potato blight had again caused much damage and insect pests had ravaged some turnip and mangold fields.[2] Harvesting done, ploughing began again, but there were days when John Boaden let the horses graze at the hedgerows whilst he re-read letters that had just reached him from faraway Australia.

They were not at all happy letters, for his old friend, Eleanor Jane's brother, had died. Edward Oates Orchard had been seriously ill for some time before they had sailed, but his family had hoped that the change of climate would save his life; his death must have

---

[1]William Jay (1769-1853) had been Pastor of the Argyle Independent Chapel, Bath, ever since 1791.
[2]*West Briton*: September 12, 1851

made them wonder whether the sacrifices involved in emigrating had been worth while. Other letters gave exciting news about the gold rushes, but Eleanor Jane dwelt longest on the lives and affairs of her family circle. Both Clare Orchard and the sweetheart of Edward Oates Orchard had broken their engagements and had married two other Mawgan emigrants in Australia – news that must have made young Boaden wonder whether or not Eleanor Jane might, ten thousand miles away, look once and again at another lad. She had, however, left Adelaide and found work in a Melbourne draper's shop; trade was brisk there, thanks to the gold rush, and wages had soared with so many men flocking off to the diggings.

There were changes at home, too, for in 1852, Sir Richard Vyvyan offered the Boadens the least of Skyburriowe and the adjoining holding of Burnoon. With two grown-up sons, John's father did not hesitate to take over one of the best farms in Mawgan, and the family moved to Skyburriowe at Lady Day, 1853. It meant more work, but the Boadens were now to be reckoned among the 'bigger' farmers with all the rural prestige that conferred. Their move coincided with a revival in corn prices; trade was better; shadows of depression seemed to be lifting off the land.

The Californian and Australian gold discoveries contributed to the general improvement in trade. Unfortunately, however, the British agricultural revival of the mid-fifties, even if the actual seasons were rather more kindly than for some years past, came just at a time to give support to the adage that it took a long and bloody war to make British farming prosperous. Despite all the pious hopes of world peace propagated at the time of the Great Exhibition, and all the talk of Cobdenite manufacturers about free trade and world interdependence, France and Britain had got involved in the Crimean War; almost immediately British farmers profited by the cutting off of grain supplies from Russian Poland and the steppes north of Odessa. A little grain and flour was already coming into Britain from America, but for several years British grain growers were to enjoy moderate prosperity. When the Crimean War ended the economic and social dislocation caused by the emancipation of the Russian serfs meant reduced supplies of corn from Eastern Europe; there followed the American Civil War, an insurrection in Poland in 1863, the feud of Austria and Prussia in Germany, and, finally the greater conflict of France and Prussia. With the world in such a state, times were 'looking up' for British farmers. The Boadens took over a bigger holding just at the right time to benefit from this new period of farming prosperity. Yet all John Boaden wrote were the few words

'We did a great deal of extra work when we came to Skyburriowe; new buildings were erected, and a great many hedges taken down in Burnoon, and other improvements at which my brother and I worked heartily.'

The actual move from Bojorrow presented few difficulties, for Skyburriowe was only about half a mile away. At the time, just before farming recovered, there was apparently not such keen competition for land as there had been in 1839 when the Boadens had been forced to leave Trease; landlords were seeking tenants rather than tenants seeking farms, but Sir Richard made the offer because he was more than satisfied to have the hard-working Boadens as his tenants and with three men now in the family they could manage a larger farm than Bojorrow. Possibly Vyvyan had promised the elder John Boaden the first chance of a bigger holding when he renewed the Bojorrow lease in 1851. At all events, the Boadens came to Skyburriowe and stayed many years; long tenancies were the rule on Trelowarren lands in Sir Richard's time, and when he died, in 1879, many of his tenants were living on the same farms they or their fathers had occupied when he inherited the estate in 1820.

Skyburriowe was, in 1853, a family farm, employing at most a labourer or two with some extra casual hands at harvest and other busy times. The hedges the Boadens removed at Burnoon doubtless separated small enclosures which had, in times past, been reclaimed by the Vyvyans and their tenants from the heath and downlands. The merging of Skyburriowe and Burnoon provided yet another reason for large fields. It was not, as yet, a question of enabling and facilitating the use of an increasing variety of mechanical implements so much as one of making the fullest use of the land, since for years to come, much farmwork was still to be done laboriously by hand. Whatever their origins, the small fields had been necessary in the past on small farms; holdings of twenty acres or less had had to be cut up for what was really a six-year crop rotation, with three years under grain or roots and three under leys, and to keep sheep and cattle out of the growing crops and hayfields. Other farmers in the Meneage and elsewhere were pulling down hedges as they gradually turned from arable to cattle-farming, for bigger fields were much more convenient in the management of large flocks and herds.

With all these changes the working day was as long as ever; there still was not and never was to be any real limit to the hours a farmer and his family might have to toil in their fields and farmhouses. In Mawgan, too, as in many other places, the bad days of the 'forties had led to the dismissal of employees; now, when prosperity returned, farmers found that many labourers had left the district. The disappearance of many smallholders, too, meant that men who did not have enough to keep them fully employed on their own farms and were willing to work two or three days a weak for their 'bigger' neighbours had also gone. There seemed to be no end to the troublesome problems incident to the farming life.

11

Marriage and Trelowarren

Letters from Eleanor Jane continued to come from Australia. Any forebodings John entertained were dispelled early in 1855 when a letter came telling him that she had sailed for England just five years after the Orchards had emigrated. By the time this news came she was nearly home, for she had sailed from Melbourne on the last day of the Old Year, had already passed the Cape, and on May 10th her ship anchored at Gravesend. James Boaden, then a schoolmaster at Purfleet, was 'telegraphed for', and went down to meet her as he had promised John he would. Eleanor Jane spent a few days in London, then came down to Bristol on the railway, thence, like John and James Boaden four years before, took a steamer down to Hayle, arriving there on May 23rd. There she was met by her uncle and aunt who took her and her luggage down to their home Gwallon, near Marazion. They had hardly got there before John Boaden arrived, in his own stilted phrse 'to receive the long separated and faithful girl.'

Five years and half had changed both of them. Eleanor Jane probably thought that she had left a stripling youth behind her and had now found a man. What John Boaden thought was rather quaintly summed up

'Her appearance was somewhat changed beyond a little by the Australian sun and sea air. She had also a new set of artificial teeth, quite an uncommon thing in those days, given her by her father, costing sixteen pounds.'

He added, however, that she was 'substantially the same'. The days of their second courtship began. Eleanor Jane seems to have thought that having waited so long they could wait a little longer;

before they married and she settled down as a farmer's wife she wanted to visit her many relations and friends to tell them all the family news from Australia. On some of her journeys John Boaden managed to get away from the farm and go with her. One day they went to Redruth on a special errand, to get the girl's 'likeness taken', presumably by some enterprising townsman who had already set up a business as a daguerrotypist; this was to be taken back to the orchards in Australia by another Cornish emigrant, the father of Fanny Moody the famous singer. Eleanor Jane then spent some time with an aunt in Mawgan before going to stay with her grandmother in St. Martin. There was another lover's meeting on Mawgan Feast Sunday, and it was on that day that Eleanor Jane first stepped across the threshold at Skyburriowe where all opposition to her marriage to John had vanished. Then there were other visits, but a farmer's son had little time to spare for courtship in the busy farming summer. Still, when Eleanor Jane was staying with her Uncle John at Stithians, John Boaden

'went to meet her on a Saturday evening after carrying hay at Burnoon, leaving Skyburriowe about eight o'clock, and it was my first visit to Stithians. It was a beautiful summer night in early July. I rode a pony. I arrived there about eleven o'clock. The village was all alive. Mr. Johns shoemaker's man was still working and his daughters out collecting for the Sunday School. On the Monday we went to Redruth and thence to Truro to get some dental work done.'

Maybe those Australian dentures required some adjustment: John Boaden did not say. There is an element of prosaic matter-of-factness in his accounts of these summer days disappointing to any with sentimental romantic leanings. The same trait appears when he mentions that Eleanor Jane came to Skyburriowe to help at harvest time; she must have convinced Father Boaden than, however, that she would be an exemplary farmer's wife, for not only did she acquit herself well in the monotonous although hardly highly skilful task of sheaf-carrying, but in driving a horse roller and coping with other tasks on the farm.

The final preparations for the wedding enlivened the Yuletide of that year. Eleanor Jane's aunt at Gwallon took charge of all those things which the bride's parents would normally arrange.

At Skyburriowe John and his friends made up a large 'hunting party', which succeeded in catching a hare which forthwith was sent down to Gwallon to form part of the wedding dinner. On the marriage morn, John along with his cousin James, brother Will and the latter's 'intended' went off to Helston in a borrowed market cart, for a wedding breakfast at the house of another of the bride's aunts. Whether or not it was a lively meal the bridegroom did not say; probably it was, but all the old Methodist wrote half a century later, was that they made their way thence to the Wesleyan Chapel where the Rev. Edward Watson tied 'the indissoluble knot'. The service over, they went off down to Gwallon in two carriages. Festivities did not end there, for that very evening the newly-weds, and probably some of the others bidden to the marriage feast, came the long way back to Skyburriowe for the 'usual New Year's party'.

It was a crowded day, but on the morrow John Boaden was back at work on the family farm, laconically writing that 'there was not the money to spend (then) that there is now'. Honeymoons, save for the affluent are only a modern development in social life, and are mainly the result of the swift, cheap, and popular transport provided by the railways and by the development of the tourist traffic in mid and late Victorian times. Eleanor Jane, too, probably had had more than enough of travelling for the time, whilst his trip to the Great Exhibition had left John Boaden with rather mixed sentiments about life and manners in the great cities and other places away from home. Both bride and groom felt that they had left youth behind them; their romance had developed and ripened into comradeship and helpmeetship, although it is psychologically interesting that, during the next few months, when there was again an outbreak of religious revivalism in the district, the newly married pair underwent the spiritual experience of conversion. Revivalism and emotional religion have since fallen into some discredit but whatever scenes of unrestrained emotion took place in the Methodist chapels of the Meneage in 1856, it is certain John Boaden and his bride were kindred souls, and that their youthful love, set in a background of chapel life, had been the sure foundation of happy marriage.

For the time John and his wife lived with the rest of the Boaden family at Skyburriowe; that year there was in the old farmhouse a manifestation of the female epidemic of 'spring cleaning', and changing times and the revived fortunes of farming started the Boaden women wall-papering – lime-washed walls no longer sufficed. The garish and even extreme ornamentation of the Victorian age had invaded even the remote Meneage farmhouses and

'Eleanor Jane before leaving Australia (had) collected a number of interesting natural objects and brought them with her, viz rich ores, beautiful pieces of malachite[1], gold in quartz, and a rather large number of prepared skins of birds of beautiful plumage for stuffing, including parroquets, laughing jackdaws, Australian magpies and others . . . They ornamented our bedroom for many years but were ultimately destroyed by moths.'

Such objects would hardly be found in a modern bedroom, and probably some older people in those days passed crude remarks about sleeping in a stuffed hen's house.

Naturally, however, the young married couple wished to get a home of their own. Before long the first of their own family would arrive, and plans were made for them to occupy the farmhouse at Burnoon. Still the two farms, Skyburriowe and Burnoon, were not reckoned enough to support two families, and so when the leasehold of Bojorrow again fell vacant the Boadens acquired it from Sir Richard Vyvyan, so young John could farm it with Burnoon. There was still, however, the younger brother, William, to be provided for, as the older John Boaden, a hale man of sixty, had no immediate inclination to retire.

Then an unexpected opportunity was offered to John Boaden, best related in his own words

'We had just sown a field of seeds on Bojorrow, when Mr. Shaw called one day to say that Sir Richard Vyvyan had sent him to offer me a situation as an assistant to Mr. Foote in managing the large farm then occupied by Sir Richard, which then included along with the Trelowarren Home Farm, Relewas, Carleen, County Bridge, Garras Moor, Nancefields,

[1]A green mineral, basic copper carbonate.

126

Trease,[1] Carvellack, and Gear. We thought that as we have not bought any stock, we might as well try it, and there was a day appointed for me to go and see Sir Richard who then reigned as a prince in this district. It was a day when we were carrying corn at Skyburriowe. I told him that I was a tee-totaller and a Methodist; he said all his servants could have their own religion. It was agreed that I should enter on the duties at Michaelmas, and that a house should be got for me ... At Michaelmas Day I went to the Granary at Chybilly where the fortnightly grists of the men were being measured out, the Miller carrying away two cartfuls of corn in the workmen's sacks to be ground and carried to their homes; he was paid for grinding. I had to keep a particular account of corn winnowed and sold, and of the stock in the Granary, with an account of all stock on the farm with all changes such as births and deaths and sales (of stock), etc.: see all the men at work every day and see the cattle, be the local market man, and prepare a monthly account.'

In short, John Boaden was given a most responsible position on an extensive farm which the squire of Trelowarren was running on modern commercial lines, with fair success. Boaden's account shows that Sir Richard kept up the old custom of paying wages partly in grain at less than market prices to his employees, but on the enlarged Trelowarren farm, much attention was paid to live-stock, possibly because it was more profitable than grain farming. It seems that most of the farms mentioned had been merged into the home farm during the past decade when leases had expired or had simply been thrown up by tenants who could no longer afford the old rents during the agricultural depression. At Trelowarren, in brief, there was, in the late fifties, an example of 'high farming' on an extensive scale, nine farms being operated as a single unit, a development that can be related to the decline in the population of Mawgan parish from 1,084 in 1841 to 895 in 1861.

[1]Trease, apparently had been bought back by Sir Richard Vyvyan some time before 1856; this might be taken as an indication that he had regained some of the capital he had lost electioneering twenty years before; it was also a sign of the declining fortunes of the Lyles.

John Boaden was provided with the farmhouse at Gear, about a mile from Trelowarren House and rather less than three miles from Skyburriowe. Thither John and his wife moved soon after Christmas, 1856, with their six weeks old firstborn daughter, Mary. It was the first home which they could call their own, and they had the pleasant excitement of furnishing it, going around to local auction sales to find and 'pick up' chairs and tables, beds and crocks. Like the move from Trease seventeen years earlier this was a move into another parish, and the parochialism of the times is shown by the way in which, whilst he lived at Gear, John Boaden identified himself with the life of St. Martin's parish. Garras was barely a mile and half away, yet he immediately joined the Methodist class led by his new neighbour Pascoe of Mudgeon, which met every Sunday morning in the house of Eleanor Oates, one of Eleanor Jane's relations. John also became a Sunday School teacher in St. Martin, and rather quaintly he recalled how he had 'tried to promote the unheard of Teetotalism on rather unwilling ears'.

The Boadens only lived at Gear about three years. In that time there were two further additions to the family. A son, also called John, was born in February, 1858, and a daughter, Emma, in May, 1859. In his reminiscences John Boaden referred to this period as that when he was 'out in the world for the first time', adding that he found the situation to be 'a good school'. He gained much experience in farm management, was brought into contact with men outside the limited family and chapel circles, and got to know ways and means whereby farming might be made to pay in the economic world of free, even of cut-throat, competition.

Writing many years after Sir Richard Vyvyan's death, Boaden drew a shrewd picture of the old Tory squire

'I found Sir Richard a sharp but in some cases not a very reasonable man; he always must have his way in spite of any other person's interest, yet he was a very refined man and on the whole an indulgent master; he rather liked a system of espionage. I only one had an opportunity of a long chat with him, which was one summer evening in Chybilly Church; he came out after dinner and we talked till dark. At this time he kept pretty much company certain seasons of the year, often neighbouring clergymen; everyone seemed to stand in more or less awe of him. He came out early as a public man, must have been in Parliament when about thirty, soon began to be recognised as a future leader, was addressing the House of Commons on the historic occasion when King William came down to dissolve it that an appeal should be made to the country on the question of Reform; was afterward re-elected as the man to move the rejection of Lord John Russell's Reform Bill. He sat previous to 1832 for the county of Cornwall and, I think, for the city of Bristol, but after 1832 was defeated in contests in both places. He afterwards sat for the pockct brorough of Okehampton till 1837, and was then out of Parliament till elected for Helston in 1841 mainly by the liberals. His attendance in Parliament during the latter part of the period when he represented Helston was very poor, and I think about 1857 at a dissolution of Parliament he did not offer himself again. He must have been a man of great application, never married, and the latter part of his life lived much to himself. For some two or three years previous to his death his mind quite failed.'

Vyvyan was certainly a man with strong convictions, but he was never a 'good party man'. He had nothing in common with the industrialist Peel who, in his opinion, had betrayed the Church over Catholic Emancipation in 1829, and then, in 1846, had, in Wellington's phrase, got into a damned fright over rotten Irish potatoes and had thrown the agricultural interests over by abandoning the Corn Laws, and it is quite possible that Vyvyan, with others, believed that the extension of Peel's much vaunted police to country districts was another mistake and another intolerable burden on the rates. He certainly distrusted Disraeli, but in that he was not alone. As for Derby, Vyvyan must have remembered that he had opposed him when in Grey's Reform Ministry in 1834 'the Rupert of Debate' had introduced the law for the gradual abolition of slavery throughout the British Empire. If, as Boaden suggests, the Liberals at Helston returned him as the representative of that borough in 1841, that did not mean that Vyvyan had changed his views; it may have been the result of local respect and esteem, although Helston politics, long after 1832, were still in the unreconstructed Eatanswill tradition of Dickens' 'Pickwick Papers'. When Vyvyan retired in 1857 two

Liberals and a Conservative canvassed the borough; the latter withdrew, and then the second Liberal, leaving the way clear for the unopposed return of a 'foreigner', Charles Trueman, known only to Helston as the man who had taken over and started re-working the nearby tin mine of Wheal Vor. Once more, in Cornish politics, a landed squire had made way for a mining magnate. Parliamentary politics and public service at the highest levels was becoming too costly a hobby for landed gentry, although they could still play a very useful and valuable part in local affairs.

John Boaden concluded his description of the Squire of Trelowarren with a tribute to Vyvyan's public spirit as an active local magistrate and, in his last years, as the first chairman of the Mawgan School board. True, Sir Richard was a martinet, expecting the ready obedience of his servants and tenants to his commands, yet in religious matters he was entirely tolerant, albeit personally delighting in the company of Anglican clergy. He was a man of considerable learning, and might easily, but for his youthful love of politics, been an ordained clergyman himself as was his nephew and heir.

When working as the Trelowarren farm bailiff John Boaden came into close contact with the 'permanent' staff of Vyvyan's estate. There was Mr. Foote – the title is an indication of the social divisions of the day when, in truth, the servants of the gentry were the most snobbish of all sticklers for dignity, suffering no man to address them by their Christian names. Foote

'a native of the parish of Northill came down as hind (to Trelowarren) when about twenty years of age, became the principal agent in carrying out his master's plans. He was an able man, but rather inclined to be tyrannical. Mr. William Hollocombe, who was house steward and managed the tradesmen on the estate, was a very different man, having a very honest, frank, and kindly disposition. Henry Skewis, the clerk, had good qualities, but was narrow, suspicious, and proud. Such were the men I had to deal with, but on the whole I got on with them pretty well, though the post was in some respects a little trying and required much prudence. I frequently met the principal servants at tea in the house-keeper's room; these gatherings I much missed when I left.'

John Boaden could probably have told some tales of 'life below stairs' at Trelowarren in the late fifties, although there could have been little scandal in the establishment of an elderly bachelor squire, with no daughters seeking marital connections with other county families and no boistersome and scapegrace sons chasing after and 'ruining' the farmers' daughters and village wenches.

Apart from the responsibilities of his position at Trelowarren and occasional difficulties in getting on and along with the other members of Sir Richard's staff, John Boaden had other troubles during his three years at Gear. There were family upsets and worries, and Eleanor Jane had more than her share of sickening family anxiety. Her second child and eldest son, John had teething convulsions, and then, when he was first crawling about upset some scalding water on his foot. John Boaden himself, who had hardly had a day's illness in his life, caught measles from his children, and a little later went down with small-pox. When all was well, the working day was a long one, whether or not daylight lasted seven hours or seventeen, for

'I had to go to the yard in the mornings, then return to breakfast, then see to the St. Martin's side of the farm before dinner, and the cattle and men on the Mawgan side in the afternoon.'

Nowhere did John Boaden in his reminiscences give any indication of the farm acreage under his supervision, but the estate then farmed by the squire embraced practically all the eastern boundary of Mawgan parish from the shores of the Helford Creek down to Dry Tree, being rather more than two miles in length from north to south and rather less than a mile a half at its greatest width from west to east. There must have been many days when, on horseback or, more likely, afoot, John Boaden travelled a score of miles without going outside the Trelowarren estate, and every time he stopped there was a job to do or some business to which he had to give prompt and painstaking attention.

John Boaden never regretted his years at Gear. It was a comfortable house and there was something to be said for a regular salary which was paid him no matter if weather damaged the crops or cattle sickened and died. Instead of helping to run and sharing the profits or losses of a family farm, however, he was a paid servant and responsible for not one or two farms but for nine, including the home farm which probably made the whole estate equal to a dozen average farmholdings. Nevertheless when his father decided to retire, John Boaden left Sir Richard's service in March, 1860, and went back to Skyburriowe. His brother moved to the 'off-farm', Burnoon, having recently married Susan Davies, the daughter of the farmer who leased Tregadjack which separated the holdings of Skyburriowe and Bojorrow. The brothers continued to work together, and for some time were joint owners of a flock of sheep; still as the years passed they tended to go each their own way, for there was a limit to the size of a family farm and growing families of their own lessened their dependence on each other for help; a day would come when, like their father before them, they would seek more land to 'keep' their own boys under their own roofs, or, failing that, seek farms elsewhere on which to settle grown-up sons. Neither John Boaden nor his brother seem to have even entertained the notion that their sons would not choose to follow their own calling than had their own father before them. For generations they had been farmers, and they did not anticipate that later generations would abandon the traditional family calling; if they were crowded out of the Meneage their sons and grandsons could do as cousins of varying degrees of affinity had already done – find farms in Australia or elsewhere.

12

Harvesting

John Boaden's decision to leave Sir Richard's service may also be ascribed partly to changes that were taking place in agricultural practices. Whatever his politics, Sir Richard was a progressive landlord, but his autocratic nature made him much less than patient with new methods which did not prove immediate successes. Boaden did not always get on easily with his fellow employees at Trelowarren, and the hint that the squire was a little enamoured of 'a system of espionage' charitably described the talebearing and backbiting prevalent at Trelowarren. John had never worked before for another man save his father; being born and bred in the family farm tradition, and now with agriculture moderately prospering, he was anxious to regain his independence; changes in farming methods might mean that the family farmer would be better off than the assistant farm bailiff of a squire, and it was not easy to bear responsibility and blame for novel methods which were not successful. Boaden's own estimate of the value of new farming methods and practices, had at times, differed from those of Sir Richard and Foote, and he seized the opportunity to take over Skyburriowe from his father. He was now a man with family cares and responsibilities. At Trelowarren he saw the life of wage-earners, dependent on the whims of an obstinate master and sometimes on those of other servants who, all too often, were swayed by petty personal jealousies; he saw that men could spend the best part of their days at the beck and call of another and then be cast aside, perhaps with a meagre pension but generally with no provision for old age except their own savings. The lot of such men contrasted unfavourably with those of a retired family farmer who spent the evening of his life pottering about the fields and barns of his sons, lending a hand whenever he felt like it, giving advice garnered from a lifetime of experience which would always be considered with respect if not carried out to the letter, and never feeling that he had been pensioned off as a brokendown retainer to live on grudgingly-given charity.

The catalogue of agricultural changes which John Boaden listed was impressive, although some of the 'new' devices came into the Meneage comparatively late. In his memoirs he wrote

'During the fifties a change had taken place in some important agricultural matters. Early in the decade threshing and winnowing machines were had for the first time on most farms of any size, which superseded the flail and winnowing sheet, and corn was getting to be sold more by the load than at Helston market.'

In point of fact threshing machines were not new. Almost forty years before Richard Trevithick of Camborne had made a machine worked by steam power which was used on the estates of two or three landowners, and since then several horse-driven machines had been devised by relatively unknown inventors, and were fairly widely used. In the Meneage district a lead had probably been given by 'squire' Davey of Bochym, who in 1844 had been using a machine designed and constructed by a St. Agnes miner, Michael Harris which was forty times as efficient as the old hand flail. This engine was portable and could be worked by a small pony. Even then it was by no means the first machine of this type for threshing, for, describing it, a local contemporary newspaper referred to its being a 'vast improvement' on former threshing machines and on those 'now generally used'.[1] Despite the experiments with steam power by Trevithick and others practically every machine employed in agriculture was still worked by horse, and Boaden recalled

'Steam threshing began about this time, but no-one anticipated that it would become general. I recollect two men belonging to a steam threshing machine coming down from the neighbourhood of Truro the last summer I was at Trelowarren (i.e. 1859), to see if they could get work in this

[1]*West Briton*: August 16, 1844

district, but they could not; there were no machines in the district.'

Meneage farmers were probably not particularly progressive but there were many others who resisted. Thus in East Cornwall in 1850 one of the most prominent St. Germans farmers, E. S. Tucker, of Tregannick, asserted that some of the best farmers were still using and would go on using flails.[1] Several believed that mechanical threshing damaged seed-grain; others, rather more justly, that it damaged straw 'reed' for thatching, a consideration of some moment in a district where storm damaged and beaten down grain fields were all too common, whilst often in a 'catchy' season even if tolerably good grain crops were saved, the straw was poor.

The change to mechanical threshing was accelerated by the repeal of the Corn Laws; this also accounted for the other change Boaden mentioned which might be called 'marketing in bulk'. The 'Indian Summer' of English grain-growing was mainly due to the mechanical methods which made it possible to bring to market and sell the produce of the arable farmers of the homeland whilst the backward farmers of Eastern Europe were still flailing their crops and then slowly conveying the grain long distances by horse waggons and bullock-wains to the ports whence it was taken aboard sailing-ships for England. By 1860 nearly every farm in southern England was within a day's haul of a railway or seaport, and the great depression in English farming only began when the foreigners improved their methods of harvesting, transportation, and storage. Furthermore in West Cornwall the vast local mining population could consume all the produce local farmers raised.

Mechanical threshing might have come much earlier in Britain had not some farmers believed it more profitable to keep their hands, and especially their own sons, employed flailing corn in the slack season after the fall, ploughing and cultivating and root and potato-lifting than to see most of their crops in the early grain market. In was here that another change recollected by John Boaden came to be of paramount importance – the rise in wages and the scarcity of labour which revolutionized harvesting operations

[1]*West Briton*: November 1, 1850

135

'There was also a rise in wages; emigration had diminished the labour supply, and the old number of hands could not be got to save the harvest. The country tradesman who had devoted much of this time hitherto to harvest work did less and less of it, and the labourers wives, who hitherto were glad to be employed, began to be careless and many did not go out (to work). The best price paid for a harvest man for the month had been £3, but it was getting higher. So instead of reaping the wheat as had been the universal habit, I suppose from the days of Abraham, yawing with big hooks began to be practised; then, in the latter end of the decade, some began to cut wheat with the scythe which became general in the early 'sixites. This went on to the introduction of the reaping machine which became pretty general about 1868, which was the year we began to use it. This continued till the far-better sheaf-binding machines came in use about 1888. This may be said to have caused a revolution in harvesting, the farmer now with his usual hands being almost able to save the harvest. The same economy of labour had been affected in saving the hay.'

It is surprising that the scythe came so late into use in the harvest fields, and that the reaping hook and sickle survived so long despite the back-aching strain of 'true reaping'. In this Cornwall did not lag behind the rest of the country, for Richard Jefferies in 1887 recalled reaping being done in Wiltshire about 1860

'with a hook alone in the hand; all the present reaping (i.e. in 1887) is 'vagging', with a hook in one hand and a bent stick in the other, and instead of drawing the hook towards him and cutting it, the reaper chops at the straw as he might at an enemy.'[1]

It seems that the Meneage was, however, behind other parts of Cornwall in adopting agricultural machinery, for the first 'reaping' machines had come into the county as early as 1852, when the farmers' clubs of Wadebridge and Probus held trial demonstrations

[1] R. Jefferies: *Field and Hedgerow* (1948 edition), p. 165.

of the American reapers of Hussey and McCormick. There had been much local scepticism and doubt about these machines, and some farmers said they were utterly impracticable simply because they were too wide to get through Cornish gateways;[1] this difficulty could be easily overcome simply by widening the gateway, which, of course, would involve getting the consent of the landowner, few of whom were likely to object. More likely, the farmers were unwilling to go to the expense of new gates for which there would be no compensation at the end of their leasehold term. Objections on the grounds of cost, however, were more realistic in another way. Although a reaper only cost twenty-five or thirty pounds it was horse and not ox-drawn, and if a farmer decided to use them he often had to buy at least one more horse, although the sale of a redundant ox-team to the butcher might help to pay this expense. In the early days, too, few farmers had the mechanical knowledge to operate and maintain the new reapers in the best way, let alone carry out small but essential repairs,[2] and there were some 'old timers' who asserted that the 'American' reaper, however much labour it saved, did not make up for the labour shortage caused by the emigration of farm-hands from certain districts.[3] For many years the machine only reaped; not for nearly another generation was the binder and binder-twine to be introduced, till then the swathes had to be gathered up and bound into sheaves by hand with twisted straw 'binds' into sheaves.

Gradually the reaping machine proved its worth and even the most conservative farmers were converted. Its introduction transformed the harvest fields, and John Boaden graphically wrote of the bygone days

'In saving the corn up to this period (i.e. about 1860), the farmer and his own hands would first begin by reaping up any wheat that might first be ripe along the hedges. Early in the harvest we have been days reaping laid[4] oats. Then when

[1]*West Briton*: February 13, 1852.
[2]*West Briton*: May 21, 1852.
[3]*West Briton*: August 20, 1852.
[4]i.e. oats beaten down or 'lodged' by heavy rains or twisted and battered by tempests.

the bulk of the crop would do to cut, help was sought for; any extra hands that could be procured, and on final days most of the population that could work, would be in the harvest field. The regular hands would be in the field at six o'clock, often using the scythe on spring corn till (the dew was gone and) the wheat was dry enough to cut.[1] Breakfast was at 7.30, the fare being barley-bread and milk. Somebody with a boy (to turn the handle of the grindstone) would grind the reap-hooks; then off to the harvest field, each one having his ridge; this would often cause emulation among the reapers, and some would make bad work rather than be left behind. Ten o'clock was 'crowst';[2] previous to the advent of teetotallism almost all the farmers in this neighbourhood made sufficient cyder to save the hay and corn, but since then the way changed to coffee and cocoa in many cases. Then a good plain dinner at noon, everybody employed all had their food at the farmhouse. About six, reaping would stop; then the carrying of the sheaves and mowing[3] would be done and it was often the case that the light was nearly and sometimes quite gone before it was finished. You could see the white glint of the moon on the top of the mows when little else could be seen, and the rustle of the feet through the arish[4] would sound through the still evening air, and the smell of the wild thyme would shed a perfume all around.'

The work in the fields at harvest time presented a busy scene with the reapers trying to see which of them could cut their way to the head of the field first, none of them wishing to lag behind and if they did blaming the grinder for not putting a good, sharp edge on their reap-hook or declaring that the local blacksmith was not so good a man as his father before him had been in making a

---

[1]Naturally men would not, if they could avoid it, handle wet grain crops; the later crops wre only fit to handle when the dew was gone, and in late August in Cornwall the dews are often especially heavy; this consideration accounted often for much anxiety in the spring to get the sowing done in good time.
[2]A West Cornish term for a snack.
[3]i.e. erecting into hand-mows, described below, p. 139.
[4]Stubbles.

finely-tempered blade. Some of the older ones, too, doubtless, grumbled at crowst-time when, instead of cider they were given a mug of milky cocoa or a sickly-looking greyish brown beverage that passed for coffee. By noon, with the sun scalding down, they were glad to go to the farmhouse for a meal. There would be more refreshments brought out to the corn-fields in mid afternoon, and then, again perhaps before they stopped reaping to spend the rest of the day, as evening shadows drew on, gathering up the sheaves and putting them into the massive hand- mows which were a peculiar feature of Cornish arable husbandry. These mows, containing some eighty or a hundred sheaves, called for considerable skill in the making. Night often overtook the labourers before they had done, especially when in the earlier part of the day there had been many hands reaping and binding sheaves in the field, some of whom had had to leave early to attend to live-stock or, in the case of the women, to do their household chores; before the introduction of 'summer time', the daylight saving ordered by Act of Parliament during the first World War, which many farmers criticised as contrary to the will of God, there was barely two hours of daylight left between six o'clock and sundown at the beginning of August and less than an hour at the end of that month. The fewer labourers in the field at the end of the harvest-day must be emphasised. Not only had the womenfolk gone indoors to help prepare a supper, put infants to bed, and help milk whatever cows were kept on the farm, but there was no knowing if or not the men sent off to see to the livestock would be able to return to the cornfield; they might find a sick animal and have to spend hours treating it, or they might find that during a sultry day cattle tormented by flies had broken out and strayed far away; on the farms where sheep were kept there was even more trouble, for the worst ravages of maggot coincided with the earlier harvest-time. Casual workers, too, tended to drift away as the shadows were lengthening; the townsman who had dropped in to give a farming relative a hand, and had to walk back four or five miles to his home, went as soon as he thought or was told that the others could manage to finish before dark; if the local carpenter had been there he might be called on to drop his reap-hook and return to his shop to make a coffin; the village blacksmith might be summoned to shoe the horses another farmer wanted to carry corn next day, their owner having only discovered at the last moment that they had cast shoes or worn them too thin and smooth for safety on the rough and slippery stone trackways; now and again the farmer himself, known to be one of the best amateur farriers in the district, would be called away by a worried neighbour to do what he could for a heifer whose first calf was not coming the way it should, or to diagnose whether or not a sickly-looking steer had contracted the dread murrain.

So they toiled on, day after day, when there was a prolonged spell of dry weather. In West Cornwall it was harder still in 'catchy' seasons, when the farmer and his helpers had to make the most of intermittent dry spells, and not infrequently attempted to race a deluging thunderstorm. There were mishaps; a hook would slip and a hand be cut or a leg gashed in reaping, but the more serious accidents generally occurred when the corn was being carried from the fields; a man might be stabbed with a pike as he was building a waggon-load or a rick; a horse, tormented by flies or frightened by a barking dog or children racing about, might bolt and upset a load; on steep hill-slopes a waggon might overturn, or the man making a load on it slip and fall headlong. The harvest-field had its perils no less than the mine or fishing-ship, and the pages of almost every burial register of a rural parish record such tragedies. Still none, apparently, occurred on the Boaden farms, nor did John Boaden mention any that occurred on neighbouring farms. He might have forgotten when he wrote that nearly thirty years before there had been a fatality at the neighbouring farm of Tregoose, when William Mayne fell off a half-laden hay-waggon and was killed outright. Helping Mayne get in his crop had been one of John's relatives, Joseph Boaden who then occupied the old Boaden farm of Millewarne. Mayne, a big man aged sixty-four, slipped and fell back heavily when the horse, tormented by grey flies on a hot July afternoon, had jerked away.[1] Many other incidents and accidents occurred from time to time on the farms of the Meneage, showing that farming is not an industry unaccompanied by occupational risks.

John Boaden, concerned with the more normal routine of

[1]This account of William Mayne's death is based on reports of the accident and inquest which appeared in the *Cornish Telegraph* on July 18, 1876, and in the *West Briton* of July 20, 1876.

old-time farming, went on to describe the picturesque old West Country harvest-custom of 'crying the neck'.

'As the end of harvest came we could hear the calling of the neck at the various farms around which was observed when the last of the wheat was cut. A tolerably-sized bunch of corn was bound together near the head before it was cut which was left to be cut last. After all the day's work was finished the farmer and his harvesters would gather around, and with this 'neck' in hand call the neck. The farmer would begin by calling three times at the top of his voice "I have 'em!" followed by a harvester calling, thrice, "What have 'ee?" then another repeating in like manner "Have a neck"; then all the party making a united "Hurrah!"; this would be repeated three times, and then all repaired to a good supper which was much appreciated in those times. In some times each harvester had his or her own neck fuggan[1] for tea. Neck-cutting in Trelowarren the harvests I was there must have been attended by seventy or eighty persons, including children, who had their tea and beer in the great office and singing after.'

The custom varied from district to district in the west country but died out in the Victorian era when the scythe superseded the sickle while the reaping machine dealt it its death blow.

In older times than those of John Boaden the neck was taken to the farmhouse and there kept until the next harvest. In some places, too, the neck was cut by each reaper hurling his sickle at the last standing bunch of wheat, and then, when it fell severed to the ground, there would be a rush to seize it, and the first to grab it would dash off to the farmhouse with the trophy hotly pursued by the rest. The custom may have been the survival of some pagan rite, but to Boaden and his generation it was the triumphal conclusion of long and weary days and weeks in the harvest fields.

If the coming of the reaper caused the disappearance of this rite, the great harvest suppers Boaden also described vanished for

---

[1] A small cake or bun.

similar and other reasons. Reapers and then sheaf-binders, meant that the farmer and his regular hands along with one or two casual labourers did the whole work of harvest: it was no longer an enterprise in which the whole community – man, woman, and child – participated and shared. Then, in the early 'forties, the religious harvest festival rapidly spread after its first introduction by Parson Hawker of Morwenstow, especially among the various Methodist sects; instead of the supper in the farmhouse or barn there was a chapel tea, followed by a service, and the sale of the harvest produce given by all members as a thankoffering for the continuing bounty of the God of harvest. The final blow, however, was the prolonged agricultural depression beginning in the 'seventies. One of the last of the great harvest-home suppers held in Cornwall was in 1873, when a Lelant farmer, Laming of Trevathoe, after carrying a hundred and thirty acres of corn, entertained seventy of his work-people and friends to a lavish supper in his great barn, which was decorated for the occasion, followed by a dance going on till about four o'clock the next morning to which all the young people in the immediate district came.[1] Hospitality on this scale was beyond the means of tenant farmers and even of most small landowners when the dark days of depression came a few years later, a depression which caused the Lamings to emigrate to the United States.

The cutting of the corn, of course, was but a single phase of harvesting; it still had to be carried to the mowhays or rickyards and stacked, and in the days of John Boaden

'Corn carryings were great times, begun usually about three o'clock in the morning and continued till dark. Almost all the corn was carried by wains; the load was tipped off and pitched (on to the ricks) from the ground; the use of waggons and (the practice of) pitching (directly) from them is comparatively new.[2] I recollect my brother Will and myself bringing in eight wainloads of corn from Park Bronc to Bojorrow

[1] *Cornish Telegraph*: September 10, 1873.
[2] Pitching directly from a wain, which was nothing more than a cart-bottom balanced on the axle of a single pair of cart wheels, particularly when drawn by a restive horse, was a difficult and ever dangerous practice, unlike pitching from a four-wheeled waggon.

mowhay before breakfast when we got (a meal of) flour and milk. It used to be the custom for each man to have a glass of brandy before he began to work; then in temperance farms they had cocoa and cake.[1] My dear wife used to rise at this early hour and get and give out (these refreshments) mainly by herself, and did so till we gave up farming. In those days labourers did not often get meals of beef, so corn-carrying was a feast to them. I have been out at three in the morning nearly every day for a week in the busiest (time) of corn carrying. Farmers helped each other and (harvest) parties were large.'

Even with modern summer-time this meant getting up at four – before dawn towards the end of August. The Cornish practice of putting the sheaves of corn into huge hand-mows made such early hours practicable; had the shocks of corn been small, the six or eight sheaves ones which were most general until the coming of 'combines', heavy dews would have delayed the start of carrying, although there are many late summer mornings when there is little if any dew at all, and since this was generally regarded as a sign of coming rain or storm the farmers hurried on with the work all the faster. With some justification many of these farmers were regarded as veritable slave-drivers by their hands but if they hustled on their men they certainly did not shirk work or spare themselves whilst Boaden pointed out the Meneage farmers helped each other out so reducing the amount of hired labour employed on their holdings.

There were times when John Boaden looked back to his days at Gear with regret, as having been 'almost a holiday'. He had been paid forty pounds a year for the rest of the time he was in Sir Richard's employ. If his position had carried a burden of responsibility, yet there had been subordinates to do the heavy manual work and many of them to share and ease the burden of toil. At Skyburriowe the farmer himself had to do everything and anything; there were still farm-hands, but the master was no mere overseer – if the farm was to pay he had to strip off his jacket, roll

[1] The phrase might give support to the cynical view that temperance was the consequence rather than the cause of the decline of smuggling, that it progressed when the 'trade' no longer provided cheap brandy.

up his shirt-sleeves, and set to with the rest of them. And John Boaden probably was wondering soon after Lady Day, 1860, whether it had been worth while for the sake of independence of the squire to become his own slave. There was plenty of time to think of such matters when, with the old and rather decrepit Dick Barker, a man who had been working on the land all his life and knew all the dodges of shifting the heavier jobs on to the younger and less cunning men, John Boaden found himself out in the fields of Gwealdrinkas preparing the land for a potato crop. Doubts were dispelled when the crop was lifted in the fall and sold for twelve shilling the bushel, realizing nearly a year's salary at Trelowarren from an acre of ground. With prices of other agricultural produce still generally higher than they had been before the Crimean War and despite their growing family the Boadens were able to 'put money by', which they had started doing when they had been living at Gear.

13

Wider Fields

After 1860 changes in farming were steadily progressive and Cornish provincialism was vanishing. The railway bridge over the Tamar at Saltash was finished in 1859, and the Cornwall Railway the next year, so, in Boaden's words

'we got connected with the rest of the Kingdom, an advantage difficult to estimate. There had been for some years previously some sheep and lamb sent up by steamer from Hayle to Bristol; all the rest of our produce had to be consumed in the district; the farmers' best customers were the miners.'

Within the next decade, however, the Cornish copper mining industry collapsed, thousands of miners left the county, and those that stayed were reduced to short wages and shorter commons. Still, food was wanted in bad times as well as good, and the railway had made a wider market accessible, so the effect of the mining slump on local farmers was reduced. The phenomenal migration of miners from some districts meant, however, that few farmers found it possible to get more or cheaper labour, whilst round Helston, where the main mining interest was tin rather than copper, the slump was less acute.

Besides providing means for marketing produce, the railway made cheap and speedy long-distance travel possible. Many now felt an itch to travel, among them John Boaden. Since 1851 he had hardly been twenty miles outside Mawgan. He was keenly interested in progressive farming and decided to go to the Royal Agricultural Show at Battersea since now the railway was completed 'we could get to London for the first time in one day . . . I felt a great desire to see London once more, feeling assured it would be for the last time, and even this I feared was extravagant for me to go there twice. I, however, was put in the little cart to go about three miles from Camborne in the early morning, walking to the station, got an excursion ticket, and got to London and found lodgings at a Coffee House in Newington Causeway. I tried to get a companion to go up with me but failed. I visited the show twice, and in company with Mr. and Mrs. I. W. Trounson. On a Saturday I left King's Cross Station for Southill on the Midland Railway – the Midland Railway not having at that time a London station – where my old friend and fellow companion of eleven years before, James Boaden was station master; he had given up being school-master, and qualified himself for the post, and had married a governess in Mr. Whitehead's family.'

Writing forty years later Boaden gave no details of the Battersea Show. He spent much of his time in London, as he had done in 1851, in renewing old friendships and attending religious services conducted by the most famous preachers of the day. On the day after his visit to James Boaden, John

'heard Morley Punshon preach to a large congregation in Liverpool Street Chapel in the morning, Newman Hall in St. James's Hall in the afternoon when Dr. Wilberforce – slippery Sam – was preaching opposite at the same hour, and in the evening heard Mr. Spurgeon in his Tabernacle which had not long been opened; there was a great crowd present. After wards I went to see Mr. and Mrs. William Harvey who were surprised that I had contrived to hear three such men in one day.'[1]

[1]William Morley Punshon (1824–81) was one of the greatest Wesleyan orators and administrators of his age. Christopher Newman Hall (1816–1902) was the outstanding Congregationalist tract writer of this period, and an extremely popular preacher. Charles Haddon Spurgeon, the most famed preacher of Victorian times, was a Baptist till five years before his death in 1892; his Metropolitan Tabernacle in Newington Causeway, able to hold a congregation of six thousand and costing

146

The Boaden Family 1865

Late Victorian Dairy Farming

Silver-tongued and golden-voiced these men may have been, but John Boaden must have seen and heard other interesting men during this trip to London. The Battersea Show, the twenty-fourth and largest 'Royal' yet, had nearly two thousand live-stock entries and over five thousand exhibits in the implement classes. Boaden, apparently, did not go out to Farningham to see the steam-ploughing demonstrations, nor did he describe the new potato-diggers and ploughs, reaping and threshing machines, hay and corn elevators, and butter-making machines which were commented upon in the press of the day. The weather was fair but overcast, but John did not mention it ot whether he went from his lodgings to the show ground by rail or by one of the passenger steamboats on the Thames.

Some exhibits at that Royal Show had immense future significance. The live-stock included a few 'Dutch' cattle, already reckoned among the best dairy breeds in Europe. Corn-growers must have been interested in a new 'hybrid' wheat, of which the agricultural correspondent of *The Times* commented at length, adding

'the importance of improved varieties of grain, realizing the prolific virtues of Pharoah's seven ears in one stalk without the thick bran and coarse flinty quality common to the branched or mummy wheat, has not been sufficiently considered; yet, within the last fifteen years we have spent more than £3000,000,000 sterling in imports of foreign corn; the purchase is rapidly increasing every year, and quickly as grows our hungry demand, sources of foreign supply multiply as fast. Little more than twenty years ago the whole of our foreign wheat came from the north of Europe and Germany. As our necessities enlarged, France, Italy, Canada, and the United States came forward with supplies, but the Black Sea ports and those of Turkey and Egypt – now such exporters to this country – are scarcely mentioned in the Custom House

£31,000, had been opened in March, 1861. Samuel Wilberforce (1801–73), Bishop of Oxford from 1845, later, in 1869, Bishop of Winchester, got his nickname in 1864, when Lord Westbury called his writings "a well-lubricated set of words . . . so oily and saponaceous that no-one can grasp it."

returns of the period. In 1840 London received corn from 185 foreign places of shipment. In twenty years 98 new grain-shipping ports arose, and during the last year about sixty fresh names have been added to the list. And one point not always borne in mind is that this foreign corn is better than our own, the advantages of climate enabling the rude tillage of serfs and ignorant peasantry to produce finer average samples than those of the scientific English farmer . . . For the last fifteen years, while the average values of English wheat have been somewhat above that of wheats from France, Belgium, the Rhine, and South Russia, the price of wheats from the Baltic ports, and from the United States and British North America, has exceeded by three to six shillings per quarter the quotations of Kent, Essex, Norfolk, Lincoln, and Yorkshire. While half-settling countries, with rough husbandry, can produce wheat like that of California . . . a thin-skinned, swelling grain, of exquisite colour, weighing 68 pounds per bushel, and while Victoria eclipses all with a wheat weighing 69½ pounds per bushel[1], it is hopeless for farmers in our English climate to strive after a like quality with the cargoes which all quarters of the world are sending into our ports. It is in quantity reaped per acre that we must make progress; and here lies the immense value of improved cereals which will size more vigorously whatever plant-food may be in the soil, and by natural habit deposit more of the nutriment in the ear, instead of wasting so much in building up a big bulky straw.'[2]

Many farmers realized the truth of these remarks, and British 'high farming' in the following years was mainly an attempt to meet foreign competition by growing more and larger ears of wheat to the acre; in the English climate no-one could grow wheat equal in quality to that of California or Australia.

Specimens of this Californian wheat were even then being shown in the International Exhibition at Kensington, where there was also an interesting exhibit in the rather poorly furnished pavilion of what some newspapers were now calling 'the late

[1]The average weight of English wheat was only 63 pounds per bushel.
[2]*The Times*: June 25, 1862

United States'. Cyrus McCormick, whose reaper had attracted much interest at the Great Exhibition in 1851, had failed to get his exclusive patent rights extended by the American Federal Government; he had, therefore, tried to offset this by attaching to his improved original reaper a device that turned off the cut corn in bundles ready for binding by hand instead of in swathes. McCormick was on the way to the 'self-binder', but already the rival American firm of Radstone had made a reaper which they claimed would

> 'cut, gather, into bunches, take a band of straw from the bunch, tie up the sheave, and tuck in the ends of the bond, all by the unassisted automatic mechanism of the machine.'[1]

Radstone's 'self-binder' was to have been shown at Battersea, but some parts did not arrive in time, and promises that it would be demonstrated in English cornfields that harvest were, apparently, unfulfilled; years passed before 'binders' became common in England or America; some sceptical and conservative farmers probably dismissed the Radstone claims as another 'Yankee tall story', and that they would only see binders working in those Elysian fields that were sometimes mentioned by 'Slippery Sam' and those other preachers in whom John Boaden delighted.

Boaden did not visit Parliament on this holiday in London, but attended a temperance meeting presided over by Lord Shafesbury who, in his opinion, made an interesting speech. Soon after, John returned to Cornwall, a kindly fellow passenger putting him up for the night in Camborne where the train arrived at one o'clock in the morning; forty years later he wrote that in 'all my touring I was as glad to get home as I was to go.'

John's account of his second visit to London is briefer than that of his trip in 1851, but there is no hint that he had changed his unfavourable opinions of city life. The cares of his growing family may have made him even more sober and serious-minded than he had been in his youth. Yet, although a strict, even a stern, Methodist, he was charitable towards the shortcomings of others, did not expect too much of human frailty, for in his memoirs he wrote that, about this time

---

[1] *The Times*: June 24, 1862

'We determined to have family prayers daily, which we continued and carried out till my wife's affliction and the difficulties of getting servants to attend them mainly caused our giving it up, but it ought to have been continued.'

It is to Boaden's credit that he did not try to enforce his religion on his dependants, but his remarks reveal the existence of a breach, which rapidly widened, between middle-class non-conformity and the so-called 'lower orders'. Still, Boaden was an active Methodist, and when

'Our Sunday School at the Garras, which had been discontinued, was again opened I at once became a leader, and have, by the blessing of God, continued so to the present day, I have also been enabled to be a regular attendant at the (chapel) services through the busiest periods of my life; my dear wife always valued them and attended them through difficulty and weakness that few would have done, for demands on her were great.'

The cares of farm and family possibly kept Boaden, now approaching middle-age, from taking a more active part in Meneage Methodism at this time. He had considerable administrative abilities, but he always shunned the limelight and had no ambition to 'get on the plan' and become a local preacher. He remained among the 'old-line' Methodists who were content to leave the chapel services to the regular ministers as much as possible. He disliked the numerous splits and schisms with which Methodism had been rent through personal conflicts and jealousies, although, at times, he could be as critical of ministers as any other man inside or outside the Connexion. His religious views might have been different had he lived in a parish where the rivalry of Church and Chapel was more acute, but in Mawgan the only violent antipathy was that of the Wesleyan and the Methodist Free Churches.

With a working day often lasting from six in the morning to ten at night 'without much stop', John Boaden had little time to do much outside the farm. The burdens on his wife were even heavier. By the summer of 1865 she had a family of seven children, the eldest not yet nine years old. The ordinary farmhouse work

150

made such a large family a considerable care. John's mother helped a fair amount, and there were some servants, but they

> 'as usual gave trouble, so about the beginning of 1866 we engaged Nurse Margaret Bishop to teach and take charge of the children; she continued with us two and a half years.'

The labour-saving devices of a 'slab-oven' was installed in Skyburriowe kitchen, but Eleanor Jane's health broke down. She became pale and listless, and local Helston and Falmouth doctors seemed unable to say what was wrong. Then the weary farm-wife rallied a little, and went down to her relations at Gwallon, near Marazion, for a change. There she was suddenly taken worse, and a new doctor who was hastily summoned held out little hope for her recovery. She was too ill to be moved back to Skyburriowe, and John Boaden took his young family in the farm trap down to see her as he feared and thought for the last time. One night she seemed to be dying, but then she rallied although her recovery was slow and months passed before she was well enough to go home.

Despite these family troubles Boaden was prospering in those years; he recorded that he

> 'commenced about 1865, from information which I got from Mr. William Johns and Sam Jope, to purchase different kinds of securities on the Stock Exchange; this I continued till 1880 when I bought Trenarth. I bought the bits of leasehold belonging to Mr. Lincock and the old Millhouse near Gweldrinkas Gate for £5 of Mr. Lincock. I began my building career in the beginning of 1868 by building Worval House for Father; Mr. Eva (was the) mason and Harry (the) carpenter; (it) cost irrespective of our labour and building stones £175. Father went there to live from Burnoon, where he had resided with Will, having (had) to leave Boscawen Cottage about thre years before. He went to Worval the same day that John Bright visited the Lizard . . . It was about 1860 (that) I bought the leasehold of Worval Tenement of Henry Dale's agent for I think, £35, and then gave £15 for change of lives from H. Dale, wife and daughter to myself, Will, and my daughter Mary.'

Far-sighted business acumen was shown in these transactions, for he was buying property that would be of use to him and his family. Worval was only across the narrow valley from Skyburriowe on the road to Garras, and in the house that he built there both John's father and himself were to end their days. He might have preferred to buy freehold property, but at that time of moderate prosperity landowners were not selling, preferring to let farms on seven and fourteen year leases and to lease cottage tenements out for three lives for a moderate sum, perhaps about ten or twelve years' valuation, and a very small quarterly or yearly rent. The naming of the three lives to be inserted in such a deed of lease was, of course, a gamble by the lessee, and John Boaden aware of the normally longer female expectation of life named as his third 'life' his eldest daughter, Mary, who had safely passed the first five critical years of childhood.[1] The Boadens bore the entire cost of building the new house, and there would be no compensation for their family when the three lives they named all died and the tenement reverted back to the owner of the freehold. It is possible that the older John Boaden had left Boscawen Cottage when a third life on it had lapsed, but more likely through a quarrel, for it probably belonged to the Davies family of Gwealeath.

This quarrel rose from other dealings in property affecting John's brother, Will, who some years before had married Susan Davies. The older John Boaden had then bought Tregaminion Farm, near the Lizard, from her father, John Davies, for Will, and this transaction had

> 'led to a very unpleasant affair, in father's house at Boscawen being broken into and the agreement which was signed by Mr. Davies for the sale of the farm cut out of the account book; it led to an estrangement between us and the Davies family that was never quite healed.'

A lawyer would have advised Boaden to have got a more regular and orthodox agreement. A promise to sell on certain terms, written into an account book and probably unwitnessed, was unwise, but farmers were very chary about consulting lawyers and

[1]She died in 1939.

152

generally distrusted them. The elder Boaden may have thought that such an agreement would save him legal fees, besides thinking that he could rely on a family as prominent in local Methodist circles as his own.

Such feuds often arose in rural society, and many farmers held the cynical view that, where money was concerned, no man could trust another. Even the squire was not above suspicion, for John Boaden write

'At Michaelmas of 1869 Father took Tregadjack for Will. He had done so about seven years before, but was rather dis-honourably done out of it by Sir Richard in favour of Sam Trounson, but seven years was enough to satisfy each other that they had better part. So now we had Burnoon added to Skyburriowe, a farm double the size. My dear wife had a plenty of cool courage; she shrank from nothing that she thought would benefit her family.'

Despite lawyers and squires a progressive farming family was steadily getting control of more and more land; that they were also speeding the departure of the smallholder, as they did by buying Worval, passed unnoticed by John Boaden. The Boadens did not shrink from extra work, and they were still saving and investing money against the time when their young sons and daughters would have to be set up in a position in the world that would do the family credit.

John Boaden's concern with material well-being may seem odd, but Wesleyans rarely emphasised the virtues of apostolic poverty – save, perhaps, for their lowly-paid ministers. Methodists were not alone among dissenting sects in forgetting the scriptural warning about the amassing of worldly wealth subject to the corruption of moth and rust and the depredations of thieves; like earlier Calvinists they might meet criticism on this by reciting the parable of the talents.

Even more strongly at variance with popular notions of the ascetic puritanism of mid-Victorian nonconformity was the trip John Boaden made to Paris to see the Exhibition in 1867, at the suggestion of 'Cousin Tom'. The cousins left Penzance at eleven one morning, and going by London, Newhaven, and Dieppe, reached Paris at six the following afternoon. Their stay was brief, and John's impressions, though interesting, were laconically recalled

'Saw the Exhibition, much like all such exhibitions are. Paris is light, clean, and beautiful; the colour of militarism seemed to prevail everywhere; the Frenchmen do not seem to be so very strong and robust, nor so well clad – though very clean – as the English. The effect of their land laws are very apparent in the small patches in which the land was divided; the people seemed to live out of doors. In going to Paris the train stopped where we could see Rouen in the distance. The weather was beautiful; it looked like a living poem. Paris was never more gay than this summer, and Napoleon III, whom Tom saw, was at the height of his popularity.'

There is no doubt the two Boadens enjoyed their excursion abroad. Tom, a younger man than his cousin, may have been tempted to see some of the wilder night life of Paris, but in those memoirs there is not an echo of Offenbach and the mad whirling music of the dance-halls where the can-can was then the rage. Returning to London they stayed with the Trounsons with whom John had gone to the Battersea Park show five years before. On a Saturday night Tom went to see the Moore and Burgess ministrel show; the next evening his more sober cousin went to hear Spurgeon preach from the text 'Though I am poor and needy', and wrote in his memoirs that it was the finest sight he ever saw, a rather strange judgement from a man who had just returned from the great exhibition in Paris; still John had a taste for sermons and liked nothing better than the sight of a chapel thronged to its doors.

John also saw James Boaden again, though now this meant a journey to Cambridge where James, having given up his job on the railway, was studying to enter the Church

'having got a B.A. degree while schoolmaster. Found him and his wife quite well. He put us through some colleges and the very beautiful grounds surrounding them. I came back that night and Tom next day; the following day we went home.'

These few remarks leave a suspicion that Boaden was one of those hustling travellers who galloped along seeing the sights and passing quickly on to see more. Cambridge was too much to see in a single afternoon, even if his time was limited and he had to get back to Skyburriowe for the harvest and the rest of the farm work. Still these hasty trips were typically those of men of his calling; no farmer worth the name has ever been truly happy for long away from his fields and his stock; he cannot believe that another knows them and can manage them and their foibles as well as he does – and often he is right.

Even these brief remarks on Cambridge show that it was the gardens and lawns rather than buildings which most struck the Meneage farmer. He brought back from France a more lasting impression of tiny field and small peasant holdings than of the Exhibition which he had gone to see. Furthermore, the moving spirit behind this venture abroad was not John but his go-ahead cousin who went with him, but stayed a night longer in Cambridge and, while in London, had enjoyed a minstrel show but who, apparently, had not gone to a sermon given by the most popular preacher of the day. Tom Boaden, one can be sure, made the most of his comparatively brief life – he was to die when only forty-six; for he made a fairly large fortune, amounting to several thousands of pounds, besides acquiring the freehold of the local farms of Treworgy and Nantithet. It was little wonder that his cousin described him as 'one of the most successful and able men our family has produced'.

John, himself, however, was 'no fool' in business matters, and about this time, he recalled that he

'Devoted much attention to the Stock Exchange and invested all my moneys as soon as I got them but did not speculate in the usual sense. I must have held – different kinds of stock . . . (by 1879) mostly of a very good class, including a great share of railway and telegraph shares. I had, I should think, about this time an increase of about £300 a year, built up by saving and investing. I had some losses in Peruvian, Egyptian, Spanish and Portuguese stocks, but other stocks had increased in value sufficiently to quite balance these losses and the interest was high.'

155

Obviously John believed in 'spreading the risks' by investing in such a variety of stocks that, some twenty years later, he could not remember the exact number. It does not seem that he risked anything on local mining ventures which, in 1866, slumped. Wise foresight and a keen appreciation of the value of speedy transportation led him to invest heavily in railways and telegraphs, but it is difficult to surmise why he bought exotic foreign bonds unless attracted by a high rate of interest; even then, he did not risk considerable sums.

Reckoning an average interest of five per cent, the 'increase' of £300 a year in 1879 or 1880 represents an invested capital of at least £6,000, over and above his stock and possessions at Skyburriowe. The basis of this fortune, including what he inherited from his father, was the land; it suggests that in the first twelve or fifteen years that he farmed Skyburriowe, John Boaden saved between three and five hundred pounds a year, although he could have put by little in the bad farming years after 1875. His rent was comparatively low, for Sir Richard Vyvyan had not raised rents to anything like the extent that some other Cornish landowners had done;[1] an ultra-Tory, the squire of Trelowarren held fast to the old ideals of the relations of landlord and tenant which elsewhere has passed away, the ideal of a fair return from the land, the ideal that neither the land nor the man who worked it should be ruthlessly exploited to swell rent rolls.

Still even in Mawgan there were acute divisions in rural society. It was tenant farmers who had to bear most of the troubles, worries, risks, and losses in agriculture, not their 'sleeping partners' – the landlords and tithe-owners. There were murmurs against landlordism and local squirearchical tyranny; not until the introduction of the secret ballot in 1870 was it possible for a tenant farmer to vote without the fear of being told that if he did not support the squire's 'man' his lease would not be renewed. In local affairs the whim of the squire was law, and in Mawgan the aged Sir Richard had become a tool in the hands of some Anglican Tory attorneys, a clique which still dominated Helston borough politics although no longer able to control its

[1] Most Cornish farm rents rose by a third or a half in the period between the repeal of the Corn Laws in 1846 and the onset of the great slump in 1875.

parliamentary representation as in the 'good old days'.

John Boaden clashed with these men when Mawgan elected him to the Helston Board of Poor Law Guardians in 1870. The Board was not conducted in the best interests of the rate-payers, and was

'ruled to a great extent by the wire-pullers, of whom Richard H. Cade was most active, in the interest of the great office. There was a great influence brought to bear on the independence of the Guardians. I found myself before the second year (for which I had been elected) had ended at variance with this party, and had to unmask a very dishonourable affair; but the party had power and daring enough to manipulate our parish vestry, so that two others who would better suit their purposes were nominated instead of Mr. J. T. Davies and myself. I was nominated after, but finding that Sir Richard had been gained over by this combination I withdrew; the two other guardians were my cousin, Edwin, and Richard John. This determined me to buy a farm that I might be independent of landlord coercion which, up to this time, had been largely exercised on tenants, and looked on generally as one of the prequisites of landed property.'

The local Guardians had wide powers in those times, but in many places besides Helston they were controlled by small cliques and pressure groups. There was little flagrant corruption, but rate-paying farmers wre suspicious of the ways money was spent; often a favoured ring of tradesmen and contractors monopolised contracts to supply provisions to the Union workhouses; some Unions, were badly managed and much money wasted. Some farmer guardians, however, were selfish, mean, short-sighted and uncharitable, though old John Thomas, a staunch Methodist from Mullion, was not a lone voice when he said Guardians should not pay for the elementary education of pauper children beyond the fifth standard, declaring that the rudiments of reading, writing, and arithmetic were enough, and that 'fancy' subjects only made children discontented with their predestined lot and made them bad workers.

Many farmers felt themselves caught between landlord autocracy and discontented labourers. Grumblings about labourers not being what their fathers had been had been voiced in every age and were common enough; even more vocal, and to some extent new, were complaints that landlords had not realized that times had changed. Tenant farmers now claimed a voice in politics and a say in running local government; they demanded their 'rights' and a fairer return for the labour and capital they spent on the land. The unpaid services of landed gentry in Parliament and on local benches of magistrates was not valued at all highly by their tenants, especially when, in the early seventies, there were signs of agricultural recession.

In the times of 'high farming' prosperity many landowners had taken too much in the way of rents from their estates, while the standard of living among tenant farmers had risen, and the luxuries of a previous generation had now become necessities to them. When prices began to drop tht new standard was menaced, but they would not abandon it. The imports of foreign produce into Britain did not, as yet, seem to threaten their prosperity since the repeal of the Corn Laws, nearly thirty years before, had not ruined British farming as the protectionists had prophesied. The slight recession in the early seventies was too easily attributed to their not raising and selling all they could from their farms, and they believed they could raise more if their landlords did not preserve so much game and sell more if their leases were less stringent. Anyone could see that twenty quarters of wheat selling at fifty-five shillings the quarter made less than twenty-five at fifty shillings or even thirty at forty shillings. Then, too, the farmers, argued, they could produce more if their men worked harder and more conscientiously.

Older men inevitably declared that workers and everything else were inferior to those of their young days, but the Cornish farmers in the eighteen-seventies had reason to think that their labourers were not the men their fathers had been. The best had saved money and become farmers themselves; more had worked diligently to make enough money to emigrate, and some farmers admitted that they had been justified in quitting the 'Old Country', for their wages were but little higher than they had been two or three generations before and their chances of saving enough to become farmers themselves, in view of the keen competition for holdings in Cornwall, were far less than they had been; the towns, too, offered better wages, more opportunities for advancement, and better living conditions.

Farm wages were low, rarely exceeding fourteen shillings a week, but many rural labourers lived in rent-free cottages, usually with gardens in which they could grow most of the vegetables they needed, and sometimes free 'potato ground' in their employers' fields; many of them could keep a pig, and milk they got free or for next to nothing. In fact, many farm labourers spent little on the necessities of life, and their employers were fairly generous with 'perquisites' besides paying higher wages at harvest time. Comparatively few rural labourers ended their days when 'past work' in the 'Unions', for any analysis of workhouse inmates over a number of years reveals the greater proportion of them to have been not aged labourers but waifs and orphans, 'fallen' women, unemployables, and aged spinsters and widows. Moreover, only rarely did the numbers of those in the Unions get anywhere near one per cent of the total population in the predominantly rural districts of England.

While squire, tenant farmer, occasionally even the parson, and labourer all contributed to the illegitimate birth rate, the great rural social problem of mid-Victorian times was the housing question. Many have criticised the 'tied cottage' system, but the effective working of a farm demanded that the labourer lived near the place where he worked. In the Meneage at this time, however, there were complaints of time and energy lost in travelling to and from work. Such cottages as did exist were small, often consisting of only two rooms, besides being utterly insanitary; against this must be reckoned numerous cases of labourers trudging to work anything from two to five miles in drenching rains or withering north-east gales, unable to change sodden clothing when they arrived, risking and not infrequently contracting pneumonia – then more often than not a fatal disease – or gradually becoming afflicted and crippled with rheumatic complaints.

The rural cottages, whether 'tied' or not were often as insanitary as any slum-dwelling in Victorian industrial towns. Large families were forced to live in hovels consisting of a kitchen and a solitary bedroom; windows were small, ventilation poor, and often no provision whatever was made for sanitation. Unfortunately, contemporaries said more about the indecency and immorality which resulted from such rural housing conditions than about the incidence of infectious diseases that was fostered.

These problems, however, did not affect John Boaden to any

great extent, for by the mid-seventies he had sons old enough to do a full day's work at Skyburriowe, while his older daughters were able to help their mother with many household chores. True, the time would come when his sons would want homes and farms of their own, and to give them a good start in life he was carefully husbanding his capital. Thrift and economy were his ideals, but looking around he saw much cause for uneasiness. He got on well enough with his own landlord, but at almost every Helston market there was talk of other landlords screwing up rents. And there were other tales too – how Squire So-and-so had installed game-keepers in cottages hitherto inhabited by farmworkers, how labourers were becoming restive not only in the Midlands but much nearer home in North Cornwall. Those were the days when farmers were cursing Joseph Arch organiser of the National Agricultural Labourers' Union, along with the squire, the tithe-owner, the government, and, of course, the weather.

Meneage farmers, however, did not worry overmuch in the early seventies when some newspapers began stressing the amount of cheap wheat coming into British markets from America. The drop in English wheat-prices in 1874 was generally ascribed to the almost over-abundant home harvest in the year. The next year's harvest was rather poor and the season wet, but fair yields of barley and oats in Cornwall offset a further drop in wheat prices. In 1876 the wheat and barley crops in Cornwall were better than those in other parts of England, although oats were below average. Boaden and his neighbouring Cornish farmers balanced past losses against past gains and reckoned that they had done tolerably well; they did not know that they had seen out the 'Indian Summer' of Victorian farming prosperity. In the fall of 1876 they ploughed and got the fields ready for the next harvest. Christmas came, and there was no reason why they should not celebrate that festive season as they had done in the past, and then the 'usual' New Year's party at Skyburriowe.

But that New Year was 1877.

14

The Lean Years

Gathered together that New Year's Eve, the Boadens and their friends talked not only of the years ahead but also of the year now ending. A little more rain at the right time and the harvest would have been nearly as good as that of '74. Luckily rain had come late in July in time to save the roots even if it meant a 'catchy' time for harvesting the corn; had the turnips and mangolds failed it would have been hard to find winter-keep for their stock, since the cold spring and dry May had meant a very slight hay crop. They could have done with far more straw too, and if the wheat crop had been good, the barley had been poor.[1] John Boaden may have reminisced about the sights he had seen in London in 1851 and in Paris in 1867; he may already have had some inkling of the price Britain must pay for becoming the industrial workshop of the world – rural depopulation and millions of townsfolk living on foreign grain; the corn fields of the homeland could now only supply the needs of about two out of every five of her swollen population. Like other Liberals Boaden praised Peel for abolishing the Corn Laws in the hungry forties, and believed that but for free trade the succeeding decades would have been even hungrier. Perhaps, in 1875, foreigners had sent too much grain to Britain but wheat prices had risen again in 1876. True, the new troubles between Turkey and Russia might have caused this recovery, just as, in the fifties, the Crimean affair had helped end the slump which had forced some of their farming friends and relations to emigrate to Australia.

Still it was the weather, the season, which made or marred the

[1]This account of the harvest in 1876 is based on reports in the *Cornish Telegraph* of June 6 and August 1 and 15, 1876.

farming year and the farmer's career. If the next harvest was not too good and the Russians caused more trouble – though Boaden himself reckoned the Turks to blame – there were always the Americans; they had got over their slavery trouble and were fast bringing their western prairies under the plough. He, John Boaden, had no doubt that the right side had triumphed in the American Civil War; some of their politicians, were awkward and ought to be more careful what company they kept, but nearer home, only three days ago, the Helston Bank had shut its doors. Stories were circulating in the district that one lucky farmer had stayed overlong yarning with his cronies and had not been able to deposit some thirty pounds after market before the Bank closed, and that an absent-minded tradesman had forgotten to bank his Christmas take of nearly seven hundred pounds before the holiday! Others had been less fortunate though rumours had been current about the stability of the bank for some time. The crash came when a client tried to get an overdraft to conclude a deal in property; he could not get the overdraft nor could he get half the sum lying to his credit in the bank. It was not a large bank, the total liabilities being about £41,000, but there were many small depositors including farmers, local shopkeepers and tradesmen, and thrifty labourers.

When the Helston Bank closed, Boaden wrote

'There was great excitement; the depositors and others were called together at the Assembly Rooms, which were quite filled, a very excited meeting, which ended by the appointment of a committee to wind up and examine the affairs of the Bank. The committee was chosen by ballot, viz. Mr. Thomas Probert, Will Trevenen, Mr. Tresidder solicitor St. Ives representing the London Bank, which was the largest creditor, Mr. Baddeley, Mr. Woolcock, draper Mr. B. Kempthorne, Mr. Will Tyacke, myself and Mr. Henry Hocking.'

The Committee met several times; Boaden probably supported if he did not propose dispensing with the two chartered accountants who were at first called in to go through the accounts when it was found that a thorough investigation would probably

'Swallow up a large part of what was left to divide among the depositors, so after a very cursory examination and not finding anything very flagrant they were dismissed.'

Boaden himself, naturally, wanted to save as much as possible of the hundred pounds he had in the Bank; others did not want an investigation which might have shown up some dubious dealings in mining shares. The only man who came out with much credit was the director, T. H. Edwards, who, well over eighty years of age, sold all his property to help meet the liabilities of the Bank. Through him, the creditors recovered about ten shillings in the pound. The banking business was taken over by the reputable Bolithos of Penzance, although, according to Boaden, they did not 'push' the business.

A loss of about twenty thousand pounds spread over a considerable number of creditors was not large, but the loss of confidence in the district was immeasurable. Bolitho's Bank even if it did not rush business, proved a formidable rival to the other Helston Bank, the Union, which two years later was forced by the general commercial depression to close its doors in February, 1879, a month after the collapse of the Cornish Bank which had branches at Truro, Falmouth, Redruth and Penzance. Boaden did not, however, mention the depression when he wrote that in consequence of the failure of the Union Bank

'There was another large meeting of depositors in the Assembly Room. Mr. Tom Bolitho presiding, at which it was agreed to accept the Bolitho's offer of, I think, fifteen shillings in the pound. Thus ended the two old rotten banks of Helston, which had been used very largely for political purposes, to demoralize the voters of the borough and to maintain a most bitter feeling between the rival parties. The loss of the depositors was very severe . . . but on the other hand Helston political life has been a gainer by their close.'

Boaden did not indicate what political deals and manoeuvres the two old banks had perpetuated but their directors had probably formed close rings to control borough affairs for their own benefit, just as in days before the Ballot Act landlords could, and often did, get rid of tenants who refused to vote as they were told, so had small local banks refused credit to and called in loans from men who showed signs of political independence.

The losses Boaden and other local farmers incurred by these bank failures wre trifling compared to those the vagaries of the seasons now brought upon them. In the Meneage in 1877 if the weather could do anything wrong it seemed to do it. Farmers only managed to save about half their hay in a brief spell of fine weather after several bad thunderstorms in early June; then, to support the old superstition, the weather 'broke' again about St. Swithin's Day. Wet day followed wet day, the only slight improvement being a few days of summer fog at the end of July – potato disease weather according to the Meneage ancients; hopes that August would be better were quickly dashed. Corn crops were beaten down, 'lodged', tangled every way. A few acres were cut, but the rain came on again, and soon the ears of the 'shocked' grain were sprouting, and the golden sheen was leeched out of the weather-beaten straw which began to rot. Grain and straw prices rose a little that autumn, but that was no consolation to farmers who had neither grain nor straw fit to sell; indeed, some of them feared that they would have to buy fodder to keep their cattle alive before the end of winter. Rather than do this so many sold off stock and cattle prices slumped but, fortunately, the winter was mild although even the mildest winter can be too long, and this was certainly felt by Meneage farmers to be the case in 1877–78.

With a wet and cold May and a broiling, thundery June, weather troubles continued in 1878; disease appeared early in potato crops, and turnips and cabbages were ravaged by caterpillars. Still, despite 'catchy' weather the harvest was reasonably good, and with a fair amount of fodder and winter keep stock prices rallied. But winter came early and lasted long – right to the end of the following April,

Even before the disastrous season of 1879, British farming was depressed. Since 1869 the general level of grain prices had dropped by a quarter, and as the foreigner now supplied over half the grain consumed in Britain the home harvest no longer determined British market prices. Some farmers may have anticipated a drop in grain prices when the troubles between Russia and Turkey were settled in 1878; a year or two later Disraeli's 'Peace with Honour' could have been called 'Peace with Bankruptcy' where British farming was concerned. Some Cornish farmers with relatives in the States may have expected that American supplies of wheat would increase rapidly, not so much on account of phenomenal developments in rail and steamship transport as from the sheer necessity of struggling American agriculturists to produce more and more to pay off debts and mortgage interest on their homesteads. John Boaden told his neighbouring farmers at the Helston Christmas Show in 1878 that they should concentrate upon raising beef and mutton, for

'They were meeting every year with a competition which was increasingly severe, and by the infinite skill of engineers and mechanics it appeared as if the fields of America, Portugal, and Spain, were practically being brought every year nearer and nearer to our own. What the result might eventually be he confessed that he did not know; but, if importations from abroad continued to increase, as some supposed, it certainly would be a very serious matter for English Agriculturists. He hoped, however, that the depression would soon pass away, and that with a general revival of trade many of their fears would be dissipated.'[1]

Other speakers at that meeting agreed that farming was suffering mainly from the general trade depression, and hoped for better times soon. Most of them believed they could stand up against foreign competition, but one or two hankered after protection, advocating restrictions on the importation of live cattle, especially from Spain into Cornwall, alleging that this was the cause of outbreaks of foot-and-mouth disease and might even bring the more dreaded rinderpest to England again.

In other places critics, saying that British farming was in a bad way, were blaming farmers for 'living too high', for spending too much on food and dress, for 'cutting too great a dash' at fairs and shows, and for overhard drinking. A few, farmers mostly, retorted that the land was too heavily taxed, which meant taxing British farm produce to benefit foreigners. Wages had gone up, but for every farmer who hinted that they pay their men less half a dozen openly declared that farm-labourers were badly paid; scores, however, did, in fact, cut wages by only employing some hands

[1]*Cornish Telegraph*: December 17, 1878.

part time and dispensing with others altogether. Rents were high, but one prominent Cornish tenant farmer, Thomas Olver, declared that

> 'three per cent is not too much for the owners or occupiers of land to expect to realize on their capital in this wealthy, highly taxed country, while its money-ocracy, regardless of its general prosperity send their capital abroad to improve foreign lands, in Peruvian, Egyptian, or even Satanic Bonds, could they be funded simply with the view of getting a high amount of interest. What the agriculturists of this country chiefly require is a fair adjustment of taxation. Trade and commerce, which have been enriched at the expense of agriculture ever since the repeal of the Corn Laws – or what is falsely called free trade – should bear a larger amount of taxation for benefits received; but the reverse is the case. Farmers formerly received higher price for grain after a bad harvest like the present; then the whole community shared in the calamity; but now, the British farmer had to "tread the winepress alone." '[1]

Olver's last argument might be called a little selfish, for farmers had never showed eagerness to drop prices in gratitude for bountiful harvests. Yet in times of agricultural prosperity land-lords and farmers had not put back the profits they had made into their land and farms but, directly or indirectly, invested abroad. John Boaden, for one, had some of those Peruvian Bonds which Olver put in such bad company, and had made many other speculations on the Stock Exchange; true he had done so with the ultimate purpose of buying land for himself or his sons, but while the money was invested it was helping the development of potential foreign rivals and competitiors. Many other farmers did the same; their investments, some small and others not so small, probably far exceeded sums manufacturing magnates and mine owners 'invested' in land property not so much to promote British agriculture as to enhance their social standing and prestige. Furthermore, with little security of tenure and less for improve-ments if they spent their surplus capital on another man's land,

[1] *West Briton*: November 28, 1881, quoting from *Mark Lane Express*.

tenant farmers naturally invested their money elsewhere. Some tenants and many landowners spent part of their profits on the land in the prosperous days of 'high farming', but these sums fell far short of the returns then being made from the land. Yet everything taken from the land has to be paid for and for many years great profits had been taken from the land and but a tithe of the reckoning paid.

Payment was to be bitter indeed, and for a long, dreary time it seemed that fortune had deserted British farmers completely. The talk of depression late in 1878 could easily have been dismissed by outsiders as farmers merely grumbling as usual. But then came 1879, which, so far as Cornwall was concerned, was 1877 and 1861 put together for bad weather. Without saying how he himself fared at Skyburriowe, John Boaden wrote

> '1879 was the wettest season on record. The losses of stock throughout the Kingdom were enormous; most farmers lost some of their sheep and nearly all others sold at ruinously low prices; crops were very poor; even the turnips were a bad crop.'

He mentioned that he had gone to the Royal Show again this year, and that the Kilburn show yard was a sheer muddy morass. On this trip he saw the Salvation Army Barracks in Whitechapel, stating briefly that the religious movement was then in its infancy, and went on to sum up farming fortunes in the eighteen-seventies, writing

> 'I think, however, that this decade, with the exception of the last year, was the best for farming in my experience. The price of cattle, sheep, and pigs was very good. Beef for a short time reached £4 a hundredweight, but at several times touched £3.10s. But the excellence of the market here (i.e. in Britain), with increased facilities of transit began to attract animal food from different parts of the world, which has kept its comparatively low ever since. This, combined with the disastrous season of 1879 and the continued fall in the price of corn were the causes of the severe depression which then began and has more or less continued to affect agriculture ever since.'

167

Many British farmers in 1879 admitted that the nation would have starved had it not been for foreign wheat. Their own cereal crops had been utter failures or, at best, only fit for animal-feed. However, supplies poured in from Russia and America, and grain prices slumped instead of rising. Having once found the British market wide open, foreigners continued 'dumping' grain into Britain, and in years of good harvests, with prices still falling, the home farmers began to complain that it no longer paid them to grow wheat. Even in 1879 few British farmers looked to the years ahead with much hope. Cornish farmers, however, unlike 'up country' ones, had not seen devastating floods sweeping the hay and corn out of their fields, although what hay and corn they had 'saved' was barely worth the trouble of carrying when the rains eased off in autumn. Hay lay rotting in the fields and ears of corn were sprouting green from black shocks and handmows in the corn fields where the farmers had managed to reap and bind a few tangled sheaves. The grain that was carried was small and shrivelled, hard to thresh, and nearly unsaleable and useless when threshed. Since the oat crop was not too bad many farmers in Cornwall decided to grow more of it next year and less wheat and barley. Down in the Lizard that autumn arish-mows were being sold off the fields for fifteen shillings instead of three pounds which had been an average price in former years, and this at a time when many farmers were already wondering and worrying how they were going to feed their live- stock through the coming winter.

Bills had to be met; rents, rates, tithes and taxes paid. Many landowners remitted part of the rents, but there began a persistent and prolonged outcry that farm rents were much too high. Cases were quoted of farms in midland and eastern counties being let with rents reduced by a third or even a half, but it still seemed that every time a Cornish farm was to be let, despite depression, a dozen or score of prospective tenants wanted it, offering rents which they thought would secure the farm against all their rivals rather than being based on any sober estimate how much income might be reasonably expected from the particular holding. Some tenant farmers in the past had put their sons into prpfessions like dealing, land agency, or auctioneering, but now, to keep labour bills down, they kept them at home on the farms; knowing no other trade or averse to slipping down the rural social scale by becoming farm labourers, these young men, when they married and wished to get up their own homes, aggravated the demand for farms; few of them wished to go far from the district where they had been born and reared. Too many older farmers had treated their sons as 'boys', never seeming to realize when they were grown up and should be entrusted with the full responsibilities of running a farm. Generally, too, where a son wanted to marry and start on his own, his father could not offer him any capital save livestock which could not easily be moved far or, in depressed times, sold; fathers, too, would share working equipment with a son who got a farm reasonably near 'home', and to get such a holding men offered higher rents than were economically justified, and often estimated the value of staying near the old district far too high. Competition for farms was further intensified by men who came back to Cornwall with a little money they had made as miners, bent on setting up as farmers in the 'old country'; and many of them knew next to nothing of farm management and economy in good let alone in difficult times, while none of them were as young and strong as they had been when they had gone away. Landlords could not be blamed for accepting the high rents offered by these men; for one thing, the existing law of distraint made the rent the prior and first charge on the asset of any tenant who failed; then, too, many landlords held entailed and encumbered estates, and were often bound to provide annuities to the younger sons, unmarried daughters, and widows of their predecessor and even of the predecessor a generation back, and at the same time were debarred, by the laws of entail, from selling a single plot of land to meet such charges against their estate; so, forced to mortgage their possessions they had to pay high rates of interest regularly and, for that reason, rarely thought twice about accepting the highest tenders of rent.

Many Cornish landowners, too, were not living on their estates, but were merely taking rents from them and spending them elsewhere, so, it was said, increasing local unemployment and rural distress. This was true in many instances, but many landlords already could not afford to live on a lavish scale in the old family mansions, 'cutting a dash', and lording it over the parish; instead they went to live in quiet obscurity in some distant place where the family name was less well-known. Their dealings with tenants were carried on by agents and stewards; there were always lawyers ready to collect rents not for a fixed salary but on a commission basis, and such men almost invariably let farms to the highest tender and were quick to enforce the law of distress upon a tenant in financial difficulties.

The regular charges of rates, taxes, and tithes were certainly burdens in hard times. Rates had in recent years increased considerably, mainly to pay for elementary education and the upkeep of the roads. Farmers started asking why they should pay for the education of other people's children besides for their own. Many of them, although not John Boaden, did not believe in education anyway, saying that children kept at school beyond the age of ten or eleven grew up lazy and bad workers, that the place the farm-hand learnt his trade was in the fields, and that if he started by picking up stones and scaring rooks when he was seven or eight years old the better farm worker he was likely to be. If children learnt too much, these diehards argued, they became discontented, moved off to the towns or the Colonies, or did as little work as they possibly could, besides getting the idea into their heads that they were as good as their masters. When the road rates were discussed, farmers asked why they should pay for the gentry and tradesmen who used the roads much more alleging that the narrow iron-tired wheels on the traps and vans which the latter used cut road to pieces whereas the wide-tired farm cart and waggon helped bind the road together. Rather less was said about poor rates – although they were heavy – but among the first advocates of old age pensions were members of Lord Winchelsea's National Agricultural Union which, early in the eighteen-nineties, proposed to raise the money for such a scheme by an import duty on foreign flour, thereby reducing foreign competition and the rates at the same time.

Tithes, perhaps, were the thorniest issue of all. Farmers were asking why disestablishment, like charity, should not begin at home instead of in Ireland, especially as by this time the English taxpayer was helping Irish tenants buy out their landlords and acquire their own freehold farms, and then to proceed to flood English markets with cattle and, later, with butter; often too, local outbreaks of foot-and-mouth disease were alleged to have been brought in by imported Irish cattle. Many farmers, like John Boaden, were not Anglicans and had to support their own non-conformist chapels as well, while those who were churchmen asked why the cost of the Established Church should fall almost entirely upon the land. Furthermore, no one could say what proportion of tithe went directly to support religion. In many parishes the great tithes of corn and grain had long been in lay hands, actual vicars only receiving the 'lesser' tithes of pigs, geese, honey, and the like, or their commuted money equivalent since the Act of 1836. Just what, if anything, original lay impropriators of tithe had done for the Church had long been forgotten. To embitter and complicate controversy still more the Tithe Commutation Act of 1836, superseding the payment of tithes in kind, had laid down that the amount of tithe be assessed on the average value of corn for the seven preceeding years. That had been a reasonable way of balancing good seasons against bad but in such years as 1879, for instance, farmers, with less than a quarter crop of wheat and a barley crop nearly as bad, were asked to pay a sum calculated on the average price a normal harvest would have brought them during the seven preceeding seasons; the 'averages', too, were not calculated from local market prices, but on those in certain up-country markets where prices, especially for barley, were usually much higher than in Cornwall.

True, when a man took a farm he took it knowing encumberances were attached to it. He knew what rent he had to pay and that he had to pay rates, he knew a certain amount, based roughly on the market value of his crops had to be paid to the tithe-owner. Still, when prices of agricultural produce fell these things did not fall with them. In many Cornish districts, particularly in mining areas and near towns, rents hardly fell at all, while in bad times, rates and taxes seemed to go up rather than down. Tithe in one respect was worst of all; even if in a few years it did fall with, or rather after, prices it was a direct levy on productive farming, a levy which may have been originally intended for the support of religion but which now, for the most part seemed to be going into the over well-lined pockets of a privileged class of laymen who did nothing to earn it and who had not the slightest obligation in return to the farm lands from which it was levied.

A succession of bad harvests and wayward seasons would have made things hard for British farmers in any case, but in the late eighteen-seventies they had another cause for discontent – increased foreign competition. In time past, as Thomas Olver had said, a bad harvest had meant high prices which compensated the farmers to some degree. At the end of 1879, however, wheat was down to forty shillings the quarter, the lowest price for many years. For the greater part of his farming career John Boaden must have made at least fifty shillings the quarter for his wheat, and several years it had been above sixty shillings. He was never to make such prices again; before he retired from farming there were to be times when he was to find it difficult to get thirty or even twenty-five shillings per quarter for his wheat; oats and barley slumped too, and wool in some seasons was only to fetch six-pence a pound instead of fourteen or eighteen pence as in the 'good old days'.

The old 'Sheep and corn' husbandry of England, through weather and foreign competition, was reeling under nearly mortal blows. To the losses of a ruined harvest were added epidemics of foot-rot and liver-fluke decimating flocks on some of the colder and heavier clay soils. Losses in Cornwall were, perhaps, not so heavy as they had been in the 1860 epidemic, but still amounted to one out of every eighteen or twenty, and were much more severe on some farms than on others. The farmers of eastern England certainly suffered far more than those of Cornwall, many of whom had adopted a rather different and more mixed farming routine which was less dependent on fair weather. Several Cornish farms had already adopted a six-year rotation in which half the cultivated land was under leys, instead of the four-year rotation with only one year in grass. Farms like Skyburriowe, and Burnoon, too, had acres of uncultivated croft-lands or 'moorland runs' for summer cattle pastures. With grain prices down they turned more and more to stock raising as the mainstay of their farming; they still ploughed land to keep it in good heart, but when labour was scarce or dear the ley might be for four or five years instead of three; it was more profitable to feed what grain was grown to their cattle than sell it to corn factor or miller. By the end of John Boaden's farming career in the Meneage wheat and barley had, in that and most other districts of Cornwall, been supplanted by mixed or 'dredge corn', and what wheat was grown was grown for a double purpose – as a crop in a rotation which was particularly effective on heavier and colder clay soils and for the reed or straw used in thatching; no longer was it grown with the sole or even primary purpose of furnishing 'bread corn'.

This period in English farming history has frequently been summed up in the phrase 'Up horn: down corn'. Certainly the area under cereal crops did decline and in places there was an increase in the number of cattle. Sheep diminished in numbers partly on account of the decline in wool prices, more perhaps on account of heavy losses through liver fluke and other diseases, but also, to no inconsiderable extent to the belief of many farmers that close-grazing by sheep destroyed good cattle pastures. True, as John Boaden wrote, there was a fall in the price of beef and of store cattle in the era of the great farming depression, but it was a drop of barely a quarter compared with the disastrous slump in grain and wool. It was in this period that John Boaden spent the last part of his farming career and in which he used the capital which he had been so carefully accumulating during the good years to set his sons up in life, four of the five becoming farmers like their father.

Note to Chapter XIV
The following Agricultural Returns from Mawgan in Meneage for the years 1867 and 1894 give some indication how farming changed by the time Boaden retired in the latter year:-

	1867	1894	Decline	Increase
Wheat (acres)	318.5	268	50.5	
Barley (acres)	297.25	303		5.75
Oats (acres)	203.25	336.5		133.25
Turnip & Swedes	167.5	171.25		3.25
Mangolds	60.5	50.25	10.25	
Bare Fallows	221	38.5	182.5	
Rotation Leys	861.25	874.75		13
Permanent Grass	89.25	910		820.75
Numbers of cattle	1,239	1,181	58	
Numbers of sheep	2,513	1,667	846	

Some of these figures are rather surprising; the vast increase in permanent pasture may be attributed to the inclusion of much reclaimed land and rough grazings in 1894. The decline in fallowing is also significant. The reduced number of cattle was largely the result of keeping beasts longer either for dairy purposes or for beef, since the numbers of cows and heifers in milk or in calf rose by 42 from 309 to 353, and that of cattle over two years increased by 81 from 254 to 335, cattle under two years declined by 182 from 676 to 494. Furthermore, compared with 1881 the Mawgan returns for 1894 saw the decline in wheat acreage over those thirteen years being not less than 101 acres, that of barley being 103.5 acres, whilst oats too dropped slightly by 2.25 acres; turnips and swedes dropped by 26 acres and mangolds 27.25 acres, but bare fallows only by 4 acres, the rise in permanent grass as much as 471.25 acres, but leys dropped by 25.75 acres. The total cattle in 1881 was 1,017, *i.e.* 222 less than in 1867 and 164 less than in 1894, whilst sheep in 1881, after the losses through disease were down to 1,178, i.e. 1,335 less than in 1867 and 489 fewer than in 1894. The returns for 1867 may not be as complete as those of later years, being the first year in which the 'farming census' was taken.

15

Farming Goes On

In 1880 John Boaden had a family of five sons and four daughters, the eldest Mary, being twenty-three and the youngest, Laurie, eight; the two eldest sons were twenty-one and nineteen respectively; Edward the third son had died of scarlatina early in 1871. It was a fairly 'long' family even in those days, but the older generation had passed away, John's father dying in September, 1875, and his mother in March, 1879, both near four score years of age.

It was not easy to give the children a good start in life. The girls had been weekly boarders at a school kept by their former 'nurse', Miss Bishop, in Helston, and the second daughter, Emma, went on to Dunheved College at Launceston. Boaden did not mention where his sons attended school, but they probably left as soon as he thought they could do a good day's work about the farm. Only young Laurie showed no disposition for farming, but Boaden had to think about ways and means of setting the other four lads up as farmers. By 1880 it was impossible for all of them to live much longer at home and Boaden was looking for a holding where the two elder sons could farm in partnership, as he and his own brother had done, till both could find farms of their own; the youngest sons might take over Skyburriowe when he himself retired. If possible, he would rather buy than rent a farm for his boys but despite the depression it was still very difficult to buy or even rent farms in Cornwall. Boaden knew of opportunities in the 'Colonies' and in the Midlands of England where, by 1880, many farmers had already thrown in their hands. He had, however, made up his mind to find a farm in the neighbourhood where he could keep a helpful and friendly eye on his sons, running it with Skyburriowe as a bigger family farm, concentrating on livestock, feeding what crops

were raised to the cattle and thus selling the produce of the arable
'on the hoof'. In any case, a stockman wanted more acres than
men who formerly had struggled so hard to make the corn mows
pay the rents and make a living. Since, however, many other local
farmers shared this opinion, the competition for land was as keen,
even keener, than when 'corn was king'.

Boaden's experience as Mawgan guardian some years back had
made him think of escaping 'landlord coercion' by buying a farm
of his own if possible. By thrift and cautious investments he had
now capital to buy land when any came on the market. He
seems, however, to have missed a chance when in August, 1879,
some Cury farms were sold to meet the liabilities the owner
incurred through the failure of the Helston Union Bank. Perhaps he thought that it was not a good time to buy since the
cheapest of the Cury farms, Trevorgey, made £3,340 or £33 per
acre, and another, Colvennor, of about 93 acres realized £4,750.[1]
Nevertheless the Cury sale did show that the big landed gentry
were no longer prepared to push up land prices to 'fancy' levels
merely to add to their broad acres or even to round off their
estates.

Moreover about the time the Cury farms had come on the
market, Boaden had spent much of his available capital. Some
time previously he had bought

'the leaseholds of the five cottages in Mawgan Cross of the
executors of Mr. T. Rowe, Tregdalle, who held the mortgage.
I afterwards bought the freehold, improved them, and sold
them to Henry Lugg, tailor, for £110; he sold them soon after
to Mr. Andrew.'

More recently he had purchased some cottages in Mawgan village
and, for £2,000, the freehold of the small farm of Choon, about a
mile from Manaccan Churchtown, the Boadens having owned the
leasehold of Choon, which had been let out on three lives, since
1849. Neither of these purchases helped solve the problem of
finding land for his sons or for him and his sons to work together;
Choon was already let to a tenant, while one of the Mawgan
cottages was let to a close friend of Boaden's wife after she and a

[1]*Cornish Telegraph*: August 19, 1879.

village tradesman spent several days putting it into reasonably habitable condition.

John Boaden at this time was in a strange position. To the Vyvyans and their agents at Trelowarren he was only one of a number of tenant farmers; to several other people in Mawgan district he was a landlord. His family may have reminded him that not only he but his father had talked often enough of owning the land which they spent their laborious days in farming, and as yet not a thing had come of it. The opportunity to remedy this came a little later when, in the summer of 1880

'Tregonwell in Manaccan and Trenarth in Constantine were advertised for sale. (My brother) Will, Mr. John Ralph, and I went first to Tregonwell and then to Trenarth. The fine house and homestead with such a good-sized farm struck me. I had been long wanting something desirable, and so had my father before me, but hitherto, every bit of land would be bought by some of the great landlords and such as I might spend a lifetime without a chance. I put (my sons) John and William over to see it; they, of course, liked it. Then I met Mr. John Boase as agent, at St. Columb then, and eventually at a meeting with him at Truro bought the farm for £6,000, Mr. E. Lawrence then renting it for a term expiring at Michaelmas, 1884, at £155 per year.'

The purchase included the small holding of Trewince and a lodge; the lease of the latter, which had been let out on three lives, had just fallen in, although that fact cannot have added a great amount to the selling price of the pleasant estate on the north-eastern side of Port Navas Creek.

Apart from writing that he was struck by and that his sons liked Trenarth Boaden did not give any reasons why he bought it rather than the Manaccan farm, which actually adjoined the holding of Choon he had, only a year ago, bought outright, and which was only six miles from Skyburriowe whereas Trenarth was nearly ten – and very much an up and down road at that. The prices of the two places may have had something to do with Boaden's decision. Tregonwell, a holding of rather less than forty-five acres which could easily be worked as a one-man or small family farm, was the type of holding in greatest demand in West Cornwall, and John

177

Boaden would have been lucky to get it for much less than £2,500, or maybe £3,000. There may have been, too, a sitting tenant with a longish period of a lease still to run, whereas the Boadens could take over Trenarth in four years, by which time John, the eldest son, would be twenty-six, and his brother twenty-four. It is most likely, however, that acreage determined Boaden's decision; even had it been possible to merge Choon and Tregonwell it would have been a holding of little more than seventy acres, smaller than Skyburriowe which, even in better farming times, had not been big enough to keep John Boaden and his brother. Trenarth ran to a hundred and thirty seven acres of meadow, arable, and pasture land, besides twenty acres of woodland which might be 'reclaimed'. The price ran out to rather less than forty pounds per acre, which was reasonable in Cornwall at that time, though not cheap; it might be added that a year later, the top bid for Tiptree Hall, the model farm of a hundred and thirty two acres, in Essex on which John Joseph Mechi had spent more than a fortune, was only £3,750.

Having agreed to buy Trenarth, John Boaden had to find the money to pay for it. His brother took over Choon for the same price as he had given; the rest, save for a mortgage of £1,000 which was paid off some years later was paid by transferring the railway shares John had been accumulating during the past twenty years.

Even before the purchase was completed and the sitting tenant's term expired, Boaden started transforming the estate. In his memoirs he wrote

'I began to repair the cattle houses, and throughout the eighties was often employed in building and other improvements at Trenarth. We widened roads and made anew hedge and entraance, rebuilt the dwelling house at Trewince with a new barn and other (out) houses and drained; took down two acres of firs and cultivated the land; put up new gates, and did much to improve the tenement. At Trenarth Bridge (we) demolished five old cottages, and built a good new house with buildings complete for the tenant; put in posts and hung gates, did hedging – poor old Willie Thomas doing the latter, almost the last work he ever did; he was a noble man; I had known him from a child, he was our nearest neighbour at Trease. We also built a new dwelling house at Trenarth, and

Original Skyburriowe rebuilt as a barn

Skyburriowe in 1995 after rebuilding in 1891

built a cart-shed, turnip house, fowls' houses, and much improved other (out) houses; also uprooted three plots of wood and after tilling the piece at the bottom of Little Trenarch for some years planted it to an orchard . . . We did most of the labour ourselves going from Skyburriowe at Trenarch sometimes with two carts, leaving about six in the morning, and returning home between 8 and 9 p.m. sometimes in winter . . . We were busy in 1884 in purchasing and preparing for John and Will to commence farming at Trenarth. It cost all told over £900. John was married in the fall.'

That was the only allusion John Boaden made to the marriage of his eldest son. He may or may not have approved of the marriage, although he probably took it as a matter of course and did not oppose the match as much as his own father had at first opposed his own marriage to Eleanor Jane. Nevertheless, whatever the vagaries of human emotions and affections, to the Boadens and to all the farmers of that time the land came first. Youths might be smitten by the charms of a potentially unsuitable mate, but that danger was minimized by keeping them hard at work at home on the farm so that in the evenings they were too tired to go off to the neighbouring villages and towns. True, by the time Boaden's sons were growing up a few 'bone-shaker' bicycles had already appeared on the scene to make farms less isolated than they had been in earlier times – or would have done had the roads been better for it was the roads of those days rather than the machines that shook and jarred cyclist's bones. When farmers and farmers' sons went abroad they mixed with other farmers and their families, and more often than not a farmer's son met few of the opposite sex save farmers' daughters in his most impressionable years. When they attended church or chapel on Sundays it was with farmers and farming families that these people mixed, and when there was more than one chapel in a village or hamlet there was a tendency for farmers to go to one and for village tradespeople to attend the other. If farmers' sons thought of marrying they were advised to find a girl who would be a good farmwife. Romance may have played some part in their matches, but the demands of the farming life came first, while families were brought into the world and reared with the unsentimental aim of ere long reducing the labour problems on the holdings. Marriages were deferred, like that of the young John Boaden, till a farm and farmhouse was available. In the case of the Boadens, too, no sooner had the improvements at Trenarth been accomplished and the young brothers moved in with the elder's bride to housekeep for them than John started building a house for Will 'against his marriage'.

All this activity and speculation, albeit speculation in labour rather than in capital, was going on while agricultural depression was worsening. It showed that even in bad times a long-headed farmer who was not afraid of work and had a family to work with him could get on and even prosper. Still John Boaden kept very tight reins on his family. It was he rather than his sons who managed Trenarth, for in 1888 he sold the tenement of Trewince to a local clergyman for £1,000, with the shooting rights over the whole of Trenarth thrown in; before that he had sold the ground he called the 'cliff meadow' to the same purchaser for £100. Possibly these deals in property helped to keep the Boaden family going comfortably during the hard farming times.

For hard years they certainly were, although in his reminiscences Boaden made but the slightest of references to the long-continuing depression. The grumbles of farmers in 1880 were more about low prices than a poor harvest, though that, too had been affected to some degree in West Cornwall by rather 'catchy' weather. Complaints began about the growing importations of foreign cattle and butter besides the vastly increased amount of American grainstuffs coming into Britain. Tenant farmers were grumbling more and more about the game laws and the preservation of game by landlords; on many farms a full tenth of the grass and corn crops were destroyed by rabbits; true, tenants were now allowed by law to trap rabbits, but in many instances they were not allowed by their lease to shoot them or even to allow anyone else to trap on their holdings. Other tenants were complaining that the conditions of their leases, in many instances based on set forms devised many years back when the farming situation was vastly different, debarred them from selling straw, hay, and root crops off their farms; such leases had, of course, been devised in order to keep the land in good heart, but farmers had come to believe that this could be done more cheaply by using artificial manures. Some landlords and agents were willing to relax such restrictions, or to allow tenants to depart from old arable rotations prescribed in their leases and to adopt longer leys or lay down permanent pastures. Still, it cost at least ten pounds an acre to convert arable to pasture and this generally fell on the tenant although he might get some compensation for it at the end of his least. Even when this was done, many landlords would not provide the additional buildings required for stock on pastoral farms, and tenants whose unsheltered cattle lost condition and sometimes died in hard winters rarely admitted that their landlord might not be able to afford the buildings they needed. For their part landlords argued that they could not abate rents and at the same time be expected to build shippens and byres. Soon yet another social stress appeared in rural society. Fencing against their own and their neighbours' straying cattle, unable to afford the money to pay labourers to put up good hedges, tenants started using barbed-wire to the horror of the fox-hunting fraternity.

Following a severe winter the harvest of 1881 brought its worries to the Cornish farmers; crops were reasonably good, but the weather was never quite right for the majority of farmers, while a slight rise in corn prices was quickly checked. The succession of wet and indifferent seasons brought fairly heavy losses of cattle and sheep through disease, although the Meneage district escaped the worst epidemics of liver-fluke, foot-rot, and foot- and-mouth. Cattle prices kept reasonably high and there was little difficulty in selling butter, but these trades were subject to wide seasonal fluctuations, and only with experience farmers learnt the best and most economical ways of feeding cattle and of managing dairy herds. In too many years, faced with demands for rents and tithes, farmers flooded the Michaelmas and Lady Day markets with cattle, markets which tended to be rather poor in any case through the prevalence of general farm sales at those times. Local prices, too, varied greatly.

Yet compared with farmers in the arable counties of eastern and midland England, Cornish agriculturists were able to make both ends meet, and usually a little more, but many of them, less energetic and far-seeing than John Boaden, only adapted themselves slowly and with ill grace to the new state of affairs. It was all very well for the more progressive farmers to cry 'up horn, down corn', and to devote their attention to stock, but there were still many who seemed unable to realise that what paid yesterday no longer paid today and was still less likely to pay tomorrow.

Views expressed by farmers in those days presented a strange medley of sheer fantasy and hard common-sense. A poor harvest in the States of 1881 led some old-time English wheat- growers to believe that their troubles would soon be over, and to derive strange satisfaction from a report that New York was importing potatoes from Europe.[1] The more long-sighted saw that in time to come, although how soon they could not tell, the rapidly increasing population of America and the exhaustion of the fertility of western prairie soils would reduce the supplies of grain coming to Britain from that country, but that, in the meantime if British farmers wanted to go on growing wheat the best place to do so was not in the rain-ravaged homeland but on the prairies of Manitoba. The stock-man, although prices still were high, had incurred some losses during the past two severe winters through lack of suitable housing for his beasts, and that did not make him feel any too kindly towards his 'niggardly' landlord, who, for his part probably, hardly knew where to turn to find the money to pay mortgage interest on his estate. Down in the Meneage men might have turned more to market-gardening but for problems of transport and its costs; the branch-line railway to Helston was not completed until 1887, and before then the gardeners of the Penzance district had found that railway charges swallowed their gains to such an extent that they combined and chartered steam-ships to take their produce to northern England. Danes, Dutch, French, and, not far behind them, New Zealanders, were getting control of the great butter markets in British cities and industrial towns. When Cornish market gardeners and dairymen complained that the 'foreigner' was getting higher prices they were told that Cornish produce was generally marketed in an inferior condition, was packed badly, and lacked uniformity in quality.

Till the end of 1882 many farmers thought that times would soon be better, for many could remember similar runs of bad seasons, and successions of poor or indifferent harvests that had followed the glorious summer of 1859, or, further back, the bad years in the 'forties. Only the eldest could remember the four bad years from 1809 to 1812, and the disastrous summer of 1816, but that and later experience showed that in farming a man could expect good and ill to alternate so far as the weather was

[1]*West Briton*: April 17, 1882

concerned. Now, at the end of another poor year, they felt that it was time for a change, that 1883 might well see things 'set fair' once more. Yet neither farmers nor anyone else seemed to be aware what the weather could do.

Things certainly continued to go wrong in 1883. February fill-dyke more than earned its name, and was followed by a cold dry, and backward spring; about the start of hay-harvesting, with a very thin crop of both seed and meadow hay to be saved, the rains came, and right through the harvesting months the weather continued unsettled with hardly two successive days alike. The wheat and barley crops were poor, although a good crop of oats was secured by many farmers, there was plenty of grass, and the roots were good especially potatoes which were said to be the best crop for forty years.[1] Still farmers went on grumbling

'one talks of mildew and of frost,
    Another speaks of hail,
A third of sheep that he has lost,
    By maggot in the tail.'

Stock-farmers, with beef prices still quite high, were fairly comfortably situated, whilst many farmers had, like Boaden, discovered that it paid to raise grain on thier farms to feed their own livestock.

Relations between landlords and tenants were still bad, the latter demanding greater security of tenure before they spent any of their capital in laying arable land down into pasture. There were no such worries at Trenarth when the Boadens took it over from the tenant in 1884; they could be sure of reaping the fruits of the money and labour they put into that farm, and did not depend upon any landlord to provide suitable outbuildings to house stock. Stock from Trenarth could be brought over to consume any crops which restrictive lease conditions did not allow to be 'sold off' Skyburriowe. In short, the Boadens could look ahead confidently when they began at Trenarth. Their first harvest there, in 1884, was reasonably good, although a dry spring and early summer meant a light shear of hay, poor root crops and a short straw yield although the grain was good. Stockmen were particularly

[1]*Cornish Telegraph*: September 20, 1883.

apprehensive about the scarcity of hay and straw, and by this time only cattlemen could easily pay the rents then ruling for Cornish farms, rents determined by the keen rivalry for farms rather than by the returns that could be expected from such holdings.

Until the disastrous seasons of 1877 and 1879, most Cornish tenant farmers had based tenders they made for rents on the old idea that the corn mow would pay the rent, although often higher offers were made to get 'a place near the old folk', or to come under a landlord who was known to be easy on the tenants in bad years. Many, however, failed to foresee that the rock-bottom wheat price was not forty shillings a quarter, whilst the size and quality of the corn mow in Cornwall always represented the outcome of a gamble with the weather.

The alternative to high rents in Cornwall, if freehold farms could not be bought was to go elsehwere. In the midlands and eastern counties landlords were desperately looking for men to occupy farms which had been abandoned by the previous occupier and which were fast tumbling down into dereliction. Much could be said in favour of moving out of the western county. If they all stayed in Cornwall and their sons with them, they would only be pushing each other into bankruptcy courts merely to fill the pockets of the squires. Up in the eastern counties a farmer could now tell a landlord what was what, while if they went further afield and took themselves off to the American prairies they would have no landlord to consider at all.

At the very time the young Boadens went to Trenarth two local farmers, Bolitho of Trevider in St. Martin, and Treweeke of Ankey in Gunwalloe, went to Warwickshire. They were by no means the first nor the last to leave the Meneage to farm elsewhere.[1] 'Up country' besides lower rents offered easier and cheaper access to the big urban markets. Accounts sent to relatives and friends by the 'emigrants' made others less ready to struggle on in Cornwall to scrape high rents together for their landlords, but there was much to be said for staying in districts they knew well, besides they believed that things would, most, improve. Only the hardest-pressed and most restless ones went, and found just how hard and costly it was for a farmer to move long distances to a new home.

[1]*West Briton*: July 3 and July 17, 1884.

Those who looked for a break in the clouds of depression and the Boadens who started farming in Constantine with such drastic improvements were, however, to suffer many disappointments. The small hay and straw ricks secured in 1884 were not enough to tide over the winter which, though not severe, was rather long; the spring of 1885 was cold and backward; dust said to be worth a king's ransom in March was not so valued in May. Rain then came and hindered rather than injured the hay and corn harvests, but Cornish farmers were well used to that. None of the cereal crops turned out very well, and a plentiful supply of straw was not valued so highly when letters came from old friends up-country boasting about the fine crops they had saved. In 1886 it was much the same, a dry spring and a damp summer, somewhat better crops, perhaps, but an even catchier harvest than in 1885, and then came a stormy autumn, snow before Christmas, and by the New Year, some farmers were wondering if they had enough hay to see them through the winter.

Such weather troubles were, however, not at all abnormal in Cornwall, and when farmers talked of bad times now their theme was low prices. Several had already given up growing wheat altogether save for a small field or two of thatching reed. Oats had done fairly well, but barley was the most difficult crop of all during these catchy seasons; cold springs delayed its sowing, and it seemed to get more damaged by rain and wind than other crops. Worse still, however, was a drastic fall in the price of mutton and beef through 'foreign' competition. By the end of 1886 the average price of the best beef had slumped to fifty-five shillings a hundredweight; a few cattlemen got more, but many less.

Many Meneage farmers had started selling butter on a fairly considerable scale, and for the first few years his sons were at Trenarth John used to go over every Friday evening for the butter and eggs which

'Eleanor Jane packed and sent to London with ours . . . We were frequently going to Trenarth to work during this period.'

With eggs, however, rarely making a penny each and butter scarcely averaging a shilling a pound, there could not have been a great deal of money in it, although the Boadens seem to have gone in for poultry on a large scale at Trenarth, since they had built special poultry houses there; when the younger sons, Howard and James took over Skyburriowe from their father, they specialized in Golden Wyandottes, obtaining prizes for that breed at Royal Agricultural Shows.[1] John Boaden had probably some arrangement with a London dairyman to take his produce, but other local farmers were not so fortunate, and occasionally in early summer butter in Helston market only fetched eightpence a pound, half the price that Danish and colonial butter was making in British markets throughout the year at that period. Many said that Cornish butter was cheap because it was inferior in quality and often badly made, and in the early 'nineties Boaden's old friend, R. G. Rows, and a few others, started advocating the establishment of 'dairy factories' in Cornwall to ensure the production of a more uniform or standard quality of Cornish butter. Cream separators were coming into use, the first in Cornwall being installed on a Buryan dairy farm in 1886,[2] but Boaden does not mention getting one either at Skyburriowe or at Trenarth, though he probably had done so by the end of the century.

Nevertheless, mixed farming enabled the Cornish agriculturists to survive and to live in reasonable comfort during these difficult years. Wage bills had been cut to the bone. The Boadens, of course, were able to farm both Skyburriowe and Trenarth without hiring much labour, and the increasing use of machinery was rapidly eliminating the cost of extra labour at harvest-time. The new 'binders' enabled three or four men and a boy or two to cut and 'shock' a field more quickly than twenty or more could have done in the old days, when half a dozen hands might be reaping, the same number following behind binding the sheaves, and others putting up shocks or hand-mows. Harvest suppers, with a score or more around the long kitchen tables, became a thing of the past, thereby lightening the work of the womenfolk. Labour was reduced in other ways, besides at harvest, but the majority of farmers themselves and their families were working harder and

---

[1]This interest in poultry as a branch of farming economy should be stressed, coming as it did a generation before the success of the Hendersons at Oathill Farm, Oxfordshire, described in George Henderson's *The Farming Ladder*. (1944).
[2]*West Briton*: August 26, 1886.

longer hours. The growing importance of eggs and butter in the income of many Cornish farms meant that the womenfolk were contributing more directly to that income than in the past.

Mixed farming meant less risk of heavy losses in poor seasons. With wheat and wool prices down it was wise to have other resources, and if one thing did badly, another might compensate it. Come wind, come rain, come mist or fog, come frost, snow or hail, as they had all being coming during the past ten or fifteen years, a Cornish farmer and his family could still get a living from the land. If they grumbled, well that might lead landlords to abate rents, might even lead a government to shift the burdens of paupers and clergy, of education and roads on to those 'better-off' sections of the community who could afford them. Only one thing did not enter their calculations and speechifying when they met in mutual admiration and grumbling societies at the Christmas shows in 1886. Many talked of the 'good old days', said things were not nearly as good as they used to be, but admitted that that was no reason to enter Victoria's Jubilee year with utter dejection. Some even reckoned that they had weathered the times of depression and would do much better in the coming year. They might have done had they not been destined to experience the weather's unkindest trick of all – drought.

16

Trials and Tribulations

John Boaden's brief allusions to the prolonged agricultural depression give little idea of the troubles besetting farmers in the late nineteenth century. After describing the acquisition of Trenarth, he began to discuss his public life, but then suddenly digressed, writing

'I should have said further back that when I gave notice to the tenant to quit Trenarch for my own sons, I had letters from Mr. Charles P. Rogers, my old friend, that had left Nanswann[1] in 1879 to be a commercial traveller (telling me) that he had taken a farm at Studley in Warwickshire, about eighteen miles from Birmingham, at a very cheap rate, and that there were several fine farms near without tenants. I went to see them before settling my sons. It was in the beginning of December, 1879.'

This suggests that he considered finding farms for his sons outside Cornwall. In Birmingham he attended a mid-week sermon commemorating the fourth century of Luther's birth, commenting that the theme whether Protestantism was the cause of the 'scepticism' of modern Europe was 'very interesting to me'.

In those days Protestants of John Boaden's stamp were certainly confident enough in matters spiritual, but the plight of the farming districts of south-west Warwickshire late in 1879 was a chastening

[1]Possibly Nanceloan, a farm adjoining Mawgan Cross.

188

experience for any husbandman. Boaden stayed a few days with Rogers, who

> 'accompanied me around to see the derelict farms which were numerous. The soil almost everywhere was heavy clay but a good corn soil, fine farms with a fair proportion of pasture and good outbuildings . . . The wet seasons and the low price of corn had ruined the tenants; it did not take long to do this; they could not turn readily to cattle farming like we (Cornish farmers) could and did; these farms could be had for a very low rental and began to attract tenants from Scotland and other districts; several from Cornwall came to this district. These remarks hold (too) for the counties of Essex, Hertford, Oxford, and Sussex, when for the first time many Cornish farmers began to migrate to all these counties; they no longer confined themselves to their own districts. When I came back scarcely anybody (from Cornwall) had yet gone up, and I have reason to believe that my report gave an impetus if it did not at that time initiate an upward movement; but I decided not to send my sons up; I wished to keep them together as much as possible, and to sell all and go up was a very big job and I felt that I should never be as happy again as in the neighbourhood of my birth.'

Boaden, of course, was no longer young and had been at Skyburriowe so long that the wrench of uprooting would have been severe. After all, he and other Cornish farmers had survived the slump; if they went they would have to adapt themselves to different types of land and farming methods. The vacant farms were holdings on which previous tenants had failed; many of them had been mercilessly racked in vain efforts to make ends meet by those tenants; a few were already derelict and reclamation charges would be very high. Practical farmers would think twice about taking them even with their rents slashed to half what they had been ten years before, and John Boaden, too, was cautious and wary, not the man to take risks like more venturesome and restless younger men.

In 1887, however, he might have regretted his decision to stay in Cornwall. A fine spring and dry summer proved ideal for the arable farmers in the Midlands and Eastern England, some regarding it as the best season they had ever known.[1] To Cornwall, however, it was a year of drought. Hay was only a third of a normal crop, though good in quality. Wheat and barley were excellent in grain, but the straw was pitifully short. Oats were a total failure, although in the recent succession of wet summers it had come to be regarded as the best crop in Cornwall.[2] On light soils and hill-slopes everything scorched; some farmers declared that in their ripe barley fields a mouse could be seen running the whole way from one hedge to the other.[3] A dry spring meant 'thin' barley and oat crops in any event, but with the drought persisting till September[4] the straw was only six or nine inches high when the grain was ripe, and it was hard to cut it with a sickle, scythe, or modern 'self-binder'.

All over Cornwall farmers were grumbling that if it did not rain soon they would be ruined; fine weather could be harmful, even

[1]S. G. Kendall: *Farming Memoirs of a West Country Yeoman*, (1944) pp. 187-9, describing farming on the borders of Somerset and Wiltshire.

[2]The area under oats in Cornwall in June 1872 had been 545,402 acres, and in June 1887, 57,355 acres; over the same fifteen years the wheat acreage dropped from 55,475 to 31,212 and that of barley from 55,949 to 40,404. The wheat and barley acreage returns in Cornwall in 1872 were the highest recorded, but the returns only began in 1867.

[3]Richard Pollard told the Wadebridge Farmers' Club in January, 1888, that he could have 'whipped a mouse through a corn field, a grass field, or a green crop field, and never have lost sight of it.' (West Briton: January 12, 1888.)

[4]West Cornwall has an average yearly rainfall of about 45 inches; in 1887 only 30 inches fell, the normal total fall in the seven months February to August is 20 inches, but in 1887 only 8.5 inches were recorded. In 1893 West Cornwall had 34 inches of rain, and only 2.5 inches instead of the average 10 fell in the four months March to June, but for the seven months from February to August, inclusive, nearly 15 inches fell. A contrast between Cornwall and Eastern England for these two 'drought' years cannot be made without stressing other considerations than amounts of rain recorded; allowance should be made for the proportion of land under winter and spring-sown crops in the two areas compared, and, still more, the nature of soils, although even in a single parish some soils may retain moisture far more than others. Only one general statement can be made: in 1887 the Cornish pastoral farmer had to endure a period of six months in which grass could hardly grow at all; in 1893 that period, at most, was fifteen weeks.

disastrous. With hardly any grass in their pastures, dairymen had very little butter to sell, and got no consolation from butter prices remaining as high as in winter months.[1] Sheep and cattle had to be turned into the fields that should have been unstocked for hay; later some farmers turned their animals into the grain fields, consoling themselves with the thought that the corn was too short in the straw to be worth the trouble of cutting. Summer dearth was bad enough, but still worst were forebodings about the coming Michaelmas rent day and winter keep. Normally cattlemen and sheep farmers sold off some stock at Michaelmas to pay their rents; in 1887 they had to sell more in any case because their animals were in such poor condition, while at the same time prices slumped because so many were selling off animals which they could not keep through the winter without buying hay and straw; indeed, there was little hay to be bought at all even at seven pounds the ton, three times the usual price. So, in the autumn of 1887, stock prices were disastrously low, with almost every farmer wanting to sell and hardly any wishing to buy.

The plight of Cornish stockmen at this time would be contrasted with momentary revival in the fortunes of 'up-country' corn-growers, including some of their own friends and relations who had left Cornwall. An arable farmer could reasonably expect the deficiency of one season to be made up by the next, but it took a stockman fully three years to recover from one bad season, since forced to sell off so many beasts at rock-bottom prices, the size of his flocks and herds would not be made up by natural increase for two years to come, and he had not the capital to make up his deficiencies by purchase.[2] Two seasons later, in 1889, with

[1] The normal range of butter prices per pound in the 1880s in Helston market was 8d to 1/5d.

[2] The agricultural returns, made every June, reveal how drought affected the numbers of cattle and sheep kept in Cornwall:

	1887	1888	1889	1890
Cattle	190,574	183,904	180,215	189,271
Sheep	440,591	418,495	414,821	442,140

and for the later drought of 1893:

	1893	1894	1895	1896
Cattle	201,258	190,749	193,900	199,825
Sheep	445,732	415,031	421,443	427,666

good crops of hay and grass, and a fair corn harvest, Cornish farmers were seeking everywhere for grazing stock to consume the surplus of their farms, so stock prices soared, and sheep sold for breeding in 1887 for 28s. were now being sold by those who bought them then for nearly double, despite their age; hay in July 1889, was only 25s. a ton, a quarter of what it had been in 1887 – and the 1887 price would have been higher had not some American hay been imported and sold at about 70s. per ton.[1]

A long, severe winter followed; not until the end of April was there a little 'pick' in the fields, and when the cattle were turned out to grass a local newspaper reported

'The lean and ill-fated kine of Pharoah's dream could not have presented a more spectral appearance . . . Nothing so humiliating has been seen within the memory of man. It is true that a few farms tell a different tale, but the number of fat and well-fed kine is as nothing compared with the living skeletons that now stand in our fields.'[2]

The Boadens may have not suffered as much as some Cornish farmers from the drought and later shortage of winter keep, although the sons at Trenarth may have been glad to drive cattle over to Skyburriowe, where the fields did not parch so badly as those on the hill-slopes north of the Helford estuary. At Skyburriowe, too, there were the Goonhilly crofts, and winter fodder was eked out by cutting and crushing young furze shoots and putting them through the chaff-cutter with what straw they had. Stock hardly grew fat on such 'balanced rations', which, however, helped keep them alive.

(cont). Such statistics, of course, do not show the considerable variations between different localities in Cornwall, notably that the Meneage suffered less than the north Cornwall district between Padstow and Bude. Together loss in numbers, loss in condition of animals, and the slump in prices meant a capital loss of at least a third and, in some cases, of one-half to individual farmers. The reduction in the flocks of sheep shown by the returns of 1888 and 1894 should be associated with the poor root crops in the preceding seasons of drought.

[1]*West Briton*: August 11, 1887, December 12, 1889, *Cornish Telegraph*: July 11, 1889.
[2]*Cornish Telegraph*: May 3, 1888.

The cold, dry spring of 1888 roused fears of drought again, but it was to be a very different season from that of the Jubilee year. The dry summer of 1887, however, led many Cornish farmers to plant more wheat; through a catchy season they got an indifferent crop, and oats too, normally a good crop in such damp summers, was poor, largely through the ravages of the frit-fly.[1] The following season brought other problems; it was genial and bountiful, but with an abundance of grass, hay, and straw, many Cornish farmers were at a loss to find stock to consume the crops, whilst it was even, not entirely facetiously, suggested that the farmers were now grumbling that the harvest was so heavy that they could not afford to pay the labour needed to save it.[2] The Boadens weathered these seasons quite comfortably, and in 1889 John bought out his brother's interest in the Mawgan farm of Tregoose, which they had jointly purchased in 1885 for about £5,000. Such land purchases show that, by thrift, wise investments, and his own and his family's industry, Boaden made both ends meet and more in these difficult times, and also won him the respect and esteem of his neighbours, which, early in 1889, was shown by his co-option to the first Cornwall County Council, as an alderman and by his return to the Helston Board of Guardians to represent Mawgan.

His life-long friend, R. G. Rows, was mainly responsible for Boaden's being co-opted to the County Council; chosen again in 1892, he served nine years before failing eyesight led him to retire. In his memoirs he mentioned that he served on the Contagious Diseases (Animals) and County Rates Basis Committees, besides the controversy whether the Council should meet at Truro or Bodmin and several meetings with the County Surveyor about improving the roads in his own Meneage district. He found the work new but congenial, and seems, at first at least, to have pleased his neighbours and a local journalist who summed Boaden up as

'a Home Ruler, a prominent Wesleyan, total abstainer, practical agriculturist, of sound judgement, unpretending in

[1]*West Briton*: June 21, July 5 and 26, August 8 and 23, and December 6, 1888; *Cornish Telegraph*: June 21 and 28, 1888; *Journal of the Royal Agricultural Society of England*, Vol. XXV (1889) pp. 332-334.
[2]*West Briton*: July 29, 1889.

manner, slow to speak, but capable of saying something worthy when he does speak; indeed, is just the man to sit on a County Bench.'[1]

Yet honours like these bring disadvantages. Thrust before the public eye John Boaden was soon feeling the lash of criticism, especially when he changed his politics and followed Rows into the Liberal-Unionist camp; some local tenant farmers, not so prosperous as the farmer of Skyburriowe, hinted that he had gone over to 'the side of the squires' with whom he hobnobbed on the County Council and its Committees, forgetting that the man they criticised – and envied a little – was quite a substantial landowner himself, even if he did not own the farm he occupied.

Most critical of Boaden were those radical sectarians in Mawgan who, forty years back, had led his wife's family to migrate to Australia. The inauguration of, first, the County, and later, of the Rural District Councils marked the passing of the old rural order in which squire and parson, sometimes more and sometimes less benevolently, had ruled all. Early in 1889 Mawgan's well- liked Rector, the Rev. William R. Bluxsome, died. A tolerant man and a good friend to the poor as one of the Helston Guardians, he had run into financial difficulties by rebuilding the Rectory; he had not been the type of man to demand that farmers pay their tithes in bad times to the day or to the last penny. Bluxsome's widow and her young family left Mawgan in July 1889, and at a farewell garden party it was John Boaden, the 'nonconformist alderman', as some had already begun to call him in not altogether friendly tones, who read a letter written out by Mrs. Bluxsome thanking all the parishioners for their kindness to her dead husband, her family and herself. One or two resented John's remarks stressing the friendly relations which had existed in Mawgan betweeen Church and Nonconformity during the past twenty years, and it was rather cynically reported that the 'sterling orthodox' disapproved of a gathering in which 'Churchmen and Dissenters, married and single, saints and sinners, Home Rulers, Liberal-Unionist, and Conservatives alike took part.'[2] Local and sectarian jealousies were already reviving like those which had

[1]*West Briton*: February 14, 1889.
[2]*West Briton*: July 25, 1889.

harassed Will Orchard so many years before and, ere long, were destined to trouble Boaden sorely.

Meantime farmers had other troubles. Complaints about the weather assumed yet another variation in 1890, with May for once the wettest month of the year recording a rainfall over thrice the average, whilst June was not much better. Although there was plenty of hay the problem was to 'save' it; straw was abundant, but it was beaten down, twisted and tangled, and the grain was poor in quality. There were some fine days scattered through July, but not until early August did a few fine days rouse hopes, forlorn hopes for the heat became intense and sultry, and those farmers who called it a storm-breeder were right. With the passing of Swithin's days, as if to justify the superstitious, there was some improvement and it was possible at last to get on with the harvest. Good root crops hardly compensated for the hay and corn damaged and spoilt by rain, whilst butter and wool prices were about as low as had ever been known.

The weather, however, seemed to have made good resolutions for the New Year of 1891. A splendidly dry February, sunny, and not very cold, enabled farmers to get well ahead with the preparation for their spring tillage, whilst March came in 'like a lamb'. The wiseacres who, then as so often, instead of being grateful for good weather never wearied of shaking their heads and remarking 'We'll pay for this later,' for once were right. The Boadens and other farming folk may have stopped a few moments chatting outside Garras Chapel after Sunday evening service on March 8th; it was too chilly, however, to linger long, though someone may have said that now the days had lengthened out so they must surely have got through the worst of winter. Monday morning dawned colder than ever and the wind was cutting like a knife; snow began to fall, a few flakes at first and then thicker than leaves in a late October gale, and went on falling for the next night and day with the wind lashing and howling up into a tempest. Many Cornish farmers had heard about the blizzards which had afflicted the farmers on the great plains of North America only a few years before; now they had a blizzard of their own to talk about and remember for the rest of their lives. The local train from Gwinear Road to Helston was lost in a snowdrift, driver, fireman and solitary passenger managing with difficulty to find their way to a nearby farmhouse. Losses of sheep and lambs on the more exposed farms of central and north Cornwall were heavy; the Meneage suffered less than most districts, but it was no easy task there or anywhere else tending sheep and cattle, carrying fodder and water to byre and shippen, through snow-drifts shoulder high, and facing the blast of a wind that seemed to be coming from the Pole. There followed thaw and slush, a wet spring, and tillage late. Early in July a short spell of fine weather made it possible for most farmers to save a resonably good shear of hay. The late tillage meant a late harvest, and the season was so catchy that several farmers upset their neighbours and the ministers by harvesting on the last two Sundays in August that happened to be fine.

Still by Michaelmas most Cornish farmers were ready to attend harvest thanksgiving services. Crops had been generally heavy, and where some corn had been spoilt the farmer concerned was told by his neighbours that he had only himself to blame, either for not getting on betimes when the sun shone, or, more often, for putting the sheaves up in small shocks in a slovenly fashion instead of spending the care and labour of putting his corn into 'arish'-hows.[1] With the increasing use of the self-binders the old practice of 'mowing' was vanishing in Cornwall, and now in catchy seasons farmers were more concerned, while the weather held, to cut down as much as they could before rain and storm could batter the standing corn even worse than it was already than they were to make secure what had already been cut. It took less labour, too, to put a field into shocks of from seven to ten sheaves apiece than to put up arish mows, an important consideration to those farmers who were forced to cut labour costs to rock bottom. In any case with corn prices so low and with so many Cornish farmers only growing corn to feed to the cattle on their own holdings, they were less concerned about producing a 'first rate sample' than in the old days.

The weather was not the only calamity to afflict John Boaden in 1891. On the last afternoon in April the sitting-room chimney at Skyburriowe caught afire, and the thatched roof of the farm-house was quickly ablaze. The fire spread rapidly and the dwelling house and the adjoining outbuildings were almost totally destroyed. The Boadens managed to save some of the furniture,

[1]*West Briton*: October 1, 1891.

although it was badly damaged, salvage work being hampered by thick and choking clouds of smoke and by fluttering fragments of blazing thatch. For some time the family had to live and sleep in the barn while a new house was being built away from the older farm buildings in the old orchard.

Years back prudent John Boaden had taken out a fire insurance policy, and in his memoirs he paid a tribute to the fairness of the West of England Insurance Company. The companies which undertook the insurance of farm premises in those days took great risks. Many of the older buildings, dwelling houses, stables, barns, and shippens were still roofed with thatch, and such buildings were often very close together, even with 'out- buildings' and farmhouse 'semi-detached' – to use a term beloved of later house agents – and that had been the case at Skyburriowe. A chimney fire was dangerous, and the destruction of some hundred and fifty feet of roofing there was attributed to rat runs in the thatching that, in places, was nearly a yard thick creating draughts which quickly fanned a smouldering chimney flue into destructive flame. A few years later John Boaden's birthplace, Trease, was also destroyed by fire, whilst it was nothing uncommon in catchy seasons for hay carried damp to catch fire although, whenever possible, the farmers kept their rick-yards and mowhays away from the main farm buildings.

Fire-fighting apparatus, too, was still very inefficient. There was a fire engine in Helston, but for some years it, along with its amateur brigade had been a local standing joke. This engine was far from new having been originally provided in the eighteen-twenties by the Norwich Union Insurance Company which had a large clientele in the town; about thirty years later it had been presented to the corporation. Whenever a fire broke out on a farm outside the town those who required its services had to provide a team of horses to take it to the scene of the conflagration. In 1889, the old engine had been the talk of the Meneage when it had been called to a rick fire at Trenance in Mullion. When news of the fire reached Helston, the Mayor took charge of the volunteer fire-fighting force, and, in the rush, the harnessing tackle for the horses was mislaid. They found it after some delay, and then the Mayor accompanied by a police sergeant and constable led the way in a light waggonette. Built somewhat on the lines of Mr. Pickwick, and with not a little of that character's ebulliance of character, known, too, as a man who rode hard to hounds whenever he could the Mayor set a furious pace, which was too much for the ricketty old engine following in the wake of his waggonette. Barely half a mile on the road a wheel came off; then rounding a corner too quickly in Cury Churchtown two more wheels trundled away in different directions; to cap all another wheel went adrift in Mullion itself. Little wonder was it that the engine reached Trenance too late to save the rick and a mow of straw that had also caught alight; still the fire ws checked from spreading to the farm buildings, and the Mayor, police, and volunteers managed to get back to Helston by breakfast time the following day. On other occasions this engine did succeed in dealing with fires, and whether the Boadens had its help or not they did manage to save some of their buildings and belongings. Luckily for them during that wet summer the barn had good walls and a moderately sound roof, though they must have been glad to move into the new farmhouse.

Prices were still low, and therr was little relief from depression in 1892; the weather was rather more kind than in the previous year although the spring was cold and dry, and the hay, while good in quality was very light. There was fine weather to secure the corn crops, and some heavy rains late in August stilled the apprehensions of those who had begun to worry about their root crops and the scarcity of grass. The rain, however, caught many with harvesting only half done, and there was again some criticism about farmers ruining good yields of oats and barley by trying to save themselves the trouble and cost of putting up arish mows. Yet those who blamed farmers for trying to reduce their harvest labour force to a self binder, two men to 'tend' it, and a boy or two to 'shock' did not consider the levels to which corn prices had now sunk. A Meneage farmer who sold wheat off his farm barely got 36s. the quarter for it; in 1896 the rice was down to 25s. If he fed it to cattle, the best fat stock made 55s. a hundredweight in 1892, but the price was falling. Rates, tithes, and taxes were taking about a sixth of the total produce of his land, and rents were just as high as ever. Long years of adversity had led many farmers to believe that the extra trouble and expense of farming well was hardly worth while. Economists might try to prove that farm labout was still cheap, but it now took twenty quarters of wheat to pay a man's yearly wage as against eight quarters or less a generation ago.

Few farmers looked to the new year of 1893 with much hope, and it was to be later remembered as yet another year of farming calamity, the cause this time being drought. In Cornwall there were fewer complaints about the weather than in 1887, which most up-country farmers had regarded as a good season. Showers at the end of June broke the long drought in the south-west, and a wet July followed by a warm August and September enabled the saving of a second hay crop to eke out the miserable shear saved in early June. Straw was short but not so short as six years before, although some arish-mows in the Meneage were no bigger than a 'pook' of hay;[1] the grain samples of barley and oats were poor, and if winter wheat had done comparatively well the grain was fetching barely 25s. a quarter.[2] It could, however, be used to feed stock, and, as in 1887, it was the problem of winter keep that most concerned Cornish farmers. Even in summer a number had been compelled to sell off cattle since they had no grass, nor hay either, and could not afford to buy what hay was on the market and fetching anything up to £10 a ton. With some snow and sleet falling in November fears of the approaching winter were aggravated, but apart from a bitterly cold week in January the winter was to be mild.

John Boaden left more of the work and management of the farm at Skyburriowe to his younger sons in 1893. He had decided to retire next Michaelmas, and in many ways it was a good season for young farmers to find their own feet. Prices were alarmingly low, but farmers bought as well as sold. The early spring was very good for getting on with the tillage, and there was no risk of rick fires through carrying damp hay that summer. Younger men were better at operating and maintaining the new reaping machines than the generation that had grown to manhood in the days of the sickle. Boaden gave more time to the County Council and to the Board of Guardians, besides speaking now and again to temperance gatherings, attending a Methodist class meeting and superintending the Sunday School at Garras Chapel. A complicated lawsuit over a will involving some of his friends made heavy demands on his time, and finally, in February, entailed a

[1]*West Briton*: August 17, 1893.
[2]*West Briton*: September 28, 1893.

week in a London law court, which, since his friends lost the day after spending two thousand pounds or more led John to express the conviction that it was utter folly to 'go to law'. Still it gave him the chance to attend a Methodist service addressed by Lady Henry Somerset and Miss Williard at the famous City Road Chapel.

Later in 1893 he revisited his friends in Warwickshire, going on, after attending the Royal Agricultural Show at Chester, to Lancashire. It was rather an eventful journey, for a passenger jumped off the train when it was going through a tunnel, receiving fatal injuries, and John was called upon to give 'an official account' of the incident 'to the railway'. In the district around Birmingham he was struck by the damage done by the prolonged drought, but

> 'all the farms around that were vacant at my visit ten years before were now let; though rents were less there was an improvement; despondency had given away.'

He remarked that around Chester the land was heavy, and the Prince of Wales visited the Show on the day he was there, but wrote no more about one of the most successful 'Royals' on record.[1] A visit to Manchester was similarly dismissed with a brief mention of the 'tremendous works going on making the canal from Liverpool to Manchester'; he went on to Southport, after an allusion to the end of the drought suggests that, even in 1893, Manchester was living up to its wet reputation. At Rochdale he visited John Bright's grave. This tour was typical of the man. His first interest was the farms he saw, many now occupied by Cornishmen who had migrated 'up country' and Boaden mentioned one, Frederick Treweeke, who was then moving yet again from Warwickshire into the adjoining county of Oxford. The second interest – Boaden probably placed it first – was attending a nonconformist service in Birmingham and the 'pilgrimage' to the grave of the paragon of Victorian dissenting Liberalism; true, not all men and certainly not all farmers held John Bright in such esteem. Finally the ideal of material progress, the ideal behind the

[1]Sir James Scott Watson: *History of the Royal Agricultural Society of England 1839–1939*, p. 63

Great Exhibition of 1851, was still as highly regarded in Victorian England as ever, and the great Ship Canal could be regarded as one of its greatest achievements.

Briefly in his memoirs Boaden remarked that the rain at the end of June saved the Cornish farmers from ruin. Other areas were less fortunate, but by Michaelmas many thought that the depression was passing. Boaden farmed Skyburriowe another year, and then left his younger sons to bear the heat of the day – though he was within call across the valley at Worval. That season, 1894, was rather an indifferent one; the winter was not severe, but in March there were again fears of drought; abundant showers, however, came in April with promise of bountiful crops; then a chilly May with thunder, hail and even flurries of snow followed by an intense but brief heat-wave early in June soon broken by violent thunderstorms led to the renewal of the old stories that the seasons were out of joint. A short, fine spell late in June and early in July enabled many farmers to save a good shear of hay, but others were caught by the rain, and even in the comparatively early Meneage district there was some hay still uncut at the beginning of August. There was some talk of St. Swithin once more; a fair spell at the end of August following some violent thunderstorms, enabled most harvesting to be done by the first week of September, the quantity of straw being good even if the quality was indifferent. Still there was no shortage to worry the stockmen, and cattle prices were much higher than a year before, although good samples of wheat were fetching less than twenty-six shillings the quarter in Helston market.

So, John Boaden's active farming career ended just when there was some break in the clouds of depression, but some feared that, just as with summer thunderstorms travelling in circles their troubles would quickly return again. John Boaden's example, however, had shown that by hard work, thrift, prudence, and by faith a farmer could survive the tribulations which beset him. Just as starkly and as loyally as he had worshipped his God in his chapel and in his home did Boaden believe in farming as a way of life which called forth and bred sterling qualities of character. Like all farmers he grumbled and complained at times, but he had courage to endure and the wisdom to adapt himself and his work to changing circumstances.

No-one could deny that John Boaden had worked hard ever since he had been a boy. Now within four years of his seventieth year the time had come for him to take life a little more easily. Still there was much to be done. His family could have the benefit of the wisdom he had garnered and harvested through long years of experience in good times and in bad. He could serve his neighbours on the County Council and on the Board of Guardians. He could carry on his work as a Methodist class leader and as a Sunday School teacher. He had seen many changes in his day, but in his view wisdom and truth were unaltering and eternal. Others, however, believed differently, and John Boaden hardly realized how much times had changed since he had been young. Like most Victorians he had believed in progress, but before his mortal course was run he felt that not all change was for the better although he was spared from living on into days of disillusionment and tribulation when the Victorian ideal of progress seemed more likely to bring about the destruction than the betterment of mankind.

17

Into the Shadows

After the harvest of 1894, John Boaden and his wife went to live at Worval. John had been looking forward to retiring, especially since Eleanor Jane was not able to cope with the hard work of a farm wife so well as in her younger days. They still spent much time, however, at Skyburriowe, helping their sons run the farm. John Boaden's public work, however, often took him to Helston or Truro, and at times he went further afield, at the behest of relatives and friends, to look over farms, for more and more Cornish farmers were being attracted by tales of cheaper farms and lower rents 'up-country' in those days of depression.

Boaden's public life sheds some light on the rise of a new governing class. In the past he, like other tenant farmers, had grumbled about local landlord tyranny, but now elected county, district, and parish councils had taken over the control of local rates from the old quarter sessions of the justices. The first step, in 1834, had been the establishment of the Poor Law Unions with their Boards of Guardians; for many years, however, squires and parsons had served themselves or dictated the choice of Guardians from each parish. Then, by 1875, under the new Education Act, nearly every parish had an elected school board, but long before this ratepayers had been demanding that those who paid should say how rates should be spent. There had been much criticism when a paid rural police had replaced the old parish constables and when highway boards superseded the old waywardens and turnpike trusts there were many complaints of bad management and of favouritism in the providing and repairing of roads. There had always been a burden of pauperism, aggravated by un-employment in times of depression, and farmers felt that they were overburdened by local rates, complaining most bitterly, of course, in periods of economic crisis that industry, trade, commerce, and mining were not bearing their fair share of public burdens. The new local councils took over many of the powers formerly exercised by the justices' sessions during the years of continuing agricultural depression, and retirement left John Boaden free to do all in his power to check the lavish expenditure of the ratepayer's money.

He had now joined the Unionist party, since there no longer seemed any hope of the Gladstone Liberals extending full tenant right from Ireland to England. In 1880 Gladstone had admitted that British farmers had lost over a hundred millions in three years, but neither the Agricultural Holdings Act nor the Ground Game Bill of his second administration helped much. Since then Gladstone gave his opponents a glorious catch-cry by remarking that the jam-making industry offered British farmers a great opportunity. Down in Mawgan John Boaden's views seemed different from those of his more radical younger days for, early in 1891, he defended restrictions in Trelowarren farm leases debarring tenants from shooting rabbits, arguing that the leases complied with the 1880 Ground Game Act since they did permit a tenant or his accredited agent to trap rabbits, and that if a tenant held rabbit-shoots on his farm he could disturb other game.[1] Neither Sir Richard or his successor had been unreasonable about game, but other local landlords would not hesitate to refuse to renew a tenant's lease if they suspected he was not 'preserving' enough game, ground or not.

Boaden was now voicing the opinion that squire and tenant could, by mutual forebearance, get on together. His critics declared that he had gone over to the landlords' side – as well he might since he was now a landowner himself; still they made a point that when they asked why a farmer should not enjoy a little sport himself and why parties of a few priviledged gentry should have a right to 'trespass' anywhere after game. Boaden seems to have forgotten the long memories of many of his rural neighbours, how they themselves in their younger days had been brought before the bench and fined, if not imprisoned or transported for poaching, while a squire or gamekeeper could still stop a man, sometimes on his own farm, and demand to see

[1]*West Briton*: January 15 and 22, February 5, 12, 19 and 26, 1891.

if it was a partridge bulging out his pocket or a pheasant in the sack he carried.

Boaden clashed with the 'radicals' again by suggesting in 1894 that the Mawgan parish council be chosen in an open general meeting of the parishioners which could discuss the 'names and qualifications of fit and proper persons' to serve. This, he thought, would save ratepayers' money and foster local social unity better than the process of election the Parish Councils Act prescribed. His critics denounced him for attempting to keep labouring men off the council, and said he was trying to bring pressure upon labourers and tradesmen dependent on his employment and custom to elect his own personal favourites.[1]

For some time Mawgan men had been alleging that the richer farmers, most of whom were Wesleyans, were an oligarchy controlling local affairs; Boaden and another farmer represented the parish on the Board of Guardians, and three or four others dominated the School Board, partly because the squire was now an absentee, but also on account of the bankruptcy of Rector Bluxsome's unpopular successor. Sectarian animosities aggravated local bickerings, and what Boaden called the 'Lower Chapel' party[2] managed, in 1895, to secure a majority on the new Parish Council and, about the same time won control of the School Board. Three years later they opposed Boaden's re-election to the Guardians and rural district Council' rather bitterly he wrote

'It was about Ladyday or beginning of April I had to run a contested election for the Guardianship of Mawgan. I had offended a little party belonging to the Lower Chapel about three years before; they wanted to have a cemetery while the clergyman, Mr. Wright, would get an addition to the churchyard; the land would be given by Sir Vyell (Vyvyan); The cemetery party resorted to false statements, but at a public meeting the scheme was quite upset; it would have been imposed upon an apathetic parish had I not resisted and wakened up others to do the same. But they felt very sure

---

[1] *West Briton*: October 11, 1894.
[2] These were the United Methodists and Bryanites or Bible Christians, and also the more extreme teetotallers or total abstainers.

about the Guardians' election. Though I had been returned at the show of hands of mere boys, Hugh L. Choak and Willie Johns, the day before, they went and with Willie Hosking as candidate with whom I had some disagreement in a question of veracity, ran the parish into a contest. I and Will Collins were returned by 85 votes with Hosking 61. The parties responsible for the contest besides those mentioned were William Reed, Henry Choak, and Samuel Johns. Hosking had support from Trelowarren men and some female house-holders customers to Hosking.'

Reading 'between the lines' it seems that Boaden resented hints that he make way for younger men, and that he did not approve of women in public affairs. The Trelowarren men who supported Hosking were the servants rather than the squire.

Boaden's re-election was challenged by men who believed that he was trying to 'run the parish' as autocratically as any squire had ever done, and that his aldermanship, followed by his com-mission as a local magistrate, in 1895, had 'gone to his head'. When he suggested that the Parish Council be chosen not by election but by an open meeting he failed to see that many would sooner pay the cost of an election than have a council imposed upon them, as it might have been under his plan, by the 'bigger' men in the parish. The new Parish Council, however, precipitated the cemetery dispute in Mawgan, by trespassing in a field in which they had no right.

The old churchyard was practically full, and the Parish Council discussed the provision of a new burial ground, but then deferred the matter since the clergyman in charge, Wright, said the churchyard could be used for another two or three years. Before the Council met again, however, Wright called a parish meeting and told it that the squire had offered to give a plot of land adjoining the churchyard to the parish, or rather to the church, provided that ground be consecrated by the Bishop. Although this was a church and not a parish matter, the Council declared that Wright was usurping their powers and infringing the rights of the people of Mawgan and their elected representatives. The root of the trouble, however, was sectarian animosity. The Lower Chapel folk wanted their own ministers to bury their dead, and resented the payment of burial fees to another Church declaring that the

Anglicans were imposing a tax on the dead. They suggested that only part of the ground be consecrated, ignoring the fact that Vyvyan had offered the land to the church and not to the parish and that he had a right to lay down any condition he chose. By so doing they admitted that the site was suitable, which weakened their later argument that the new burial place would pollute the water supply of Mawgan Churchtown. Cynics asked why consecrated ground was more likely to pollute water than unconsecrated, and said that since Churchman and *Methody* could not worship together in life in death too they must be divided. At all events up to this time Anglicans, Wesleyans, Bryanites, and all the rest had been buried in Mawgan churchyard without sectarian discord and strife. Finally a general meeting was held at which the radical sectarians were outnumbered. It was easy to blame them for raising local strife; it was even easier to stress the cost which a separate cemetery would entail on Churchman and Dissenter alike. In the end it came down to the fact that only Vyvyan was ready to give any land in Mawgan for a burial ground; no dissenting landowner was prepared to give any land at all or any money to buy land nearer the two rival chapels at Garras.

Resentment, however, lingered, and since Boaden had supported Wright the Lower Chapel party went on talking about the 'unholy alliance' of the Anglican parson and the 'Nonconformist Alderman'. Then in 1897, John clashed with William Hosking, a village shopkeeper, and aroused the opposition of those 'female householders' he disparaged.

A young 'up-country' man, Hibberd, had been appointed master of the Carrabane school by the Board of which Hosking was chairman, Parson Wright vice-chairman and the other three members Methodist farmers. Hibberd's strong Anglican views and over-rigorous discipline offended the more extreme dissenters. One winter evening some lads, whose younger brothers he had caned, pelted him with mud as he was returning from church. He threatened to take legal proceedings against them, but Boaden intervened, and persuaded him to be content with an apology from the lads, telling Hibberd that if they were brought before a court it would harm their future prospects in life. Some parishioners, however, were determined to drive Hibberd out of Mawgan, denounced Boaden as an interfering busybody, and turned up in some force at the monthly meeting of the school board in

February, 1897, to complain that the master had been using the cane far too severely.

A garbled account of this meeting appeared in a local paper, suggesting that Hibberd had defied the Board, had refused to meet the parents of boys who complained that he had treated them brutally, and had vowed that there was no point in using the cane unless it was felt. This report was contradicted by Wright and Hosking a week later, but the other three members of the Board, then published a letter stating that Boaden had been at the 'meeting' in the school when Hosking and Wright signed the first letter to the press, going on to state that Hosking did not know what he had signed and that when he found it out he had thought of telegraphing the paper to stop its publication.[1] This was probably the 'question of veracity' that led to Boaden's quarrel with Hosking. The Board then gave Hibberd a month's notice, and he, again acting on Boaden's advice, promptly sent in a letter of resignation and demanded testimonials from the Board. He quickly found a teaching post at Chacewater, possibly through Boaden's County Council connections.Boaden probably thought that the Board was interfering too much with the daily routine and discipline of the school. He did not, however, approve of Hibberd's method of punishing some refractory lads by relegating them to lower classes, which kept them at school longer; for, in 1901, he declared that one of the main causes of the scarcity of labour in rural areas, and of the migration of so many to the towns, was keeping children at school till they were in their fifteenth year, instead of allowing them to leave when they were twelve or thirteen;[2] the law then, of course, allowed a child over eleven years old to leave school if it had a 'labour certificate' stating it had received a certain standard of education.

Hibberd left Mawgan, but Boaden's critics sarcastically suggested that the School Board stay at home and allow the 'alderman' to manage the parish without let or hindrance, and then opposed his re-election to the Board of Guardians. The challenge failed, for the majority in Mawgan knew he was honest and always did his best to serve the interests of the parish. He was, perhaps, too concerned to keep the rates down, as when in

[1]*West Briton*: February 18 and 25, March 4 and April 22, 1897.
[2]*West Briton*: December 12, 1901.

1897 he resisted a proposal to increase the staff of the Helston Workhouse by appointing a married couple, at £35 a year, in place of a single man at £20 to undertake the duties of a porter. One man who had been appointed had died before he took up the post, and another resigned after a month when he found he was expected to carry coal and potatoes, do gardening work, keep an eye on the infirm when they walked abroad, and a score of other odd jobs besides recording the arrival and departures of 'casuals' and locking up at night. Boaden reckoned one man could do all the work, and countered arguments that the workhouse was understaffed by declaring that less infirm inmates should do more daily work. Another time he stated that public employees should not be given retirement pensions, saying that this not only imposed extra burdens on the rates but discouraged individual thriftiness. Memory of his own youth led Boaden, in 1901, to oppose a proposal that inmates of Helston Workhouse be given a mid-morning lunch of bread and cheese, saying this was luxury unknown among working classes and that they would turn the union into a second-class hotel. A little later he was almost alone among the Guardians in opposing a grant of £12 to an orphanage to send a Mawgan lad to Canada; he was told that if the grant was not made the boy would be kept in the institution another two years, costing the ratepayers at least another sixteen pounds, but he was adamant, declaring that such a policy hastened 'denuding of the rural districts of the working population', and was not one whit moved when asked if he really believed that it was in the boy's own interests to bring him back to Mawgan to work for, at most, a shilling a day whilst in Canada he might become a prosperous and substantial citizen. It is easy to surmise what Boaden's view of the welfare state, already coming into existence, would have been.[1]

Only the habit of boldly facing adversity, bred of long years of farming depression, led Boaden to seek re-election to the Helston Guardians in 1898, when he had already given up the County Council. He fought the election under severe physical disability

---

[1]The above paragraph is based on reports of the meetings of the Helston Board of Guardians published in the *West Briton* and particularly in the issues of July 29, August 12 and 26, September 9, November 4, 1897, and of January 24 and February 21, 1901.

– the threat of blindness. He had discovered early in 1896 tht the sight of one of his eyes was nearly gone; a local oculist could do nothing, but a London specialist, after getting a second opinion, operated on the eye in August that year, although not very successfully, for Boaden 'never saw but little in that eye again'. The sight of the other eye then began to fail, and Boaden, a keen reader all his life, did not improve matters by reading by candle and lamp light far into the nights for he also suffered from insomnia for many years. By the spring of 1898 he was almost blind, and after winning the election he went, in April, to London for a second operation which, in his opinion, checked rather than cured the trouble, although four years later he wrote that he was able to find his way about and could still read a little.

Even these visits to London to get the best treatment of the day for his failing sight served other purposes. While waiting to go into a London hospital for his first operation, in 1896, he went to Radnorshire to see James Boaden once more; finding him half-incapacitated by a stroke, but still carrying out his clerical duties. John's sight was good enough for him to remark on the colour of the Shropshire harvest fields, whilst in Radnor, he and James went to see the tunnel being cut through the mountains to take water to Birmingham. That was the type of engineering work in which Boaden ever took an interest; it was Victorian materialistic progress at its best, yet the old farmer believed that many of the thousands in Birmingham and the other great cities would have served themselves and their country better by staying on the land. Boaden left his old friend to go to hospital, probably wondering if they would ever meet again in this world but he saw James twice more before the latter died in July, 1899.

In December, 1896, John Boaden accompanied his son-in-law, Carter Thomas, to look for an 'up-country' farm. A relative, who held an Essex church living, had written Thomas that there were some farms for sale near Stambourne on the Suffolk border. The great agricultural depression had been felt most severely in that district; rents had fallen a half or more since 1875; landlords were desperately seeking tenants lest their estates become utterly derelict, and many rather than lose more capital were quite willing to sell land at prices which, compared to those in Cornwall, were extremely low.

Old style reaping

Steam threshing set, about 1900

Carter Thomas took his father-in-law with him because he had a high opinion of Boaden's judgment and thought the old man might make a better bargain than he could himself. John's account of the trip to Essex and its outcome suggests that a gipsy horse-dealer might well have come off second best in any dickering with this 'methody' farmer. After reaching London and visiting Carter's brother there – another case of that migration from the land which Boaden deplored – they went on to

'Mr. Frederick Thomas's parish of Stambourne . . . We got there one night; a sprinkle of snow covered the roads; we had a four miles walk from the station through the Essex lanes; young Fred had come to the station to conduct us . . . Our object was to buy a moderate sized farm as it would not take more capital to do this than to stock a large one. Saw three or four farms for sale the next day; one we liked. The following day Mr. Bonner who keeps the inn drove us to Dunmow,[1] and old-fashioned country-town; saw a farm for sale and another on the way back; we had a very dense fog for most of the day. Christmas Day we went down with Mr. Frederick and looked over some land of the Old Hall estate of which Wildings forms a part.[2] We went there again . . . next day. Went back to London. Carter went down to Sussex; the farms he saw were poor. I went to see the owner of the farm which we liked near Stambourne, a Mr. Bennett, a Marylebone Police Magistrate, a very sharp man. We continued correspondence with him after getting home, till we accepted the farm by telegram, but no details or terms were settled. I went to London in Spring, 1897, took Mr. Frederick Thomas with me to a Solicitor's Office in Chancery Lane where he had agreed to meet Mr. Bennett to settle terms; by asking terms that he professed to think unreasonable, he rose,

---

[1] A distance of about thirteen miles. Boaden's description suggests that the Essex parson did not have a gig or trap of his own; if this were the case it is a commentary on the poverty of rural livings as a result of the great agricultural depression.
[2] This suggests that neither Boaden nor the Anglican parson, whatever their views on Sabbath observance, had any religious scruples about observing Christmas Day, which, in 1896, fell on a Friday.

put on his hat, and had gone through the doorway; then Mr. Thomas and I rose and left; the bargain had been disowned which was the very thing I wanted; a clerk ran after us to bring us back, but I was glad to get rid of the bargain. In less than an hour I was on the way to see Wildings again.'

It was Wildings which Boaden finally secured for his son-in-law, the deal taking some time since the estate was heavily mortgaged. A minor complication was an annual charity charged upon Wildings, but Carter Thomas got a farm of over a hundred and seventy acres for less than a thousand pounds; twenty years earlier it would have cost three times as much, and in the Meneage he would have had to pay more for a thirty-acre smallholding.

Before concluding the deal Boaden was offered the whole of the estate of which Wildings had been part, over four hundred acres of good land, for less than three thousand pounds – less than half what he had paid for Trenarth which was hardly a third the size. His sons went up to see the place and wanted to buy it, but Boaden finally turned it down after reckoning costs of moving, of compensating outgoing tenants, of selling his lands and other property in Cornwall. He stated in his memoirs that he never regretted his decision, but his sons may have thought differently. Carter Thomas left the Meneage for Essex at Michaelmas, 1898, the occupier staying at Wildings an extra year as his tenant.

The Thomases were not the only farming family to leave the Meneage that quarter day, for with them went another of Boaden's sons-in-law, Nicholas Lambrick who was going to Sussex, and two Mullion farmers, the four combining to hire a special train to take their stock 'up-country'. Lambrick had been farming Tregoose, and now Boaden's second son, William took over this holding which his father owned; the third Boaden son, James, took over Skewis from Carter Thomas. John Boaden had visited Sussex while waiting for his second operation, in April 1898, staying with another Cornish 'emigrant' who was doing well on a dairy farm near Chichester; and this, apparently, paved the way for Lambrick's move six months later.

These Meneage farmers moved at a propitious time. In Cornwall, competition for farms and small-holdings was keener than ever. Wheat prices had risen, rather suddenly, to nearly fifty shillings a quarter; the hay and corn harvest of 1898 had been the best for years; it seemed tht the farming depression was ending and that the future outlook was bright. Even if war clouds were gathering in the Transvaal that mattered little and some farmers were hopeful of returning to 'Crimean prosperity'.

Four or five years later Boaden reckoned that his sons who had stayed in Cornwall had done better than Thomas in Essex and Lambrick in Sussex, though all shared in the moderate farming revival. Yet Boaden wrote

> 'throughout the nineties the price of corn was very low and farming languished, this with the ten preceding years making twenty years of agricultural depression which severely injured the farming class and ruined many.'

Prices fell towards the end of 1898, but a good season had made things easier for farmers than they had been for years, and had revived hope. Adversity had forced farmers to adapt themselves to a new order of things; although they were still raising corn they were feeding it to their livestock instead of selling grain. The area tilled, however, was much less than in 1875, and many farmers now fed live-stock with cheap foreign grain. Several Meneage cattlemen after the droughts of 1887 and 1893 had been glad to buy foreign hay, whilst in the early 'nineties British grain prices fell so low that a number of farmers, far from demanding a return to the Corn Laws, expressed fears that it would soon no longer pay American agriculturists to raise grain to feed not only the people but the farm stock of Britain.

The scattering of the Boaden family began three years before the Thomases and Lambricks went to Essex and Sussex, for, in 1895, the youngest son, Laurie, went to Johannesburg as a bank cashier. After 1898 John and his wife spent some time in the Home Counties. Carter Thomas had hardly been in Essex a week before he sent for John to come and advise him about the compensation to be paid the outgoing tenant. Practically blind, John felt he could not go alone and his wife went up with him. They stayed in Essex several days, and then went down to see the Lambricks in Sussex. Returning through London, John found time to listen to the 'Marble Arch orators', before they caught the night train. When they reached Helston station, they heard that during the night, that of October 14, 1898, the steamship *Mohegan*, had struck the notorious Manacles, off the shores of St. Keverne, and had foundered with the loss of over a hundred souls, although it had been a moderately calm and clear night.

The outbreak of the Boer War brought Laurie Boaden home towards the end of 1899, but early in 1900 he went back to the Cape, after visiting his sisters in Essex and Sussex. John Boaden, writing after Eleanor Jane's death, recalled that

> 'his mother said she never expected to see him again, but she had a wonderful power of controlling her feelings, and prepared and got all that was necessary for him, busily engaged until he was leaving the house. Ma had no time for folding her hands. Our children being nearly all settled and scattered, correspondence with them began to occupy more of our attention.'

There were family worries, too. The Thomas family in Essex had a run of serious illnesses, which took Clara Boaden up to Wildings for some time to help them out, leaving her parents to look after themselves at Worval. In May, 1901, Eleanor Jane had a bad fall, when out gathering firewood, and for some days was hardly able to get about. Boaden had another shock, the same month, when he looked up an old neighbour at Nancegollen, who did not first recognize him and then, with more candour and tact, said – 'Is this the young John Boaden? why, you're gone to look like an old man!'. The years were beginning to tell on Boaden and his generation, for, another day he ran across his old workman, Edward Downing, looking 'feeble, having palsy', but he seems to have had rather a different shock when he called on another old acquaintance, a Crowan shoemaker, whom he found 'playing cards with his landlady'. Cards, to many Methodists, were Satan's Prayer Book.

One week-end, early in the summer of 1901 was spent at Trenarth. On this Sunday morning Eleanor Jane felt too unwell to go to Chapel, but in the evening they all went to the Bible Christian Chapel at Port Navas, taking the preacher back to Trenarth with them, to 'spend the remainder of the evening with the family in singing and prayer'. When they returned to Worval,

Eleanor Jane strained her side getting out of the farm-trap too quickly, and had to stay in bed for some days. The doctor paid her a couple of visits, and then all seemed well again; there was no apparent reason why they should not go to London, and then on to their daughters, in July.

The visit to London was to see a Harley Street specialist, for Boaden's sight was now very bad, and he no longer ventured far alone. Wildings, apparently, was not a dairy farm, for they took no less than eighty pounds of butter with them for their daughter Emma to put by for the winter, and Eleanor Jane had to get it across London to the terminus of the Great Eastern besides, as John put it, 'leading me in the bargain.' Still, the long journey had not been tedious for the old man who wrote

'my defective eyesight prevented all enjoyment of the sights by the way, but does not diminish the pleasure of conversation; a gentleman, and expert in bee culture, entered (the train) at Redruth; he had been demonstrating at the show the day previous; my wife had an interesting conversation with him.'

The London visit, apart from seeing the specialist in Harley Street, was mainly spent in visiting old friends and, as on John's first London holiday nearly fifty years before, in a round of nonconformist services. Their first call was on

'Mr. and Mrs. Barker; he is a native of Coverack, foreman in a butchery business; we went to see them about some money left in Chancery by a party called Grubb, Mrs. Barker being descended on the maternal side from a Mawgan family of that name. We were (there) to dinner; we found that Richard Perry, formerly of the Garras, lived close by . . . went to see Mr. Perry . . . we had a very kind reception, and my dear wife was able to telephone with her old friend, Mrs. V. Harry (Selina Curnow).'

So the Boadens found a little Cornish colony in London, where they spent the Sunday attending at Dr. Clifford's chapel, at Westminster Abbey 'where Archdeacon Wilberforce preached eloquently', and at the Tabernacle in the evening where Boaden

215

reckoned Thomas Spurgeon's sermon was 'the most spirited discourse we heard for the day'.[1]

They stayed at a Temperance Hotel, near Liverpool Street, where Boaden said he was well-known, the legal busines of the Grubb will keeping them till Tuesday when they were glad to leave the bustling city and get up to Essex. All was well at Wildings, but

> 'the grass had suffered much from the cold spring; hay on pastures just nothing, mangolds thin and backward, turnips suffering from fly; but corn though rather short in straw looking fair for an average crop . . . Many days we went over the farm with the children, and rambled the Essex lanes.'

Boaden, however, did not seem over-enthusiastic about farming in Essex, though he did not compare it directly with conditions in the Meneage. The farm at Baythorn Bridge, tenanted since 1898 by William Henry Thomas of Mullion seemed to have good crops apart from hay, but Boaden did not seem very impressed, save by the 'good farmhouse and buildings'.

After a week at Wildings the old people and their daughter Clara went to the Lambricks in Sussex. The first evening there, Eleanor Jane complained of a violent pain in her side. Poulticing gave her little relief, and the liniment and medicine prescribed by a Rye doctor even less. She spent most of the time they were with the Lambricks in bed, but John found his way about a little, commenting

> 'the crops looked pretty well; the hay was very light; the green crops much better than in Essex. I like Sussex best; it is better for grass, and more like home.'

And, as soon as his wife seemed a little better, home they went, their daughter Jane Lambrick going with them, leaving Clara

[1]John Clifford (1836–1923) the great Baptist divine; Albert Basil Orme Wilberforce (1841–1916) fourth son of Bishop Samuel Wilberforce, Archdeacon of Westminster from 1904 jo his death; Thomas Spurgeon, (1856–1917) son of C. H. Spurgeon, who, however, unlike him, remained a Baptist.

behind to housekeep on the Sussex farm. They travelled down from London by night, and as soon as they got home their local doctor was summoned. Two days later he said he could do nothing, for Eleanor Jane was suffering from cancer. In September, it seemed to be a matter of days, or hours, but she rallied somewhat. With the doctor only providing pain-relieving and soporific drugs, the Boadens tried some of the 'quack remedies' advertised in the papers, John mentioning violet lens and 'Count Metteis so-called cure'. All was in vain, the end coming on the evening of April 8, 1902.

In those trying times John was helped by the kindness of numerous friends, and was especially moved by the numbers who came to the funeral on a dreary, wet day when Methodist minister and Anglican parson shared the duties, a reward and a tribute to Boaden's own fight for sectarian toleration and forebearance, and at the last moment the squire, Sir Vyell Vyvyan, still rector of Withiel, took the service in Mawgan Church.

More touching then the public tributes and the funeral trappings with which Eleanor Jane was mourned and buried were the words Boaden, bereft, alone, and feeling his years wrote a few months later. He stressed her staunch faith, recalled how she often read her Bible in bed and sometimes chid him for not reading it as much as 'man's works'. He said that she had been scrupulously honest in paying her debts, forgetting nothing, that

'her soul during a life of incessant attention to her duties had matured to a high state of Christian grace. She loved the world only so far as it helped us to develop for a better . . . She was also capable of defending her rights and pursuing and contriving for her family interests in every way she could. Her self-denial was great; even when weak and feeble if a child wanted her she would be out of bed at once; was always neat and scrupulously clean, but not for vain show, always had a pleasant recollection of Australia where she had received much kindness, where everybody had been kind to her. Her patience during her last illness was exemplary, often fearing she would exhaust us. She prayed almost if not always for each of her children. She liked to go to bed soon after nine, but duties often kept her up late; was very orderly and systematic, of great decision of character, could decide

217

instantly and was generally right. After we went to Worval she was almost always out of the bed before me, and sometimes would be clearing the weeds outside. I know her to be a good woman, her husband and children inherit the fruits of her industry, and it is difficult to estimate what she saved the family with her experience in buying the clothes and (in) making them, always contriving (some economy), and then in furnishing she bought much 2nd[1] was an excellent person to (go with to) a sale; I don't think I ever knew her to be taken in, but what above all else and (what is) of the greatest value to her descendants, is her example and her character; she was a good woman.'

These words were written nearly three score years after a callow youth in his teens had been drawn to a pretty face in Garras Chapel. The married life of the Boadens by modern standards – or lack of standards – was tediously respectable. A humdrum life of hard work had brought them a modicum of prosperity. Perhaps they were too hard-working, expected others around them to labour hard too; maybe they were a little over-careful in their amassing of worldly wealth, but still it was wealth that came to them the harder way – through toil and forethought. Their religious faith may have been somewhat narrow, yet John Boaden was certainly more tolerant than some of the sectarian zealots in Mawgan parish, and believed that religion should be a bond of community rather than a force of social disruption. And in the paragraph describing his dead wife there is no doubt that, for John Boaden, it was a faith that could do more than move mountains, that it was a faith transcending the bournes beyond whence no traveller returns.

Boaden lived on two years longer. His sons were not far away, and he could always walk over their farms. He had retired from the Board of Guardians in 1901, but now and again he met Rows and other old associates in public life on the magistrate's bench. Relations and friends often came to spend an hour or so talking to the old man, sometimes seeking his advice. In December, 1903, he was a guest speaker at the annual dinner which the Helston

---

[1] i.e. second hand.

Board of Guardians and Rural District Council had inaugurated the previous year, and showed that he held fast to his old ideals when he told farmer colleagues and later successors that their duty to the poor in any case of want or destitution was to give relief, but take every care in their charity lest they sap the spirit of independence and self-reliance among the poor. He declared that the people must be inculcated with the principles of self-support and of individual independence, and deplored the 'cancer of indolence' which had eaten deeply into the heart of society. He took the opportunity once more to condemn not mere drunkenness but the 'drinking habit', and to repeat again that the money of the ratepayers should be invested wisely and not carelessly thrown away.[1]

Had Boaden lived a little longer he might have added to his memoirs. He left an account of a farmer and, to some degree, of his wife, although his tribute to Eleanor Jane did not do full justice to the hard-working farm wives of those or of later or earlier times. Still, bereft and alone, half blind, yet fortified by his religious faith, John Boaden never forgot the girl who had returned from distant Australia to be his bride. It is not really surprising that he married again – a brief eventide marriage to the old friend who, when Eleanor Jane had been nearly overwhelmed by the cares of a young family, had come to Skyburriowe as a nursemaid and help and who, later, had kept a school which Boaden's daughters attended. Boaden, almost blind, could not live alone; his family save for the son in South Africa and the two daughters in Essex and Sussex, were near, but that was not enough for they belonged to a later generation than his own. As a man grows old and friends vanish from his mortal ken he clings all the more closely to those that are left who had shared his fortunes and cares in the days when he was in his youth and prime.

A later age that has known so much instability and catastrophic change can hardly understand the way survivors of Boaden's age felt at the passing of the great Queen, nor the disillusionment brought by the war in South Africa with its grim reminder that mankind had not progressed nearly as far along the road to human perfection that many Englishmen had believed for so long. For John Boaden, too, there was personal bereavement and care. He

[1]*West Briton*: December 24, 1903.

could console himself that Eleanor Jane had had a full and contented life, but when, a year after her death, his eldest son died at Trenarth after a brief illness it was a crippling blow. His grandsons there were young, and then in 1903, too, there were signs that the brief revival in farming fortune was waning.

The harvest that year was bad. In the Meneage many farmers were still carrying corn at the end of October. The following spring was cold and backward, and when John Boaden went along the lane back to Worval from Garras Sunday school on Easter Day he may have wondered if the drear cycle of seasons that had come in the late 'seventies was not beginning again. Still there were signs of spring in the hedgerows and fields, golden gorse, a fresh green in the meadows, blackthorn blossoming. Perhaps, however, he paid little heed to these things, but mused over the Easter message of Resurrection, recalling that twelve months ago the coming Wednesday his son had died, and that on Friday Eleanor Jane would have been dead two years. Ere the first of those days dawned John Boaden too had gone, and on the anniversary of Eleanor Jane's death he was buried in Mawgan churchyard.

One long life's harvest had been gathered in, one labourer's long day of toil and care was over. Still the clouds passed over the skies; shadows fell and passed over the land. Night came, with now and again the pale golden gleam of the moon and the silver glitter of stars. In the old trees by the churchyard and in those of the drive to Skyburriowe and in the dark Trelowarren plantations the owls of Mawgan called through the night. With the dawn came the song of early larks singing to the heavens and soaring high above the green pastures and the woods, the shimmering waters of the Helford creeks, the dark ploughlands and the lighter heaths and downs of the Meneage.

Epilogue

In John Boaden's lifetime the world had change much; it was to change even more. Things that were commonplace features in everyday farming life at the close of Victorian times quickly followed the flail and the sickle. Before Boaden died reaping machines had driven the gleaners from the harvest fields; in the next half century horses too had almost vanished. A succession of Education Acts banished rook-scaring boys from the fields, and women, too, were rarely seen engaged in out-door farm work in the early years of the new century, though world wars brought some of them back. Rural depopulation continued, and it was in the country districts that there first appeared an alarming social problem – the growing disproportion of old people in the total population, more and more old folk at a time when the comparative number of young people seems to be just as certainly though more irregularly declining.

In 1900 the rural farmstead was still more or less self-sufficing. Some farms were already selling all the milk they produced, keeping back just enough to make a few puddings or cups of tea, and were buying butter or substitutes for it from town shopkeepers. The day had not yet come when nearly all the meat eaten by farming families was supplied by a roundsman butcher, and for some years yet pig-killing days were still high festivals to the children of farmers and their labourers, but already some preferred 'factory' bacon to home-cured.

Yet the 'good old days' had their disadvantages, disadvantages needlessly exaggerated by some, but more often ignored and especially by those escapists who, feeling modern times to be out of joint, would whine and flee to a golden age that never existed save in their own imagination.

It is now almost traditional for the farmer turned author, and certainly for the authoress-farmwife, to dwell on the earth closet, usually treating it as a noisome convenience – or lack of convenience – to be laughed at rather than deplored. Still by the mid-twentieth century most farms had running water or had been supplied with chemical methods to ameliorate the problem of rural domestic sanitation. These were long overdue, but it is impossible to estimate the sickness and mortality, especially infant mortality caused by lack of sanitation in former times. Typhus and diphtheria were the greatest of the attendant scourges, but the lack of indoor sanitation often was the direct cause of chills and pneumonia which frequently ended fatally; only a few were as tough as that old cottager who, asked by a sanitary inspector where the 'necessary accommodation' of her home was, and then only able to grasp what he meant under a cruder name, said the moor at the back was big enough for her.

An increasing use of cement almost eliminated the old farm-yards which were bogs of dung and rotten litter reeking to high heaven. On some holdings there is still room for improvement, but on the dairy farms which were possibly the worst offenders, official intervention to secure clean milk and clean milking has brought a great transformation. Cattle shippens have also been improved by the use of cement, perhaps at the cost of some warmth and comfort, but gains in cleanliness and convenience outweigh this ten times over, and it is impossible to estimate the losses on farms where loose-stone walled buildings harboured teeming colonies of rats.

From mowhays and rickyards some old-world charm has vanished with covered yards superseding thatch. A well-thatched rick was a work of art, but many who bewail the disappearance of the thatcher realise that not one farmer in a thousand is in his business simply on account of its aesthetic or romantic appeal. Thatching only survived in the south-west and other parts of Britain because, between 1880 and 1914 and again between 1920 and 1940, few farmers could find the cash to buy Dutch barns or galvanised iron even if they thought that, in the long run, it would save them money. Thatching was cheaper, especially for family farmers who seem to have put a very low price on their own labour, but those who had to hire labour went over to the 'new-fangled' ways, and others adopted them simply to 'keep up' with their neighbours. Covering a rick with galvanised iron was quicker, but not so much quicker in the opinion of older men who could recall some very speedy thatching jobs in their younger days. As a means of keeping ricks dry galvanised iron was more effective.

Or was it?

For after a gale the farmer could find his rick stripped, and have to pick up the scattered sheets which had not been adequately secured but had been torn and tossed away by the wind. More often than not such sheets would be buckled and bent, and when put on the ricks again there would be gaps through which rain would seep into the hay or straw beneath. Then, too, the length of a sheet of galvanised iron could not be changed; if it was too short the farmer would have to leave the lower eaves of a rick either uncovered or cobbled up with thatch; if it was too long it was even worse, for a gale might then whip up beneath the jutting eaves and tear off the sheets, hurtling them with a fiendish clatter through the air scaring flocks and herds, even maiming and killing now and again. Dutch barns and covered yards were a different matter, but they were much dearer, whilst the fire risk was increased by putting so much hay and corn under a single cover, particularly in catchy seasons when so much damp hay and straw was brought in from the fields.

Skilfully-used galvanised iron had everything in its favour, but for a long time it was hard to say it was economic. It saved labour on the bigger farm, but on smaller family farms this did not matter so much; hay-ricks could easily be thatched in the slack time before the corn was ripe, whilst in years when the hay crop was heavy a farmer might not have enough galvanise to hand and would have to do some thatching in any case. In years of low prices it hardly seemed worth while covering corn with costly metal sheets, especially when thatch, either reed or rush, grew on the farm or nearby. In time, too, there was another argument for the old ways; many farmers bought inferior cheap galvanise which, in a few years, flaked and rusted, and they found that raw iron oxide in the bullock's feed often had fatal results.

Perhaps, however, the invention which effected the greatest rural change since last Victorian times has been barbed wire. It did much to aggravate the antagonism of hunting squires and tenant farmers, and brought to the countryside almost as much bad feeling as the old Game Laws. Barbed wire was both effective and cheap, and was introduced at a time when farmers wre racking their brains how to find the money to pay a hedger's wages or, perhaps more often, having the money and not knowing where to find a man who could build a good hedge.

In many places barbed wire was only used to make existing hedges a more efficient barrier against straying cattle and sheep. Elsewhere, however, it was used as a substitute for quickset hedgerows, earthen banks, or stone hedges. It was a boon where temporary fences were needed, but it led in many places to the removal of the old hedgerows and the loss of shelter offset the gain in cultivable area, for such shelter for cattle, to some extent, had shortened the wintertime when the farmer had to keep his animals in byre, shippen, and stable. No animal could find any shelter from the rage of the elements on either side of a wire fence. Barbed wire, too, hastened the disappearance of small fields, for it was easy if need arose to fence off a small temporary paddock.

Some believe that the disappearance of the old hedgerows, partly due to the introduction of harvesting machinery, partly to the later conversion of so much arable land to pasture, did not add to the productivity of farms. Although a wider acreage, amounting on some holdings to nearly fifteen per cent of the whole, could be cultivated, there was not a comparable increase in the quantity of crops produced, since along with the hedges there disappeared many of the birds which kept insect pests under control. Hedges however, had sheltered pests and parasites as well, whilst some thought that the elimination of the old hedges reduced the rabbits as well, but judging from the numbers that continued to swarm in most districts up to the great myxomatosis epidemic of 1954 this hardly appears to have been the case. Rabbits certainly did much damage, but a good farmer could keep their numbers down after the Ground Game Act of 1880 limited landlords' preserving rights, and they also provided some sport to relieve the monotony of farming and rural life, besides being edible. The coney may have been the cause of some law-breaking, but it would be asked what an enterprising poacher would do when he was deprived of opportunities to poach. If the poacher drifted like so many others to the towns when rural conditions no longer appeared to offer the chance of a living, it was hardly likely that he became a model member of urban society. Poaching could almost be regarded as a safety valve for that inborn propensity of most men to challenge and flout law and authority at some time or other.

Apart from these controversial points barbed wire brought other problems to the countryside. Fences were neglected, wire-rusted and broke and fragments were dragged some way or another into the fields, and the risk of blood-poisoning and lock-jaw among both animals and men increased. In time scientific research provided more effective antidotes for such ills, but they are not always to hand when most needed.

It might almost be asked if 'change' and 'progress' have ever really benefitted men without involving some loss. Only in one contribution of science to modern life does the balance of absolute gain seem unquestionable – the improved 'artifical' light. Many old farmers can still recall the dark 'old days' – or rather nights and how unpleasant it was to be benighted with many farm jobs still to be done. On a winter evening the cattle would be brought in from the fields, the farmer would decide that since daylight was gone anyway he and his family might as well have their tea and take all the longer over that meal since the milking and feeding of the stock would now, in any case, have to be done by the light of a hurricane lantern. The things that could go wrong under such circumstances were numerous.

Where did someone or other leave the lantern last night, or where had some tidy soul put it through the day?

When found, the lantern might be all but empty of paraffin. That could soon be fixed – if the supply of paraffin had not run out, as it sometimes did; then, perhaps, someone would be blamed for not bringing more back when they had gone to town on market-day and, maybe, had returned rather over 'lit-up' with another kind of 'oil'. There would be mutual recriminations and shortening tempers. Even if there was paraffin at hand and there was no need to stumble in the gloom of night to the nearest neighbour to borrow a bottleful, it was a messy job filling the lantern, and then the glass might smoke up since the wick had not been trimmed. Or, perhaps, when found, the lantern was broken, since last night someone had fallen over a step or slipped in the miry yard with it, or it had been left lying too close to the foot of a bullock that might have commanded a high price in the football transfer market.

Many things certainly could go wrong on a farm. Even if the lantern was all right the farmer might then go out and find an animal missing; it had not been brought in from the fields with the rest, and there was nothing for it but to go out and find it. To do so, it was best to take the dog – but where was the dog? Like every other hound in the parish gone off after old So-and-so's something or other bitch. Or the dog might be there but once in the field would be off after rabbits. Then one had to wander all over the field, and even a three-acre meadow on a dark night seems as vast as Sahara, and the lantern only cast a glimmer a few yards round the man who carried it. On a still night the noisy breathing of the animal might be heard, but usually on the night when these things happened there was a gale howling and rain or hail pelting down – and sometimes both. It was wise to search by the lee hedge first, then go round the others, but it was even wiser to look most carefully near the gate first of all. For there were times when, leaving the gate open, the farmer went all around and over the field, found no sight or sign of any animal and, at last, giving up in despair went back to the farmstead to find that the missing beast had calmly made its own way to the byre. But sometimes the animal was found sick or dead.

It was all in the farmer's day's or night's work.

Nor was a hurricane lantern the safest of objects to carry into barns filled with hay or straw, nor to carry in one hand with a bundle of fodder clutched beneath the other arm, perhaps even clambering down a ladder while thus encumbered.

Electric light and powerful electric torches have made all these things of the past, have made farming more comfortable and less hazardous. True, some carping critics say that good light has made farmers desultory night crows or morning slug-a-beds, usually the same conceited sages who derided and mocked those who called daylight saving and 'summer time' unwarranted interferences with 'God's own time'. On the farm there is no time but day and night and the seasons of the year; the rest is man-made, and having made it man has then made himself the slave of that grim-idol – the dial of a clock. The dew on mown hay cannot be compelled by legislation to evaporate an hour earlier even if Parliament says it is eight o'clock in the morning and not seven. Farm work must be geared to nature, and the farmer who tries to work always by and to the clock, and starts carrying dew-laden hay 'first' thing in the morning as soon as his hired men put in an appearance would at best get a musty heated rick, at worse a pile of ashes and the insurance people refusing to compensate a loss incurred by supine folly. It might be necessary to 'alter the time' to get urban workers up betimes in the summer so as to allow them the greatest benefit of a day divided between labour and well-earned recreation and leisure, but things do not work quite that way on the farm.

Man has changed some things; others have not changed.

Near the coastlands of England gulls still swarm after the plough even though now it is drawn by a tractor and not by horses or oxen – perhaps even in greater numbers than half a century ago since the oil which man has cast upon the waters have made the foreshores, their former happy hunting grounds, a death-trap to them. In England, in Cornwall, and down in the Meneage men still speed the plough, although some American farmers, reaping the bitter harvest of soil erosion their grandfathers and great-grandfathers sowed, have started blaming the plough for their expanding dust bowls. Artificial insemination may have transformed pedigree bulls into procreative machines producing semen at clock-geared intervals as if life can be produced along the mass-production belt, but the cow still shows its urge to maternity in the same old way. Most unchanging of all has been the wayward weather. There had always been talk that neither winter nor summer are what they used to be, but human memory is impressionistic not photographic. Exceptionally dry or wet summers and abnormally cold winters linger longest in memory till, in that time, they banish all remembrance of others. Yet in the decade following the end of the second world war there were two droughts in England comparable to those of 1887 and 1893. There were wet seasons nearly as bad as that of 1903, though none as bad as 1879, a season that only recurs about once in three or four score years; there were cold winters that reawakened the memories among older people of the Great Blizzard. And although John Boaden lived over three quarters of a century he never saw a summer that surpassed those of 1976 or 1995 nor winters as bitter as that of 1962–3.

APPENDIX

The Acreage and Farming Economy of Skyburriowe

In his memoirs John Boaden did not gie details about the acreages of the farms with which he had been associated, the crops cultivated, or the amount of stock kept. He mentioned that Trease, when Lyle bought it, had been a smallholding of twenty-four acres, and tht Bojorrow was twice that size. Changes in occupancy and still more the selling of lands and estates have, since Boaden's time, meant changes in the size of many farm-holdings.

Among the papers of Sir Richard Vyvyan at the Cornwall County Record Office in Truro, is an undated rent survey of the Trelowarren estate; it gives details of various farms round about the year 1840. The acreage of Bojorrow, split into no less than six different 'parcels', half designated 'arable' and the rest 'croft', came to 43 acres, croft-land comprising 2 acres 2 roods and 16 poles; the rent was the rather odd amount of £77-2-9d. There were separate returns for Burnoon and Skyburriowe, but it is very strange that not only were the two identical in size but that each consisted of 58 acres 1 rood and 19 poles of 'arable' and 18 acres 2 roods and 1 pole of croft. Eliminating the croft, which was probably furze and rough grazing on Goonhilly Downs, the Skyburriowe-Burnoon holding was 116 acres in extent, bearing out the statements of local farmers that the two farms which were 'always farmed together' made a holding of rather more than a hundred acres. When John Boaden's father took the double holding in 1862 the rent, excluding the old mill, was £150 a year, although earlier the rent of Skyburriowe had only been £50 and that of Burnoon £70.

Since there are no detailed farming accounts estimates of the acres-tilled and stock kept by Boaden at Skyburriowe are only conjectures. A farm of 116 acres, however, comprised about a twentieth of the 2,289 acres of cultivated and pasture land returned for Mawgan in the 1867 agricultural returns, and rather less than a twenty-sixth of the 3,096 acres so designated in the returns of 1894. The Skyburriowe-Burnoon holding can be reckoned as at least 'average' for Mawgan, most of it lying on the fertile soil of the Meneage Crush Zone though touching the poor serpentine soils to the south. If Boaden raised, as he most certainly must have done, a twentieth of the crops and stock of the parish, it seems that in 1867 he had about 16 acres under wheat, 15 under barley, 10 under oats, 15 under swedes, mangolds, and other 'roots', 11 acres lying fallow, and nearly 50 acres under leys or permanent pasture. By 1894 the fallow had vanished only about 12 acres were under wheat but nearly 15 under oats and, perhaps, 14 acres of roots.

What those acres returned to Boaden depended on the weather and the prices. In the dry summer of 1867 Boaden, like most Cornish farmers probably had better than average wheat and barley crops but poorish oats. Now with the average yield per acre in Cornwall being 29 bushels of wheat, 35 of barley and 43 of oats, the cash value of Boaden's crops that season was about £200 for wheat, £120 for barley, and £50 for oats, making a total of at least £370. In 1894, a 'catchy' season with a very wet July, the maximum value of the corn crops on the farm was less than £200, with the wheat being worth, at most £60, the barley rather less, and the oats £80. Rent, rates, taxes, and tithes together would more than swallow up the corn crops raised at Skyburriowe that year, leaving nothing for the costs of cultivation; on comparable farms in Cornwall in those times a yearly wage bill of £150 and one of nearly £100 for artificial manures was the rule rather than the exception. No wonder farmers talked of bad times.

As for live stock in 1867 Boaden probably had a herd of sixty or seventy cattle, one half being young stock under two years of age, and from 125 to 150 sheep. By 1894 he may only have had 55 head of cattle, but only about a score over two years old, and less than 100 sheep. These figures might come as a shock to those who believe that English agricultural history in late Victorian times was 'Up horn, down corn'. Possibly poor harvests in West

Cornwall in the early sixties had led many farmers to use the plough as an adjunct of live-stock husbandry while the low stock figures of 1894 were due to the drought of 1893 which forced farmers to cut their flocks and herds by fully a tenth. The decline in cattle, however, was wholly in older stock; economic necessity in the bad times, and the fact that oxen were no longer kept for seven or eight years as draught animals before being fattened off for the butcher, meant that farmers concentrated on stock fit for slaughtering in their third year; early 'cram' feeding also reduced slightly the numbers a farm could maintain. Declining wool prices had, of course, a similar result among the flocks of sheep; as the returns were made in early June, both those of 1867 and 1894 indicate the size of the flocks before many early lambs had been sold to the butcher. Five or six horses, and possibly about twenty pigs comprised the remainder of the live stock kept at Skyburriowe, and of course there were the hens which had become quite an important part in the Boaden's farming economy by 1894 although comparatively few of their neighbours attached much importance to poultry and eggs at that time.

Index

111 s per Qtr : 38 s per Cornish Bushel

So there are : $\frac{111}{38}$ Cornish Bushels per Qt$_r$

$$38 \overline{) 111 \cdot 00} \quad 2.92$$
76
350
342
80

= 2.92 ?!

or 61 s/qtr = 23/s per bushel — 2.651 ?!

$$23 \overline{) 61 \cdot 00} \quad 2.651$$
46
150
138
120
115
850

what a
difference !

see
p 88